Asylums and After

A Revised History of the Mental Health Services:
From the Early 18th Century to the 1990s

Kathleen Jones

THE ATHLONE PRESS
London & Atlantic Highlands, N.J.

First published 1993 by The Athlone Press Ltd
1 Park Drive, London NW11 7SG and
165 First Avenue, Atlantic Highlands, NJ 07716

© Kathleen Jones 1993

British Library Cataloguing in Publication Data
A catalogue record for this book is available from the British Library

ISBN 0-485-11429-1 hb   ISBN 0-485-12091-7 pbk

Library of Congress Cataloging in Publication Data

US CIP data is available from
the Library of Congress

Typeset by Datix International Limited, Bungay, Suffolk
Printed in Great Britain by the University Press, Cambridge

Contents

List of Tables   vi
Acknowledgements   vii

Introduction   1
Chapter 1   First Moves   5
Chapter 2   Moral Treatment and County Asylums   23
Chapter 3   The Parliamentary Reformers   41
Chapter 4   Creating the Asylum System   60
Chapter 5   The National Lunacy Commission   78
Chapter 6   The Triumph of Legalism   93
Chapter 7   Stagnation   112
Chapter 8   Into the Community   126
Chapter 9   A New Service for a New Age   141
Chapter 10   The Ideologies of Destruction   159
Chapter 11   The Disappearing Services   181
Chapter 12   The New Legalism   197
Chapter 13   Distractions and Placebos   214
Chapter 14   Consequences   238

References   256
Bibliography   277
Index   297

List of Tables

4.1 Capital costs of asylum building, England and Wales 60
4.2 The abolition of restraint at the Lincoln Asylum 65
7.1 Known persons of unsound mind, England and Wales, 1859-1909 116
7.2 The size of county asylums, England and Wales, 1829-1930 116
7.3 Proportions of male and female patients admitted to asylums, England and Wales, 1844 117
10.1 Mental illness: resident populations of mental hospitals and other institutions, England and Wales, 1914-1959 161
11.1 Mental hospitals, England and Wales: resident populations and admissions, 1959-70 187
14.1 Residents in mental illness hospitals, England, 1976-1991 243
14.2 Beds available for mental illness, admissions and bed turnover, England, 1976-1991 244

Acknowledgements

My debt to friends and colleagues who have helped me to evaluate the history of the care of mentally ill people has been acknowledged in previous texts. For the present text, I should like to add thanks to the following:

Elizabeth Adeboyo of the Statistics Branch, Department of Health, for assistance with statistical material.
Patricia Allderidge, Archivist and Curator of the Bethlem Royal Hospital, for help in checking facts from the Bethlem records.
Professor Jonathan Bradshaw for saving me from a sizeable error.
Professor Hugh Freeman for disagreeing with me with much tolerance and courtesy.
Dr Veronica Pearson for broadening my horizons.
Dr Pauline Prior for wanting to know why, if I was revising the text, I was not a 'revisionist'.
Sage Publications for permission to use passages from *Experience in Mental Health: Community Care and Social Policy* (1989).
Professor Andrew Scull for sending me back to first principles.

The opinions are my own. I hope that there are no factual errors in the text, but if there are, they are mine too.

Introduction

This study is the fourth in a series.[1] The three earlier volumes are now out of date and out of print. The first, *Lunacy, Law and Conscience, 1744–1845*, which was my doctoral thesis, was written at a time when there were no modern secondary sources on the history of the mental health services, but there was a rich collection of primary source material to be discovered – contemporary newspaper and periodical reports, medical treatises and asylum records. Some were found in specialist libraries, and some were unearthed in unexpected places – like the early nineteenth-century records of one asylum, which were found stacked in the boiler room, ready for burning.

The study pieced together from these sources described how the asylums were founded, taking their first patients from prisons and workhouses; the development of 'moral treatment', which replaced chains and intimidation with an appeal to reason; the long battle against abuse and neglect in the private madhouses and the work-houses; the 'non-restraint' system which ended the use of manacles, leglocks and straitjackets; and the formation of a national Lunacy Commission in 1845.

The second study, *Mental Health and Social Policy, 1845–1954*, had a very different story to tell: how the asylums grew into large, self-serving institutions, and the Lunacy Commission became increasingly bureaucratic; how the legal profession and the medical profession fought for control, and the lawyers won; how attempts were made to humanize the asylum system; how the coming of the National Health Service offered a hope of better care and treatment;

and how the Mental Health Act of 1959 reduced a stigmatizing legal framework, and made community care possible. For this period, there was an overwhelming quantity of documentation, all easily accessible, and the task often involved précis rather than discovery.

The third study, *A History of the Mental Health Services*, abridged the two earlier books and brought the account up to 1971. The additional material chronicled a period of change: of rising hopes followed by growing cynicism; the beginnings of the radical critique in the work of Erving Goffman, Michel Foucault and Thomas Szasz; the hospital scandals of the late 1960s; and the frustration of community care policies by the perennial problems of lack of finance, lack of staff, lack of training and public indifference. By this time, the available material was not only plentiful, but highly controversial.

A new and updated version in the 1990s brings the story into a period of even greater change, because both the mental health services and the literature of the subject have altered beyond recognition in the past twenty years. Mental hospitals are literally biting the dust – reduced to piles of rubble as their sites are sold off for housing estates or leisure centres. The movement against the mental hospital, initiated by Left-wing theoreticians, was ironically brought to fruition by the Right-wing pragmatists of the Thatcher era.

At the same time, there has been a steady stream of publications which present alternative views of the events of the past three centuries. Lawyers, psychiatrists, sociologists and medical historians have revaluated events in the light of a variety of concepts, ranging across the political spectrum, or stressing the contribution of particular academic disciplines (notably medicine, law or sociology). Again, the extreme right and the extreme left have joined forces, and a genre of 'revisionist' writing has developed in which it is quite possible to believe (with Dr Szasz) that only private fee-paying psychiatry is free of the threat of 'social control', while believing (with Karl Marx and Foucault) that capitalism is the sole cause of oppression.

Revisionist writers have been vehement in attacking what they call 'Whig history'.[2] Their definition of 'Whig history' would be unfamiliar to British historiographers,[3] and has been applied to some very disparate texts.[4] Readers of this text will not find in it any faith in the 'myth of progress': quite the reverse, for the whole story is one of good intentions going wrong, advance and backsliding, misunderstandings and misinterpretations. Nor will readers find any support for the notion that the best developments in the mental health field have been medical and scientific. On the contrary: the really creative developments (with the arguable exception of the development of the phenothiazines and associated drugs in the early 1950s) have been social in character: moral management, non-restraint, the therapeutic community, community care.

A new generation of scholars is carrying out more detailed work than mine on particular areas of study. They are not too troubled by doctrinaire considerations, and are getting back to primary sources. Roy Porter's extensive review of recent literature[5] shows a rapidly developing field, given an institutional basis by the Wellcome Institute for the History of Medicine in London and other bodies, and the journal *History of Psychiatry*.

The present study is what the title says: a history of the mental health services – that is, an account of the social care of people who were or are diagnosed as mentally ill. It is not a history of psychiatric treatment; still less is it a sociological study of 'madness'. The study of societal responses to irrational behaviour is valuable in its own right, but the terminology is objectionable. I suggested to one revisionist writer that the use of 'madness' in a modern context might be distressing to mentally ill people and their relatives. The reply was 'I don't think that matters'. I think it matters.

Terminology presents a difficult problem, because words tarnish quickly, and become dated. Almost any terms connected with disorders of thought and behaviour carry negative connotations; but there has to be an end to euphemism, though it is not necessary to return today to the crude terms of the eighteenth century. Without specific terms, one cannot discuss the subject at all, so I have tried to use whatever term was current in the period under discussion. For the modern period, I have used 'mental illness' – not from pro-medical bias, but to express a holistic approach to care and treatment. We still know relatively little about the interaction of mind and body. In a century or so, the current division into mind-treatment and body-treatment may seem quite primitive, and perhaps we will have evolved a new terminology appropriate to the age of community care. Today, the term 'mental illness' is the least stigmatizing term we have. It is understood by the general public, and, more important, it is a term acceptable to mentally ill people. If 'empowerment' means anything at all, it should mean that their views are taken into account. In or out of hospital, they *feel ill*, they *suffer from illness*, and no amount of semantic manoeuvring is likely to shake the testimony of experience.

The changes which have taken place in the mental health services, and in my own life, since 1972 are so great that the previous studies might have been written by someone else. In the first nine chapters, I have gone back to many of the original sources. While some passages have stood the test of time, others needed to be redrafted. At many points in the narrative, there are new secondary sources to be taken into account, and critics to answer. The last five chapters, which deal with the massive changes of the last twenty years, are new.

Earlier material on criminal lunatics and chancery lunatics has been omitted, because these are complex subjects which need separate treatment. I have also omitted the chapters which dealt specifically with mental deficiency (now known as learning disability). The issues relating to people with learning disabilities are very different from those relating to people with disturbed thought and behaviour patterns, and this is increasingly being recognized.

This is an account of the twists and turns of social policy for mentally ill people in England over some 250 years. In the 1980s, when faith in market forces and the profit motive predominated in public life, the private misery caused by mental illness was marginalized and ignored. The problems of mental illness, and the ways in which society has tried to deal with them, need to be restated in plain language, without cynicism or polemic. It is hoped that this new version will provide a guide through what has now become an academic minefield.

First Moves

England in the early eighteenth century was a country of some five and a half million people, who lived for the most part in small towns and villages. There were few towns of appreciable size – London had a population of a little over half a million, and Bristol had about fifty thousand. In most parts of England, people lived in semi-isolated communities, remote from each other and from any central stream of influence. Travel was slow and hazardous, over roads that were rutted in summer and quagmires in winter. There were few books, and no national newspapers. Some of the rich were cultured and sceptical. Most of the poor were illiterate and superstitious; and some of the poor starved.

Life for the majority was painful, dangerous and short. According to local studies, which provide the only evidence before the first national census of 1801, birth rates and death rates were very high[1]. Many children died in infancy: before the Industrial Revolution, about three-quarters of the children born in London are thought to have died before the age of ten[2]. Most women spent their adult lives in an endless round of miscarriages and childbearing. Most men spent their lives in hard physical labour. Epidemic and endemic diseases, fevers and fluxes, brought the shadow of death close to the living; and many of those who survived past forty were old before their time.

In such a society, preoccupied with the problems of sheer physical survival, many forms of mental disorder simply passed unnoticed. If people were unable to maintain themselves, or their relatives could not help, they were reduced to the Poor Law. If they offended against a harsh penal code, they went to gaol or might be hanged for quite minor offences. If they wandered abroad, they could be picked up as vagrants, forced to work for the cost of their transport, and then sent back where they had come from under the Laws of Settlement. Violent behaviour or persistent hallucinations which made people intolerable enough to be recognized as 'mad' led to extreme forms of suppression: threats, physical assault, incarceration.

The Church still believed in exorcizing demons, though it was less enthusiastic about it than in past centuries. James I's Witchcraft Act 'against conjuration, witchcraft, and dealing with evil or wicked spirits' remained on the statute book until 1736, and though by the beginning of the eighteenth century juries were becoming reluctant to convict, belief in Devil-possession was not far beneath the surface[3].

Medical competence varied. Irvine Loudon quotes the author of *The Quacks Unmasked* (1727), who complained of 'the Coal Porter, Tinker, Taylor, Midwife, Nurse etc. [who] spring up like Mushrooms in a night to be Physicians and Surgeons'.[4] Medicine was not the prerogative of a closed profession, but the sort of subject which educated men might take up as a hobby, like art or music. Clergy and schoolmasters frequently practised without any special training, and at the other end of the social scale there were itinerant pedlars offering infallible remedies and miracle cures [5]. Even well-qualified medical practitioners had little to offer in the treatment of insanity, for medical knowledge was still dominated by a belief in the four 'humours' – blood, choler, bile and phlegm. Purges, vomits, bleeding and blistering 'reduced' the excess humours, as well as the patient's capacity to disturb others. Some medical practitioners ran small private madhouses for people of means, but the only public hospital for the mad was Bethlem or Bedlam in London, which received the capital's more troublesome lunatics.

Michael MacDonald notes that in the early seventeenth century,

methods of explaining the natural and supernatural causes of insanity and relieving the suffering of the victims were marked by a traditional mingling of magical, religious and scientific concepts. Individual cases of mental disorder might be attributed to divine retribution, diabolical possession, witchcraft, astrological influences, humoral imbalances, or to any combination of these forces.[6]

MacDonald's analysis of '2,000 obscure rustics' who were treated for mental disorder by the 'astrological physician' Richard Napier gives a rare insight into the confusions of medical and religious thought.

By the early eighteenth century, a growing rationalism made the educated class sceptical of magical remedies; but whether the explanation of bizarre behaviour was religious, superstitious or scientific, the results for the patient were much the same.

The third Earl of Shaftesbury showed an unusual compassion when he wrote 'Poor mad people and naturals, how treated? The diversion of seeing Bedlam – what a better laugh? See the malignity of this . . . vulgar, sordid and profane laughter.' But he subscribed to the prevalent philosophy of *laissez-faire*: 'What wouldst thou? That which is good for the world. – Who knows what is good for the world? Who should know better than the Providence which looks after it?'.[7]

BETHLEM

The hospital which gave the English language a new and descriptive word, originally derived its name from a priory of the Order of St Mary of Bethlehem founded in London in 1247. A statement in a Privy Council inquiry of 1632 records that 'When [Bethlem Hospital] was first employed to the use of distracted persons, appeareth not. The first mention we find of it to be employed so, was in the beginning of the reign of Richard II.'[8] Bethlem existed largely on public subscriptions, though the parish of settlement was usually charged for the maintenance of paupers.

There is a tradition that up to the middle of the seventeenth century, Bedlam beggars, wearing a badge giving them licence to beg in order to pay their arrears, were a common sight in towns and villages throughout England. John Aubrey's description is a well-known one:

Till the breaking out of the Civill Warres, Tom o' Bedlams did travell about the countrey. They had been poore distracted men that had been put into Bedlam, where, recovering to some sobernesse, they were licentiated to goe a-begging . . . they wore about their necks a great horn of an oxe in a string or bawdric, which, when they came to an house for almes, they did wind.[9]

Other beggars counterfeited the distinguishing marks of the Bedlam beggars in order to escape the penalties of the vagrancy laws.[10] A poem composed by a pretended Bedlamite in the seventeenth century sings of

> The lordly lofts of Bedlam
> With stubble soft and dainty,
> Brave bracelets strong,
> Sweet whips, ding-dong,
> And wholesome hunger plenty.[11]

'Old Bedlam' was rebuilt in 1678. The new building was in the style of the Tuileries, a fact which is said to have given considerable offence to Louis XIV. Prints in the British Museum and elsewhere show an imposing frontage. On either side of the main gate stood the two famous figures of Raving and Melancholy Madness, designed by Caius Gabriel Cibber, father of Colley Cibber, the actor, and commemorated by Alexander Pope in *The Dunciad*:

> Close to those walls where Folly holds her throne,
> And laughs to think Monroe would take her down,
> Where, o'er the gates, by his famed father's hand,
> Great Cibber's brazen brainless brothers stand.

'Monroe' refers to James Monro, son of a Principal of Edinburgh University, who became resident physician of Bethlem in 1728. He held office until 1752, when he was succeeded by his son John. The medical care at Bethlem remained largely in the hands of an unbroken line of Monros, the office of physician passing from father to son, until 1852.

Perhaps the best-known representation of conditions at Bethlem in the eighteenth century occurs in the eighth scene of *The Rake's Progress*, which Hogarth drew in 1733. The Rake lies on the floor, practically naked, with his head shaven, while a keeper manacles his feet, and another, or an apothecary, examines him. Another print, dated about 1745, shows a similar scene. The patient is again shorn; his hands are chained, and he struggles violently while three keepers hold him down in order to affix a leg-lock to his ankles. A bowl for bleeding or vomit lies in front of the group, and one of the onlookers is a woman – presumably, from her clothes, a female attendant.

Before 1967, Bethlem records were not available to scholars.[12] The only secondary source was O'Donoghue's *The Story of Bethlehem Hospital*, published in 1913. The present Bethlem archivist describes this account (with justice) as 'amateur and self-congratulatory, combining historical voyeurism with an unfortunate turn of whimsy'.[13] Jonathan Andrews' *Bedlam Revisited: A History of Bethlem Hospital* now provides a full and scholarly account of a limited period, but ends in the early 1770s.

Andrews confirms the Bethlem practice of barring medical practitioners and medical students from visiting patients, but allowing casual visitors, who came in large numbers in some periods, to visit for a small fee. In the second half of the eighteenth century, going to Bethlem to laugh at the lunatics was a popular entertainment for the idle and curious. O'Donoghue describes how Swift took three hackney coaches, with children and nursemaids, to see the sights of London:

> Set out at ten o'clock to the Tower, and saw the Lions. Then to Bedlam. Then dined at the Chop-house . . . and concluded the night at the Puppet show.[14]

Jonathan Andrews makes some defence of the Bethlem practice of admitting casual visitors, pointing out that as a charity, the hospital was dependent on public goodwill, and on the fees received. A ticket system was introduced in 1770, and the practice was gradually abandoned thereafter.[15]

A note in John Wesley's journal indicates that the Bethlem ban on visiting by medical men also extended to Methodist preachers:

> I went to see a young woman in Bedlam; but I had not talked to her long before one gave me to know that none of the preachers were to come here. So we are forbidden to go to Newgate for fear of making them wicked, and to Bedlam for fear of making them mad![16]

This is perhaps more understandable than the medical ban in the context of the time: the rational order of the ruling classes was challenged by religious 'enthusiasm', and Wesley was regarded as something of a rabble-rouser.

Andrews' detailed study reveals a more complex picture than the common stereotypes of Bethlem suggest. Bethlem took the most dangerous patients in the metropolis, and they must have presented serious management problems. Some patients (those who could pay) lived quite comfortably, and without undue privation. There were periodic attempts at de-lousing. Possibly only the incontinent patients slept on straw. If the diet was poor, it may have been deliberately lowering to reduce violence. If the medical treatment was brutal by later standards, it was the common practice of the time. The good intentions of the Governors were often frustrated by the poor calibre of untrained and ignorant keepers. But when all this and much more has been said, Bethlem medicine and Bethlem practice in the eighteenth and early nineteenth centuries deserved many of the allegations which were to be made against them in 1815 (see Chapter 3).

WORKHOUSES AND POORHOUSES

The basis of Poor Law legislation was the Act of 1601 (43 Eliz. c.2). It has been estimated[17] that there were between twelve and fifteen thousand separate parishes and townships, each controlling its own system of relief for paupers. The great failure of the Poor Law lay in the apparent inability to distinguish between the 'impotent poor', who could not work, and the able-bodied, who would not. The punishments for not working, or for 'mischievous conduct', might include solitary confinement in a dark room, deprivation of food, or being made to stand on a stool 'with the Crime pinned to their Breast'.[18] Violence and excitability were sternly discouraged in institutions which placed great emphasis on orderliness and quietude.

In most workhouses or poorhouses, no attempt was made to separate lunatics from other paupers. A few of the larger workhouses possessed infirmaries, but these appear to have been mainly used for those suffering from infectious and contagious diseases, such as smallpox or syphilis.

The records of St Peter's Workhouse, Bristol,[19] show that it was one of the very few where pauper lunatics were treated as a separate class, and almost certainly the only one where they received treatment as distinct from confinement. Almost from its inception in 1696, the first building, known as the Mint, was used for the impotent poor of the city, and other premises were acquired as a 'manufactory' for the able-bodied. By degrees, the aged and those suffering from ailments of a mainly physical nature were housed elsewhere, until the Mint became the asylum for what was then England's second largest city.

The lunatic patients were placed in separate wards, an early regulation recommending that 'the lunatic ward be floored with planks', presumably on the grounds that stone floors were injurious to the patients' health. Medical attention was provided by surgeons and physicians of local standing, who gave their services voluntarily.

The authorities at Bristol established three principles which laid the foundation for the later development of county asylums: the care of the insane should be a public responsibility; they should be treated as a separate class, their living conditions being adapted to their special needs; and they should receive treatment, not punishment.

GAOLS AND BRIDEWELLS

Bridewells, or houses of correction, were built on the pattern of the original Bridewell raised at Blackfriars in London in 1555. They generally received vagrants and beggars who could not be convicted of any crime save that of wandering abroad without visible means of support, or refusing to work, together with petty offenders. The chief distinction between a gaol and a bridewell was that, in the former, the inmates were responsible for their own maintenance and the payment of gaoler's fees. Many prisoners were forced to remain in gaol as debtors long after their original sentence was served. In a bridewell, the officials received a salary, and the Poor Law authority was responsible for the maintenance of pauper inmates, who were released at the end of their sentence.[20]

Conditions were such as to deter the sturdiest of beggars. John Howard's report on *The State of the Prisons* (1777) records:

Several Bridewells . . . in which the prisoners have no allowance of food at all. In some, the keeper farms out what little is allowed them: and where he engages to supply each prisoner with one or two pennyworth of bread a day, I have known this shrunk to half, sometimes less than half the quantity, cut or broken from his own loaf.[21]

In many cases, there were no tools or materials with which the prisoners might work and earn their keep:

Some keepers of these houses, who have represented to the magistrates the wants of their prisoners, and desired for them necessary food, have been silenced with these inconsiderate words, 'Let them work or starve'. When these gentlemen know the former is impossible, do they not by that sentence inevitably doom poor creatures to the latter?[22]

When Howard undertook his lengthy and self-imposed travels on behalf of prisoners, he found hardened criminals, shiftless vagrants and petty offenders confined together with the insane. 'Idiots and lunatics . . . serve for sport to idle visitants . . . where they are not kept separate, [they] disturb and terrify other prisoners. No care is taken of them, though it is probable that by medicines and proper regimen, some of them might be restored to their senses, and to usefulness in life.'[23]

The prisoners often lacked not only medical relief and separate quarters, but even fresh air. 'One reason why the rooms in some prisons are so close is perhaps the window-tax, which gaolers have to pay; this tempts them to stop up the windows and stifle the prisoners'.[24]

THE GROWTH OF PUBLIC CONCERN

When did attitudes begin to change? Michel Foucault, searching for a peg on which to hang his account of Reason and Unreason, chooses 1656, the date of the foundation of the Hôpital Général in Paris, which he marks as the commencement of 'the Great Confinement'.

This is a very arbitrary choice. The foundation of the Hôpital Général was only an administrative reorganization of three existing institutions, the Salpêtrière, Bicêtre and the Hôpital de la Pitié, to provide for the poor of Paris 'of both sexes, of all ages and from all localities, of whatever breeding or birth, in whatever state they may be, able-bodied or invalid, sick or convalescent, curable or incurable'.[25] The measure did not apply specifically to lunatics. It did not involve any new accommodation, or any new methods of confining people.

Foucault links it to the absolutist and monarchical government of France, but concedes that 'In England, the origins of confinement are more remote',[26] and mentions an Act of 1575 covering both 'the punishment of vagabonds and the relief of the poor' in bridewells or houses of correction. As we have seen, the first bridewell was set up in London in 1555, but this was a means of keeping vagrants out of gaol rather than a Great Confinement.

Richard Hunter and Ida Macalpine's *Three Hundred Years of Psychiatry, 1535–1860*[27] suggests a much earlier starting date, but the focus of this splendid lucky dip for students of the mental health services is very largely on the work of the medical profession, and the title is possibly misleading. Psychiatry as a medical specialism has not existed since 1535: it is a twentieth-century term, and a twentieth-century specialism. Much of the early material is only tenuously connected to the theme. W.F. Bynum notes that a standard *Dictionary of Psychological Medicine*, published in 1892 does not contain an entry for the word 'psychiatry'.[28]

Psychiatry depends on taking a rational view of Unreason. The belief that insanity was the result of a compact with the Devil died very slowly, and persisted long after the repeal of the Witchcraft Act in rural and remote areas. Only the development of Reason made it possible to make a more dispassionate analysis: before the middle of the eighteenth century, the frame of reference for the study of insanity simply does not exist.

Attitude changes are often slow and patchy. All we can be sure about is that some time after the repeal of the Witchcraft Act and before the American and French Revolutions, which mark an advance in the understanding of liberty, influential people began to be concerned about lunatics. This new concern was part of a wider social change. The tide of industrial development brought an intensification of social distress in both the crowded urban areas and the depopulated rural communities. The very force of misery produced a new social conscience, a desire to tackle many problems of poverty and sickness and ignorance which had previously been taken for granted.

The change began imperceptibly, through a series of apparently disconnected events, each of which aroused a different kind of public interest. In 1714 and 1744, dangerous lunatics were specially considered in a revision of the vagrancy laws; in 1763, the public was alarmed by revelations concerning conditions in private mad-houses, and a movement to control them was initiated; in 1789, the nature of George III's illness became generally known, and the topic of madness was widely discussed in a context which excluded the possibility of moral condemnation. It was scarcely possible – at least in Tory circles – to assume that the King was being punished for his sins. It is only in the light of later developments that these disparate happenings assumed a relevance to each other.

Lunatics under the Vagrancy Laws

The perennial problems of vagrancy tended to be reviewed every thirty or forty years through the sixteenth, seventeenth and eighteenth centuries. Dr Parry-Jones points out that the provision whereby the 'furiously and dangerously mad' might be confined on the warrant of two magistrates, and 'kept safely locked up in some secure place' as long as their madness should continue, was first contained in the Vagrancy Act of 1714.[29] This is the origin of the 'magistrate's order': there was a safeguard in the requirement that, while other vagrants might be confined on the order of a single magistrate, the 'furiously and dangerously mad' required two. In 1744, a further Vagrancy Act marked another stage in development by adding the intention that they should be 'cured'. Though it did not specify the means by which 'cure' could be carried out, this is the origin of a commitment to treatment on the part of public authorities.

Vagrancy Acts no longer included scholars in the definition of 'Rogues and Vagabonds' (a Tudor Act refers to 'all Psons [sic] calling themselves Schollers going about the country begging'); but the Act of 1714 included 'Minstrels Juglers all Persons pretending to be Gipsies or wandring in the Habit or Form of counterfeit Egyptians or pretending to have Skill in Physiognomy, Palmestry or like crafty Science ... all Persons able in Body who run away and leave their Wives or Children to the Parish'. The 1744 Act omitted the references to 'crafty Science' (since witchcraft was no longer a crime) but added 'Persons found in Forests with Guns'.

Lunatics were thus added to a band of travelling showmen,

marital defaulters, poachers and other undesirables. The 'secure place' in which they were detained was usually a gaol or house of correction, since those were the only places which possessed the means of preventing escapes.

Private madhouses, 1763–1774

The question of illegal detention was raised in connection with the small private madhouses where people of property might be confined at the instance of relatives interested in the estate. Dr Parry-Jones has defended the reputation of private madhouses:

> The constitution of the private madhouse, as an institution run for profit, always exposed it to accusations of malpractice, and its history was chequered by repeated disclosures of infamous practices. The more disreputable aspects of the private madhouse system have received considerable attention, and this has led, generally, to a biassed conception of the private madhouse.[30]

Dr Parry-Jones's study is based on documents kept by madhouse keepers, who were unlikely to record their own abuses for posterity. He relies heavily, though not exclusively, on a collection of documents from two private madhouses in Oxfordshire; and he does not cover the London madhouses at all – on the grounds that they have 'always received greater publicity and documentation in the reports of parliamentary enquiries and in other publications'.[31] Not all private madhouses engaged in malpractice. There were some good small establishments run by members of the medical profession; but abuse was always possible, particularly where people of property were concerned, and often reflected family battles about inheritance.

One well-documented case is that of Dame Sarah Clerke, a rich elderly woman who supported a number of relatives. Her brothers, Sir Edward and Arthur Turnor, had her forcibly confined, 'struggling ... & railing' and 'crying out for help'.[32] She was eventually freed on a writ of Habeas Corpus from the Lord Chief Justice. The usual practice was to require that a physician appointed by the court should be given access to the patient. If he reported that the patient was sane, the proprietor of the madhouse was then required to produce the patient in court. Dame Sarah had powerful allies, including at least one member of her husband's family, Sir Talbot Clerke, and the case appears to have been primarily a dispute over inheritance between the Clerkes and the Turnors. In the case of *Rex* v. *Turlington* in 1761,[33] a motion was made on behalf of the relatives of Mrs Deborah D'Vebre for a Habeas Corpus to be directed to Turlington, the keeper of a private madhouse in Chelsea. Mrs D'Vebre had been sent there at the instance of her husband. A rule was made that a physician, together with the patient's nearest blood relation, Peter Bodkin, should 'at all proper times and reasonable hours respectively be admitted, and have free access to Mrs Deborah D'Vebre . . . at the madhouse kept by Robert Turlington in Chelsea'.

Two days later, an affidavit from the physician was read in court. It stated that he 'saw no reason to suspect that she was or had been disordered in her mind: on the contrary, he found her to be very sensible, and very cool and dispassionate'. Mrs D'Vebre was produced in court, and allowed to leave with her attorney.

In another case, *Rex* v. *Clarke* in 1762,[34] the attempt to serve a writ of Habeas Corpus was defeated by an affidavit from the appointed physician that the patient, Mrs Anne Hunt, was in an acute state of mental disorder, and had in fact been sent to the madhouse on his own advice.

The interest aroused by the Turlington case and the Clarke case caused a growing degree of public concern which was fanned by the publication of an article in the *Gentleman's Magazine* in 1763:

When a person is forcibly taken or artfully decoyed into a private madhouse, he is, without any authority or any further charge than that of a mercenary relation or a pretended friend, instantly siezed upon by a set of inhuman ruffians trained up to this barbarous profession, stripped naked, and conveyed to a dark room. If he complains, or asks the reasons for this dreadful usage, the attendant brutishly orders him not to rave, calls for assistance, and ties him down to a bed, from which he is not released until he submits to their pleasure . . .

Next morning, a doctor is gravely introduced by the master of the house, to receive the report of the under-keeper or waiter, in consequence of which the doctor pronounces the unfortunate person a lunatic, and declares that he must be reduced by physic. If the revolted victim offers to argue against it by alleging any proofs of sanity . . . he is then deemed raving mad: the banditti of the whole house are called in, the forcing instruments brought, upon which the sensible patient must submit to take whatever is administered.

When the poor patient thus finds himself deprived of all communication with the world, and denied the use of pen and paper, all he can do is to compose himself under the unhappy situation in the hope of a more favourable report. But any composure under such affliction is immediately deemed a melancholy or sulky fit ... the doctor prescribes a repetition of the dose ... until the patient is so debilitated in body that in time it impairs his mind ... What must a rational mind suffer that is treated in this irrational manner?'[35]

The article contrasts the condition of patients in private mad-houses with that of patients in the new lunatic hospitals which were being set up in London and some provincial cities by public subscription. In the public hospitals, the writer comments, 'no impatient heir can be gratified ... There are no masters or keepers to enrich, no fees for doctors, no perquisites to servants, and no deprivation of fortune'. He ends with an appeal to Parliament to frame regulations designed to prevent the imprisonment of sane people, and in the same year the House of Commons set up a Select Committee on the State of Private Madhouses.[36]

The report of this committee makes curious reading. The members apparently found it necessary to proceed with extreme discretion, since London madhouses confined the relatives of many prominent people, and a number of well-known members of the medical profession had financial interests in private madhouses. They confined their study to two houses – Miles', at Hoxton, and Turlington's, in Chelsea – and to the detailed study of only one case in each house. They stressed in their short report that these were not selected cases, and that hundreds of similar examples existed, but stated that they refrained from publishing further cases out of consideration for the families of sufferers. The two cases were relatively mild ones – a Mrs Gold, who had been confined at Hoxton for three weeks eight years earlier, and a Mrs Hawley, thought to be an habitual drunkard.

The report was notable for a clash of medical opinion. Dr Battie of St Luke's Hospital was asked if he had ever met with cases in which persons of undoubted sanity were confined as lunatics. His reply was that 'It frequently happened'; but Dr Monro of Bethlem flatly contradicted Battie's statement, and said that no such cases existed.[37]

Eleven years passed before the Act for Regulating Private Madhouses 1774 became law. It did not apply to pauper lunatics in madhouses, nor to single lunatics. No person was to take charge of more than one lunatic without a licence. In the metropolitan area ('within the cities of London and Westminster, and within seven miles of the same, and within the County of Middlesex') licensing was to be carried out by five Commissioners elected from their number by the President and Fellows of the Royal College of Physicians for this purpose. They were to visit all licensed houses 'between the Hours of Eight and Five in the Day-time' and were to make notes in writing of the condition of the patients.

> In case the Commissioners upon their Visitation shall discover any Thing that, in their Opinion, shall deserve Censure or Animadversion, they shall, in that case, report the same; and such Part of their Report and no more shall be hung up in the Censor's Room of the College, to be perused and inspected by any Person who shall apply for that Purpose.

A keeper who refused to admit the Commissioners forfeited his licence. Notice was to be sent to the Secretary of the Commissioners by the keeper within three days of the reception of a patient.

Outside the metropolitan area, licensing was to be carried out by the justices at Quarter Sessions.

The Act applied only to a limited section of patients, and had many weaknesses. The most glaring of these was that the Commissioners had no power to revoke licences on the grounds of illtreatment or neglect of patients. A keeper would forfeit his licence if he refused to admit the official visitors; but as long as he admitted them, whatever the conditions, they could take no action except that of displaying their report in a place where few could see it and none would have their attention drawn to it.

This Act remained almost a dead letter. Its significance lies in the fact that it was the basis from which the later work of the Lunacy Commissioners developed.

The King's illness

The 'madness' of George III has been the subject of much modern speculation. Macalpine and Hunter[38] have argued that the condition was not mental illness, but a rare metabolic disorder known as variegated porphyria. However, medical practitioners do not usually diagnose without examining the patient. When the patient has been dead for the better part of two hundred years, and the only evidence consists of the records of eighteenth-century medical practitioners, diagnosis is a somewhat dubious procedure. In this case the evidence is weak.

Variegated porphyria is an inherited metabolic disorder.[39] It can cause painful weakness in the arms and legs, hoarseness and difficulty in articulation, wasted muscles, giddiness, visual and auditory disturbances, sleeplessness, convulsions and delirium. So, of course, can many other medical conditions. The distinguishing feature of variegated porphyria is that the patient passes purple urine. The medical records on George III mention six instances of discoloured urine, described as 'dark' or 'bloody' or 'bilious' (not purple); but many other conditions, such as kidney failure, internal bleeding or dosing with senna, also produce discoloured urine, as any medical or nursing text-book will indicate. As Macalpine and Hunter note, the treatment administered by his doctors – beatings, confinement, purges and vomits, and blisters and bleeding – could have caused a deterioration in the King's physical condition. The 'variegated porphyria' theory is supported by John Brooke in his biography of George III; but a foreword by the present Prince of Wales, who has studied the documents on his ancestor's illness in the Royal Library, comes to the conclusion that the King was probably suffering from an unidentified form of toxic confusion.[40]

Macalpine and Hunter's attempt to extend the diagnosis back to the Tudors and Stuarts (porphyria is a Mendelian dominant, which means that about half the progeny will inherit) is unconvincing, as is the suggestion that George IV inherited porphyria from his father. George IV was, understandably, in view of his bulk and his appetite, known to be bilious. 'It is tempting to take this as evidence', record Macalpine and Hunter;[41] but it is not evidence, and the verdict must be 'not proven'.

From the historical standpoint, the real nature of George III's illness is immaterial. The debate does not affect the impact of his illness on his contemporaries. It was believed that he was suffering from mental derangement, and his treatment was prescribed according to the dominant medical paradigms of the time.

The supposed nature of the King's illness did not become public knowledge until 1788, when the attack was so severe that he became incapable of carrying out the affairs of state for several months. The Prince of Wales later described it to his friends:

> He told us that he was present when the King was first seized with his mental disorder: that His Majesty caught him with both his hands by the collar, pushing him against the wall with some violence, and asked him who would dare say to a King of England that he should not speak out, or who should prevent his whispering. His Majesty then whispered.[42]

The King's doctors, Dr Warren and Sir Lucas Pepys, were not optimistic about a swift recovery, but the fate of the administration hung precisely on this point. If the King's illness lasted more than a few months, a Regent would have to be appointed. The Prince of Wales left no doubt in the minds of his adherents that his first action would be to dismiss the younger Pitt and his colleagues, and to install the 'Carlton House set', headed by Charles James Fox, in their place.

Pitt and his colleagues needed a more optimistic opinion to preserve themselves in office. They called in Dr Francis Willis, a former vicar of Wapping who had left his living to practise as a physician and run a private madhouse in Lincolnshire. The King appears to have taken an instant dislike to Dr Willis, and taxed him at his first interview with having abandoned the Church for profit – a rebuke to which Willis rejoined that the Saviour had cured demoniacs. 'Yes,' said the King, 'but he did not get £700 a year for it.' Fulke Greville recounts that the King offered Willis any preferment he wished if he would return to his former calling.[43]

Willis's first step was to acquire ascendancy over the mind of his patient by intimidation. The King was immediately separated from his wife, and kept in fear of the straitjacket. According to Countess Harcourt:

> The unhappy patient ... was no longer treated as a human

being. His body was immediately encased in a machine which left it no liberty of motion. He was sometimes chained to a staple. He was frequently beaten and starved, and at best he was kept in subjection by menacing and violent language. The history of the King's illness showed that the most exalted station did not wholly exempt the sufferer from this stupid and inhuman usage.[44]

On 11 November 1788, Lord Bulkeley wrote to the Marquis of Buckingham, 'We have been at Windsor the last three mornings, and sorry I am to tell you that poor Rex's state seems worse than a thousand deaths.'[45]

By the end of 1788, the King's condition was being openly discussed in clubs and coffee-houses. There was despondency at White's, the Tory stronghold, and exultation at Brooke's, where the Prince of Wales and the Duke of York freely discussed their father's illness, and made it a subject for merriment. A Regency Bill passed the Commons on 12 February 1789. Whig Ladies wore 'Regency caps' and 'Regency favours', and it was said in Brooke's that Mrs FitzHerbert was to be created a duchess; but the King frustrated all these plans, whether because of or in spite of the treatment of Dr Willis, by making a recovery. In March 1789 he was much better; on 23 April, he attended a public service of thanksgiving in St Paul's Cathedral. Dr Willis returned to Lincoln-shire, the Whigs shelved their plans of political triumph, and the Prince of Wales reluctantly made his peace with his father.

There were further episodes of illness in 1801, 1804 and 1805. Dr. Willis and his sons were sent for; again the straitjacket, the cauterizing irons and the herbal remedies were produced. In 1805 – he was then sixty-seven years of age – the King's sight began to fail. The final descent into illness, from which he did not recover, came in 1810, and was attributed to the death of his favourite child, the Princess Amelia. Dr Willis had died in 1807, but his sons, Dr Robert and Dr John Willis, returned to take charge of the King. He was confined to a suite of rooms at Windsor, where he found solace in Handel's music, and hymn singing, and gradually slipped into senility.

The Regency Bill became law in 1811, and the King lived on until 1820, through more than thirty years of intermittent illness. His death was little more than a reminder of his long-drawn-out life. *The Times* provided a sympathetic commentary: 'Thus has ended a course of personal suffering, long and affectionately deplored by every honest Englishman' and referred to the King's 'escape from that dreary prison-house of the soul, of which no sane mind can fully understand the horrors . . .'[46] Public opinion was changing.

CHAPTER 2

Moral Treatment and County Asylums

In the second half of the eighteenth century, medical men began to experiment with more humane methods of care and treatment, and hospitals were set up in some cities by public subscription. St Luke's in London and the Manchester Lunatic Hospital are of particular interest. St Luke's seems to have been the first hospital for the insane to admit medical students. The Manchester Lunatic Hospital practised 'tender treatment of the insane'; but both continued to use the standard remedies of bleeding, purging, blistering and vomits. The Retreat at York, a Quaker establishment, abandoned these methods after a short period of experimentation, and developed 'moral treatment'. This gentle régime was to be adopted in a number of the first county asylums, which were set up under an Act of 1808 to provide a means of treatment for lunatics in gaols and workhouses.

ST LUKE'S HOSPITAL

Reference has already been made to Dr Battie's dispute with Dr Monro of Bethlem before the Select Committee of 1763. St Luke's, where Battie was the physician, was founded in 1751 by public subscription. A pamphlet entitled *Reasons for Establishing St Luke's,* published in 1817, makes the following points: Bethlem was overcrowded, and had lengthy waiting lists; people of means were frequently reduced to poverty by insanity, and the workhouse was not a suitable place for them; and if medical students were to acquire a competent knowledge of the forms and treatment of insanity, a hospital must be established where they would be able to observe and study cases, as they could not at Bethlem.[1]

St Luke's quickly developed into an institution rivalling Bethlem in everything but age. In 1758, Dr Battie published a pamphlet in which he gave an account of his methods of treatment. This was construed by Dr John Monro as an attack on his father, and he published a printed reply in the same year. The paragraph which chiefly gave offence was that in which Battie wrote of insanity: 'This distemper is as little understood as any that ever afflicted mankind, because the care of lunatics is entrusted to empiricks, or at best to a few select physicians, most of whom think it advisable to keep the cases as well as the patients to themselves.'[2] John Monro's reply was tart:

By a few select physicians, I presume are intended the physicians of Bethlem Hospital, whom I consider it as a duty incumbent upon me to defend against any injurious reflections.

Monro described his father as 'a man of admirable discernment (who) treated this disease with an address that will not soon be equalled'.[3]

Dr Battie spoke also of 'the impertinent curiosity of those who think it pastime to converse with Madmen and to play on their passions'. Such visitors were strictly forbidden at St Luke's. Battie advocated generally a quiet and natural form of treatment, without violent vomits and purges, and with a sufficiency of simple food 'not highly seasoned and full of poignancy'. He believed that the condition of many patients could be alleviated by diversion, and that an asylum should provide 'amusements ... rendered more agreeable by a well-timed variety'.

THE MANCHESTER LUNATIC HOSPITAL

Manchester had a comprehensive scheme for the treatment of mental and bodily illness in patients of means. The parent body was the Infirmary, founded in 1752, and attached to it were the Lunatic Hospital, the Lying-in Hospital, the Eye Hospital and the Lock Hospital, occupying contiguous sites.[4] This chain of hospitals was raised by public subscription, and largely administered by the trustees of the Infirmary. The Lunatic Hospital was completed in 1765. Physical violence was not to be used on the patients, unless it was 'necessary to restrain the Furious from hurting themselves or others'. Mechanical restraint was used, as it was also provided that 'the feet of those in straw or chains be carefully examined, gently rubbed night and morning, and covered with flannel during the winter'.[5] Treatment was otherwise mainly medical, and consisted, according to an account written by the infirmary physician in 1795, of the usual methods of blood-letting, blistering, purging and drugs. Dr Ferriar noted that tartar emetic acted 'briskly' and 'had an instantaneous effect in restoring a degree of rationality' in maniacal cases. Blood-letting was practised on 'the young and plethoric maniac whose eyes are turgid and inflamed, who passes the night without sleep, and whose pulse is quick and full', but Ferriar also gave warning that frequent repetition might prove dangerous. Opium was used in 'large doses in maniacal cases'.[6]

Although the medical treatment was no advance on the usual methods of the day, the physicians seem to have realized that other factors also affected patients' mental condition. The trustees reported in 1783 that 'Those whose condition will admit it are allowed to walk with their friends in a large adjoining garden', and Dr Ferriar wrote 'Small favours, the shew of confidence and apparent distinction, accelerate recovery.'[7]

Public sight-seeing was specifically forbidden by the rules. The physician was to see his patients twice a week, or more often if necessary, and was to keep a record of all his cases. The house visitors of the Infirmary were to visit the Lunatic Hospital daily to investigate the behaviour of the keepers and the domestic staff to the patients, and to examine the sleeping accommodation.

The Lunatic Hospital's claim to a place in the history of reform depends less on its medical treatment than on its tentative approach to what later became known as 'moral treatment', and the close connection with the parent Infirmary. For the first time, a distinct form of patient care for lunatics was recognized as being related to the treatment of physical illness, and the terms 'hospital' and 'patient' were used.

The Retreat was founded in 1792 by the Society of Friends. It was unique in two ways: first, because it was neither a subscription hospital nor a private asylum, being financed and organized on a non-profit-making basis by a religious sect; and second, because it evolved a form of treatment based, not on the scanty medical knowledge of the time, but on gentle Christianity and common sense.

The city of York already possessed a subscription asylum – the York Asylum, founded in 1777. The conduct of the asylum was wrapped in secrecy, the Governors and the physician resisting any attempt at visitation and inspection. Until 1790, would-be reformers could point to nothing more concrete than the general reluctance of the authorities to open the building to responsible enquirers, and the complaints, easily discredited, of ex-patients.

In 1790 or 1791,[8] a patient called Hannah Mills was sent to the asylum, and her relatives, who lived at some distance from the city, recommended her to the care of the Society of Friends. Friends who tried to visit her were refused admission on the grounds that she was 'not in a suitable state to be seen by strangers', and she subsequently died under circumstances which aroused strong suspicions of ill-treatment and neglect.

The project for the Retreat was a direct result of Hannah Mills' death. It was primarily the brainchild of William Tuke, a York tea and coffee merchant. The Governors of the York Asylum were a powerful and influential body in the city. Reform was impossible until some other system of treatment had been tried and found successful. The Friends proceeded to buy eleven acres of land at a cost of £1,357, and to approve a building estimate of nearly £2000. These sums were raised by private donation and covenant from members of the Society by the end of 1797.

It was significant that the new institution was named neither 'hospital' nor 'asylum'. Daniel Hack Tuke states that 'The Retreat' was suggested by his grandmother, William's daughter-in-law, 'to convey the idea of what such an institution should be, namely . . . a quiet haven in which the shattered bark might find the means of reparation or of safety'.[9]

The pleasantness of the site was described in the first 'Visiter's Book' of the Retreat by a Swiss doctor named Delarive, who visited the establishment in 1798: 'Cette maison est située á une mille de York, au milieu d'une campagne fertile et riante; ce n'est point l'idée d'une prison qu'elle fait naître, mais plutôt celle d'une grande ferme rustique; elle est entourée d'un jardin fermé.' The Retreat was built to accommodate thirty patients, either members of the Society of Friends or recommended by members. There were several grades of accommodation, the cost ranging from eight shillings to fifteen shillings weekly. Patients' servants could be accommodated for a further six shillings a week.

Samuel Tuke's *A Description of the Retreat* (1813), which is dedicated to his grandfather William, gives a very detailed account of the establishment, the reasons for it, the staff, the management and the method of treatment. For some time, William Tuke himself acted as superintendent, and Timothy Maude, 'a friend of great worth as well as medical knowledge' was appointed visiting physician; but Maude died within three months of taking up his appointment, and Dr Thomas Fowler replaced him. After a period of trial and error, he came to believe that his 'sanguine expectations' of the efficacy of medical methods of treatment were disappointed. He came to the 'painful conclusion . . . that medicine, as yet, possessed very inadequate means to relieve the most grievous of human diseases'[10] and that 'moral' methods of treatment were preferable to medical methods.

In 1797, Tuke relinquished the day-to-day control of administration, and a lay male superintendent was appointed. This was George Jepson, who later married the female superintendent, Katharine Allen. William Tuke continued to act as secretary and treasurer, and still found time to know the patients individually, and to supervise the details of their treatment in many cases. Jepson thought that an abundant diet of 'meat, bread and good porter' was more effective than a policy of semi-starvation, and that porter was as successful as opium in inducing sound sleep, and less detrimental to the constitution. Good food, air, exercise and occupation took the place of drastic medical methods.

The Tukes believed that many patients could be rational and controllable, provided that they were not aggravated by cruelty, hostility or harsh methods of restraint. Patients were never punished for failure to control their behaviour, but certain amenities were given to them in order to foster self-control by a show of trust. The female superintendent gave tea-parties, to which the patients were invited, and for which they were encouraged to wear their best clothes. There was an airing court in the grounds for each class of patients, and each court was supplied with small animals – rabbits, poultry and others – so that the patients might learn self-control by having dependent on them creatures weaker than themselves.

Every attempt was made to find occupation for the patients. Some cared for the animals, some helped in the garden, the women knitted or sewed. Writing materials were provided, and books were carefully chosen for a patients' library. Books on mathematics and the classics were recommended as 'the most useful class of subjects on which to employ the minds of the insane'. Religious meetings were held at the Retreat, and parties of patients were taken from time to time to share in the worship of the city Quakers.

An account by Samuel Tuke of the reception of a violent patient illustrates the antithesis between the old system and the new:

> Some years ago, a man of Herculean size and figure was brought to the house . . . so constantly during the present attack had he been kept chained, that his clothes were contrived to be taken off and put on by means of strings, without removing his manacles. They were . . . taken off when he entered the Retreat, and he was ushered into an apartment where the superintendents were supping. He was calm. His attention appeared to be arrested by his new situation. He was desired to join in the repast, during which he behaved with tolerable propriety . . . the maniac was sensible of the kindness of his treatment. He promised to restrain himself, and he so completely succeeded that during his stay no coercive means were ever employed towards him . . . in about four months, he was discharged, perfectly recovered.[11]

'Point de barreau, point de grillages aux fenêtres', wrote Delarive. The windows of the Retreat were specially designed to look like ordinary windows, the iron sashes being painted to resemble wooden ones. Restraint was seldom used, except to prevent a patient from injuring himself or his fellows. Chains were never used, and the strait waistcoat only as a last resort. Extracts from the case-history of a patient named Wilson Sutton give a vivid picture of the degree of forbearance which this system demanded of the keepers:

1814. 12th August. Today after a walk in the country and eating a good dinner, while the attendants were at theirs he became quarrelsome – struck Josh Whiting hurt Saml. Lays head and neck. After this he was shut up in a room to get calm.

1815. 15th January. When S.L. has come into sight, he has fallen on him furiously with his fists.

20th February ... seized Saml. Smith his attendant and threatened to throw him downstairs, breaking his watch and chain and straining his thumb.

16th September. Fecht him (Smith) a blow betwixt the eyes.

Sutton was then placed in the strait waistcoat for a few hours, but when freed, he seized an iron fender and felled the unfortunate Smith with it.

11th October. He has since conducted himself in a peaceable manner, but has not deigned to speak to S.S.[12]

The household bills for the Retreat in this period show frequent expenditure on porter, and on such luxury items as wines, oranges and figs. Samuel Tuke referred to the community of staff and patients as 'the family', and the accounts show expenditure like that of an ordinary middle-class household: in 1796, when the Retreat was originally furnished, there are bills for beds and bedding, sheets, blankets, bags of goose feathers and counterpanes; for beer jugs, coffee mugs, cream jugs, cutlery and cruets.

The Visitor's Book shows that from the earliest days, the Retreat received distinguished visitors – English philanthropists such as Robert Owen and Elizabeth Fry; medical men such as Dr Delarive and a Dr Duncan from Dublin who described it as 'the best-regulated establishment in Europe'; writers and thinkers such as Sydney Smith, who wrote his famous article 'Mad Quakers'[13] immediately after reading Samuel Tuke's *Description of the Retreat*. No fewer than three parties were sent over by the Russian royal family. One included the Grand Duke Nicholas, and another the Grand Duke Michael. Perhaps the most picturesque visitors were the seven Red Indian braves who had been brought over to England to appear in a London theatre. After they had toured the building, their chief offered up a short prayer of thanks, and Quakers and warriors remained for some few minutes in prayerful silence.[14] The Quakers, though they were a religious sect, were never bigots.

Michel Foucault's 'Gallocentric' standpoint[15] results in misconceptions about the Retreat and the Quaker way of life. He states that the Retreat was 'an instrument of segregation . . . a moral and religious segregation which sought to reconstruct around madness a milieu as much as possible like the community of Quakers'.[16] It was a community of Quakers, who were at this time an exclusive religious sect: they did not, for example, permit 'marrying out' – marriage to non-Quakers. The Retreat was established because the Quaker way was not to protest against the ways of the outside world, but to show a better way by example.

Foucault's allegation that 'the fear instituted at the Retreat is of very great depth'[17] is a misunderstanding. Samuel Tuke's *Description of the Retreat* makes it clear that the Tukes were wholly against 'the terrific system' of intimidation, beatings and physical weakening through bleeding, vomits and purges.[18]

Foucault quotes four passages in Samuel Tuke's book to illustrate the repressive nature of the system at the Retreat. The first is the case of the 'maniac' who had his manacles removed, and was invited to dine with the superintendents. The comment is 'Tuke created an asylum where he substituted for the free terror of madness the stifling anguish of responsibility'.[19] Thus a purely human gesture of trust (involving some risk to the superintendents) is interpreted as a sinister form of repression.

The second is the affair of the Lady Superintendent's tea-parties. Foucault sees the patient 'incessantly cast in this empty role of the unknown visitor';[20] but for early nineteenth-century Quakers, tea-parties would have been part of normal social life. Foucault cannot have understood the traditions of *le five-o'clock*.

The third is the allegation that 'work comes first in moral treatment as practised at the Retreat'.[21] This is simply not supported by the evidence. The Tukes arranged amusements, diversions and occupation for the patients, because it was better for them to keep busy than to sit around moping or hallucinating. Some helped in the house or the garden. Samuel Tuke notes that sedentary occupations were generally best for the 'maniacal class', while 'the most active and exciting kind of occupation' was generally encouraged for melancholy patients. 'No strict rule, however, can properly be laid down on this subject; and the inclination of the patient may generally be indulged, except the occupation he desires obviously tends to foster his disease.'[22]

Finally, there is the case of the keeper who was threatened by a patient with a large stone. The keeper might have called for help. He might have tried to subdue the patient. What he did was to look the patient in the eye, and tell him to put the stone down. The patient complied. This is construed as 'Surveillance and Judgement'.[23]

'Tuke,' says Foucault, 'reconstitutes around madness a simulated family.' This is true enough. The patients at the Retreat had been rejected by their own families in frightening and confusing circumstances. The good middle-class family, with its warmth and affection, was the best model available at the time. Of course it was paternalistic by late twentieth-century standards; but in comparison with the inhuman treatment in Bedlam and elsewhere at the time, a substitute family represented an enormous advance in understanding.

Quakers believed (and still believe) in the 'inner light' which enables every man and woman to distinguish between right and wrong action. They believe that the ability to get on with other people can be strengthened by trust and affection. Foucault evidently does not share this view of human nature, but it is difficult to see how he could regard it as repressive. Many modern therapeutic groups operate on very similar principles.[24]

Anne Digby gives a good description of the Retreat in its early days, and its policy of 'controlled openness'. It had to be closed for a time in 1832 because of a cholera epidemic. Until 1820 the patient population was exclusively Quaker, and even by 1846 only one-eighth was non-Quaker.[25] She describes the image of the Retreat's work presented by Samuel Tuke's *Description* as 'to some extent a misleading one' on the grounds that it is 'written from a reformist standpoint'; it 'neglects the Retreat's antecedents'; it is selective in describing its therapy; and it is 'optimistic about the outcome'.[26] The Retreat was certainly 'not a typical asylum'. It was small, it catered for patients of some means, and Quakers were hardly a violent section of the community; but most of Tuke's claims can be checked in the records – the case-books, the accounts and the minutes of meetings are all available to scholars at the Borthwick Institute in York.

It is hardly fair to say that Samuel Tuke 'neglected the Retreat's antecedents'. St Luke's and the Manchester Lunatic Hospital were medical establishments, and the Retreat was not. Though humane treatment was not a complete novelty, moral treatment on non-medical lines was new. Andrew Scull has a useful passage[27] in which he describes in some detail the experiments in medical treatment carried out by the physicians in the first five years of the Retreat's operation, and the decision to dispense with medical treatment altogether. After 1801, 'the visiting physician confined his attention to treating cases of bodily illness, and it was the lay people who were in charge of the day-to-day running of the institution'. Samuel Tuke was not 'selective' in describing the system of moral treatment: by 1812, it was the accepted system at the Retreat, and it had no antecedents.

Samuel Tuke was, of course, a good publicist, and all good publicists put up their best case. He had to convince the Quaker community that the Retreat was worth supporting; but he was 'reformist' because he believed deeply that moral treatment could be practised on a much wider scale in the developing county asylums, and that this humane system could supersede the indignities practised in the name of medicine.

Dr Digby dislikes the family model, pointing out that the family can be 'a more negative, even destructive force, its claustrophobic inner life inhibiting independent growth and its authoritarian parental control constraining the individuality of children';[28] but this is late twentieth-century thinking. There were few critics of family life two centuries ago, and they would not have been found in Quaker circles. She does note that the records 'suggest a tender solicitude' rather than the domineering role suggested by Foucault.[29]

Fiona Godlee, in an original and stimulating paper,[30] asks how it happened that the Quakers, an 'unruly sect' of the seventeenth century, became a model of respectability in the eighteenth. Quakers had been known for the 'convulsive trembling' which gave them their name, for religious excess, and for an insubordinate attitude to authority, the men refusing to take off their hats as a mark of respect, and both sexes using the familiar 'thee' and 'thou' in conversation with persons of authority; yet at the end of the eighteenth century, 'once the worst of madmen, the Quakers were the best of mad-keepers'. Quakers, like other Nonconformists, did become extremely respectable towards the end of the eighteenth century, and there was a considerable conformity in matters of dress, religious observation and 'preoccupation with social niceties' in the newly prosperous commercial classes. By the 1790s, Quakers had their own very clear social norms, which were reflected in the Retreat.

The Retreat catered only for a restricted section of society. It was small enough to be referred to as 'the family', and sufficiently well endowed to be run on the lines of a comfortable guest-house. To say this is not to minimize the extent of the achievement, but merely to point out that conditions were particularly favourable to success. The influence of the Retreat on less-favoured institutions was to prove immense. It removed the final justification for neglect, brutality and crude medical methods, and it proved that 'judicious kindness' was more effective than rigorous confinement.

THE FOUNDATION OF COUNTY ASYLUMS

Lunacy reform began on a national scale with the foundation of the county asylums, following the County Asylums Act of 1808; but no reform takes place in a vacuum, and it is necessary to refer briefly to the movements in thought and in philanthropic practice which bridge the gap between the small local reforms of the late eighteenth century and the parliamentary reform movement of the early nineteenth.

The ideas and ideals of the 1790s form an immense contrast to those of fifty years earlier. Reasoned apathy had been replaced by violent emotion. 'Cosmic Toryism' was challenged on all sides – by Paine, by Godwin, by Malthus, by Bentham. The Americans had rejected George III; France rejected the Bourbons; the religious became converted, the literary wrote lyrical poetry, the politically-minded talked of revolution. Out of this intellectual and social ferment, and the effects of agricultural and industrial change, arose two movements which were to have a decisive effect on lunacy reform: Evangelicalism and Utilitarianism.

The Evangelical Movement started from the Clapham Sect –
that group of 'lay saints' who gathered round William Wilberforce,
the slave trade reformer, in the years 1795–1808. They made use of
experience gained in the world of politics and business to develop a
concrete policy for social action. Societies for the reform of particular abuses became the fashion, and each cause had its small group
of parliamentary adherents who were ready to press for legislative
action.

Evangelical humanism stemmed from an emotional appreciation
of the plight of the poor and oppressed; but Utilitarianism came
from cold reason, from a fundamental love of order, a hatred of
administrative confusion. Its dominant figure was Jeremy Bentham;
his disciples were Edwin Chadwick and John Stuart Mill. The
Utilitarians were both a philosophical school and a political group.
They were without a sense of history, being characterized by 'a
volcanic desire for utter, organic, sweeping change'.[31] They were
not concerned with the plight of the insane from any sense of pity.
Bentham himself considered it right and proper that lunatics should
be kept under constant surveillance and in perpetual solitude; they
were among the social groups for whom the Panopticon was
designed;[32] but he taught his followers to detest legal anomalies,
and to think in terms of public responsibility.

In 1806, the new train of events was set in motion by a
Benthamite, Sir George Onesiphorus Paul, the High Sheriff of
Gloucestershire, who addressed a letter to the Secretary of State
urging him to take action concerning the condition of criminal and
pauper lunatics. Paul was a prison reformer who had known John
Howard, and had personally designed the new county gaol and
bridewells erected at Gloucester. He was also President of the
Stroud Society for Providing Medical Attention for the Poor, and
his experience led him to consider criminal and pauper lunatics as
two components of a single problem. Of pauper lunatics, he wrote
in his letter:

> I believe there is hardly a parish of any considerable size in
> which there may not be found some unfortunate human creature
> of this description, who, if his ill-treatment has made him phre-
> netic, is chained in the cellar or garret of a workhouse, fastened
> to the leg of a table, tied to a post in an outhouse, or perhaps
> shut up in an uninhabited ruin; or if his lunacy be inoffensive,

left to ramble half naked and half starved through the streets and highways, teased by the scoff and jest of all that is ignorant, vulgar and unfeeling.[33]

In the prisons, the position had been complicated by the Criminal Lunatics Act of 1800, which provided for the first time for detention 'during His Majesty's pleasure'. This covered persons found guilty at the time the crime was committed, those found insane on arraignment, and also any person 'discovered or apprehended under circumstances that denote a derangement of mind and a purpose of committing some crime' – a sort of preventive detention. The Act had not directed where these different classes were to be housed.

There was a case for the construction of a new type of institution where pauper and criminal lunatics could be treated as insane persons, and not primarily as paupers or criminals.

The Select Committee report of 1807

A Select Committee of the House of Commons 'to inquire into the State of Criminal and Pauper Lunatics in England and Wales, and the Laws relating thereto' was appointed in January 1807, shortly after the setting up of Charles James Fox's Ministry of All the Talents – a brief Whig episode in long decades of Toryism. The committee included members of both political parties, and some well-known names: Charles Williams-Wynn, then Under-Secretary of State for the Home Department; George Rose, sponsor of the Friendly Societies Act of 1793; Samuel Romilly, William Wilberforce and William Whitbread, all prison reformers and members of the Clapham Sect.

The report[34] consisted of a brief survey of existing conditions, together with several appendices. The committee found that the only law which might be construed to affect pauper lunatics was the Vagrancy Act of 1744, and referred to the evidence of Sir George Onesiphorus Paul in stating that the condition of those in workhouses was 'revolting to humanity'. They recommended that an asylum should be set up in each county, to which both pauper and criminal lunatics might be sent. Each asylum should have a committee of governors nominated by the local justices of the peace, and should be financed by means of a county rate: 'To this the public opinion appears so favourable that it may be sufficient at least in the first instance rather to recommend and assist than to enforce the execution of such a plan.'

The first appendix to the report comprised the returns of pauper and criminal lunatics made to Parliament in 1806. The total number of lunatics in pauper institutions in England was given as 1,755, but the omissions were considerable. Hampshire ignored the request for information. The authorities of the counties of Hereford, Stafford, Warwick, Hertford, Bedford, Cumberland and Cambridge replied that there were no pauper lunatics within their boundaries, though two of these counties – Staffordshire and Bedfordshire – were to find it necessary to construct county asylums a few years later. The East Riding of Yorkshire found only three lunatics, while the West Riding by contrast made a return of 424. Dr Andrew Halliday, who undertook the statistical compilation, personally investigated the position in Norfolk and Suffolk in order to arrive at an estimate of the proportion of pauper lunatics to population. In the workhouses of Suffolk, which had made a return of 92, he found 47 'lunatics' and 67 'idiots' confined to 'damp, dark cells'. In Norfolk, the official figure was 22; Halliday's figure was 114.

The same inaccuracies were apparent in the returns for criminal lunatics. The deficiencies of these returns might be explained in several ways: when each parish controlled its own pauper institution, it was not easy to obtain standardized information. There was a motive for concealment because if pauper lunatics were kept in conditions 'revolting to humanity', parish overseers and local magistrates would have no desire to see those conditions publicized – especially when the only practicable alternative was to send all lunatics to expensive private madhouses. Some local officials probably had only the most elementary idea of what constituted insanity. Some counties may have experienced a curious sort of local pride in proclaiming that all their inhabitants were in full possession of their faculties; but the chief causes of inadequate returns were probably apathy and dislike of central government intervention.

The County Asylums Act 1808

The Ministry of All the Talents fell in 1807 – partly, it is alleged, as a result of the Whigs' refusal to pay 'hireling scribes' to praise the

Government in the press.[35] The Act of 1808 'for the better Care and Maintenance of Lunatics, being Paupers or Criminals, in England', known as 'Wynn's Act', was passed under a Tory administration. The main provisions were as follows:

1. Justices of the Peace might give notice at Quarter Sessions of their intention to set up an asylum. Two or more counties might combine for this purpose.
2. A committee of visiting justices was to be appointed at Quarter Sessions to be responsible both for the erection of an asylum and for periodical inspection. They were authorized to contract, to purchase land, and to appoint a Clerk and a Surveyor.
3. The justices were empowered to raise a county rate for the purpose of building the asylum, and were given power to mortgage the rates for a period not exceeding fourteen years. An appeal for voluntary contributions might be made to meet part of the initial cost.
4. They were to 'fix upon an Airy and Healthy Situation, with a good supply of Water, and which may afford a Probability of constant Medical Assistance'.
5. There were to be separate wards for men and women, and also for 'Convalescents and Incurables', together with day rooms and airing grounds for the different classes, and 'dry and airy Cells for lunatics of every description'. The buildings were to be exempt from the window tax.
6. Patients were to be admitted as 'dangerous to be at large' under the 1744 Vagrancy Act, or under the various provisions of the Criminal Lunatics Act 1800.
7. The parish was to pay a charge laid down by the justices. If the parish overseer failed to notify the justices of a pauper lunatic, he became liable to incur a heavy fine.
8. Patients were to be discharged by the visiting justices on recovery. Any officer or servant of the asylum who made possible, either through neglect or connivance, the unauthorized departure of a patient, was liable to a heavy fine.

Amending Acts

The first asylum to be constructed under the new Act was at Nottingham. It received patients from 1810, and was formally opened in 1811. According to the returns of 1806, Nottinghamshire had only 35 pauper lunatics, and no criminal lunatics. The asylum was built to accommodate 76–80 patients. It cost over £21,000, and was overcrowded in the first year. By the terms of the Act, there was no way in which the asylum staff or the visiting justices could exercise discretion in admitting patients. Parish overseers were bound, on pain of fines, to notify the justices, and the justices were equally bound to send the patients to the asylum. An amending Act of 1811 gave the justices discretionary power in issuing warrants, 'particularly in cases where it shall be found that the number of applications on behalf of persons having just cause to be admitted does at any time exceed the number of those who can be properly accommodated in such an asylum, with a view to cure, comfort and safe custody'.

An amending Act of 1815 required overseers to furnish returns of all lunatics and idiots in their parishes to the justices on request, whether admission to the county asylum was sought or not, with a medical certificate for each. Two justices were empowered to discharge patients on behalf of the visiting committee.

The 'Small Act' of 1819 dealt with certification. Until this date, certificates stating merely that 'Mr — is a suitable Object for your Place',[36] or, to quote a well-known example, that 'Hey Broadway a Pot Carey' thought that 'A Blister and Bleeding and Meddeson' would be suitable for a gentleman who 'Wold not A Gree to be Done at Home'[37] were quite common. The new prescribed form of certification was as follows:

> I do hereby certify that by the direction of L.M. and N.O., Justices of the Peace for the County of H., I have personally examined C.D., and the said C.D. appears to me to be of insane mind.

The 1819 Act also gave the justices power to send patients to the county asylum without the concurrence of the parish overseer.

The effect of these three amending Acts was to place the responsibility for the admission of patients with the magistrates rather than the overseers, thus weakening the connection of the county asylums with the Poor Law.

Andrew Scull[38] challenges the view that the foundation of the county asylums was a reform, suggesting that it raises two main questions: how and why insanity came to be defined as illness; and why 'the mad-doctors and their reformist mentors' opted for the asylum as a solution. Insanity did not 'come to be defined as illness'.

Once witchcraft, sorcery and conjuration had died out, and most people lost faith in exorcism, the methods traditionally used by medical practitioners were the only ones left with any credibility until the development of moral treatment at the Retreat. The treatment of George III illustrates this very clearly. If there had been other accepted forms of treatment, Pitt and his advisers would have made sure that the King benefited from them, because their hold on political power depended on the King's recovery. In fact, the King lived on until 1820, and might have benefited from the methods used at the Retreat; but the activities of a small group of lay dissenters in a provincial city were too unorthodox to warrant consideration.

The early asylum doctors were not primarily 'medical men'. They were men with medical qualifications who left mainstream medicine to take on a demanding new kind of work, and the skills demanded of them were mainly in administration and human relations. When the asylums were first set up, the army of the 'helping professions' as we know it today simply did not exist. Medical training was patchy and unstandardized, but the alternative to appointing a medical man, as some of the early asylum committees found, was to appoint someone with no training at all. A medical practitioner was at least educated, and there was a need for basic medical attention. Many pauper patients came to hospital suffering from malnutrition, unidentified 'fevers' and 'wasting diseases', and the boils and eczema which often afflicted the poor. It was necessary to exclude physical causes before proceeding to a diagnosis of insanity – and to guard against the spread of infectious and contagious diseases in the asylum. In the nineteenth century, the risk of the spread of cholera, smallpox, typhus, typhoid and other diseases was high in closed communities, and the appointment of a medical practitioner was a sensible precaution.

Turner notes the attitudes of 'suspicion and denigration' which the asylum doctors faced, not only from the general public, but from the rest of the medical profession.[39]

The asylum was the only solution possible. Any standard social history describes the brutality and violence of the period, and the lack of social support outside the family. Charity gave only sporadic help. The only possibility when family support failed was what would now be called residential care. We should not read post-Goffman views of the pathology of institutions back into a period when this perspective was unknown, and there were no community services. An asylum was what the word originally meant – a place of refuge from a very harsh world.

CHAPTER 3

The Parliamentary Reformers

The publication of Samuel Tuke's *Description of the Retreat* in 1813 elevated a small, provincial experiment to something like a national monument. In the same year, a county magistrate, Godfrey Higgins, discovered a series of abuses at the York Asylum. Failing to obtain satisfaction from the Governors, he communicated his findings to the press. When an investigation seemed imminent, the asylum caught fire. All the records were burned, and four patients died in the blaze. Higgins sent his evidence to Earl FitzWilliam, who was then the lord-lieutenant of the county, and had it published, first in Doncaster and then in London.[1]

In London, a group of six parliamentary reformers investigated Bethlem, and discovered William (or James) Norris in a horrifying form of confinement. An iron collar several inches wide encircled his neck, and was fastened to a wall behind his head. His feet were manacled, and a harness was fitted over his shoulders, pinioning his arms to his sides. It was just possible for him to stand, or to lie on his back, but he was unable to shift his position when lying down, or to move more than one step away from the wall. He had been confined in this apparatus for nine years. The MPs reported that he 'discoursed coolly, and gave rational answers to the different questions put to him'.[2] He was able to hold intelligent conversation on political matters, and to read with comprehension any matter which was put before him. He was in an advanced stage of tuberculosis, and died shortly after being set free.

Patricia Allderidge tells us that, according to the Bethlem records, Norris's first name was James, not William. He was an American marine, 'the most violent and dangerous patient Bethlem had ever encountered', who 'made a number of murderous attacks on keepers and fellow patients'. He had a kindly keeper, who allowed him to read, and to play with a cat.³ On behalf of the Bethlem authorities, it can be argued that this suggests that he was sometimes released from the harness, which strapped his arms to his sides and would have prevented either activity. An American marine, separated from his mates and among seemingly hostile foreigners, may well have been violent and difficult to control. It was to emerge on enquiry that the Bethlem doctors simply did not know any other way of controlling him. His treatment was clearly exceptional, which is why it has become one of the icons of the history of reform. It can also be argued in favour of the Bethlem authorities that the parliamentary reformers did not see Norris in one of his murderous phases. He was dying by the time they visited Bethlem.

But this interpretation is not wholly acceptable. If Norris told the reformers that his name was William, he was probably right: hospital records are not infallible. If he had a kindly keeper who let him read and play with a cat, the implication is that he was educated and capable of gentleness; and if he was dying, he did not need to be chained like a wild animal. John Haslam, the apothecary at Bethlem, was to admit that Norris was only released from this apparatus three weeks or a month before he died.⁴

Armed with the Norris case and other evidence of abuse, the parliamentary group of reformers was able to press for the appointment of a new Select Committee with wide terms of reference. They included Charles Williams-Wynn, who had led the movement for the County Asylums Act, George Rose, Lord Robert Seymour, the younger Peel, and William Sturges-Bourne, a Poor Law reformer, all of whom became members of the Select Committee. They set about their task with much energy. In 1815 and 1816, they took evidence on good practice at the new Nottingham Asylum, St Luke's, and the York Retreat; and on abuses at the York Asylum and Bethlem and in workhouses and private madhouses.

YORK ASYLUM

An advertisement in the *York Courant* of 7 August 1772 first drew the attention of the citizens of York to 'the deplorable situation of many poor lunatics of the county, who have no support except what a needy parent can bestow, or a thrifty parish officer provide'. An appeal was made for donations from 'such Noblemen, Gentlemen and Ladies as are desirous of promoting an Institution for the Relief of an Unhappy Part of the Community'. A local historian reported that 'the building, as an edifice, was worthy of the architects',[5] and the asylum had an imposing list of Governors, headed by the Archbishop of York; but it appears that, as at Bethlem, the magnificence of the frontage and the social status of the Governors bore little relation to the conditions inside. The building was designed for 54 inmates, and by 1815 it held 103. The patients were verminous and filthy, herded together in cells with an utter disregard for cleanliness or ventilation. The first physician, Dr Hunter, had his 'secret insane powders, green and grey' which were nothing more than powerful emetics and purges. 'Flogging and cudgelling were systematically resorted to.'[6]

All this was suspected, but there was no concrete proof. After 1792, the Retreat provided an alternative system for Quakers, but most patients still went to the asylum, where Dr Hunter and his successor, Dr Best, discouraged inquisitive visitors and succeeded in evading condemnation until 1813. In that year, Godfrey Higgins began to investigate.

Higgins was a quiet country gentleman of independent means, with antiquarian interests. He had written a number of privately printed pamphlets, including 'The Celtic Druids' and 'An Apology for Mohammed', and was a member of several learned societies.[7] In the summer of 1813, a pauper named William Vickers or Vicars was brought before him in court, accused of assault. Higgins 'presently discovered he was insane' and issued a warrant to convey him to the asylum.[8]

In October of the same year, Vickers' wife Sarah appeared before Higgins to ask for poor relief, and alleged that her husband had been ill-treated at the asylum. Higgins sent the surgeon responsible for the paupers of the district to examine Vickers, and received the following report:

He had the Itch very bad, was also extremely filthy, for I saw his wife not only comb several lice from his head but take them from the folds of his shirt neck; his health was so much impaired that he was not able to stand by himself; his legs were much swelled, and one of them in a state of mortification.

There were lash marks on Vickers' back, and when Higgins visited him in the Asylum, he said he had been flogged. His friends and relatives had not been allowed to see him, being told that he was 'insensible in an apoplexy'. Higgins commented 'No doubt it must have disturbed him very much to be looked at in a state of insensibility.'

Higgins corresponded with the physician, Dr Best, but obtained no satisfaction. On 27 November 1813, he published a statement in the *York Herald*, together with extracts from the correspondence. Dr Best's defence had been a complete and unequivocal denial. He stated that Vickers' condition was 'the unavoidable consequence of the lamentable and dangerous illness under which he has recently laboured, and from which he was . . . in a state of convalescence'. He claimed that Vickers had had a fire in his room, a special attendant, 'assiduous medical treatment . . . nutritious food . . . mulled ale . . . everything conducive to his recovery'. Best urged Higgins to consider 'whether you are not lending your name as a magistrate to a purpose most foreign to your office as a magistrate, and giving effect . . . to a malicious conspiracy against myself and the Asylum'.

The asylum Governors met, and accepted Dr Best's statement at face value. A statement signed by the chairman, Archbishop Venables-Vernon, was issued, to the effect that the Governors were 'unanimously of the opinion that during the time the said William Vickers remained in the Asylum, he was treated with all possible care, attention and humanity'.[9] Higgins was less easily convinced: 'The Archbishop, the last minute before I came away, told me very politely that they would detain me no longer, they had no further use for me . . . I am very far from satisfied with what has been done.'[10]

The Governors' meeting had been adjourned for a week, and when it met again, there were forty-six new Governors. The foundation rule was that any person subscribing £20 to the work of the asylum was entitled to become a Governor, and forty-six citizens of York, including Godfrey Higgins, William Tuke and Samuel Tuke, had subscribed. The old Governors, if not outvoted, were certainly outflanked. The Archbishop bowed to the inevitable after what Higgins called 'a warm debate',[11] and a committee of investigation was formed.

On 26 December 1813, the asylum caught fire. A letter to the *York Herald* of 4 April 1814, signed 'A Governor of the Asylum' gives these details: most of the staff were absent; Dr Best was thirty miles away, attending a private patient; the apothecary and the housekeeper had 'gone out to keep Christmas'; two of the four male keepers had Christmas leave, and of the two who remained, one was asthmatic and could not bear the smoke. 'Before the flames could be extinguished, damage was done to the building and property amounting to £2,392, and four patients perished in the conflagration. This served to shut out from all mortal eyes proofs of maladministration at which the imagination shudders.'[12]

A plausible explanation was again forthcoming from Dr Best. The fire was said to have been caused by sparks falling down a chimney from an adjoining one, and 'setting fire to some flocks laid there to dry in a room locked up'. Godfrey Higgins, in his new capacity as a Governor, demanded to see the chimney in question, and found that it was built 'in a direction so far from the perpendicular' that it was impossible for the outbreak to have originated in this way.[13] Nine weeks later, he launched his second attack.

Having suspicions in my mind that there were some parts of the Asylum, which had not yet been seen, I went early in the morning, determined to examine every place. After ordering a great number of doors to be opened, I came to one which was in a retired situation in the kitchen apartments, and which was almost hid. I ordered this door to be opened ... the keepers hesitated ... I grew angry, and told them that I insisted on (the key) being found; and that if they would not find it, I could find a key at the kitchen fireside, namely, the poker; upon that, the key was immediately brought.[14]

Higgins unlocked the door, and found a series of cells about eight feet square:

in a very horrid and filthy situation ... the walls were daubed with excrement; the air-holes, of which there was one in each cell, were partly filled with it ... I then went upstairs, and [the keeper]showed me into a room ... twelve feet by seven feet ten inches, in which there were thirteen women who, he told me, had all come out of those cells that morning ... I became very sick, and could not remain longer in the room. I vomited.[15]

Higgins expressed in his letter to the press the hope that 'the public will never rest until the Augean stable is swept clean from top to bottom'. Five months were to elapse before this wish became realized – five months of urbane explanations, recriminations and constant pressure to induce the reformers to give way. In a published reply, Dr Best complained that 'Mr Higgins' attack is personally and particularly levelled at me.'[16] Best behaved throughout as though he were the victim of a monstrous conspiracy. The cells mentioned by Higgins were, he stated, reserved for women of unclean habits. They were cleaned out every morning, and it was an extremely offensive undertaking. Chains and handcuffs found in the asylum had been examined by the Governors, and found to be covered with rust, which proved that they had not been used for a considerable time. Best then shifted to a defensive position. The place was damp and low-lying, half the building had been destroyed by fire, there were too few staff and too many patients. 'If the servants neglect to perform their duties . . . if the laws and constitution are defective . . . I do not consider myself as responsible for any of these circumstances, or for the evils which may naturally be expected to result from them.'

The *York Herald* of 4 April 1814 contained a letter signed 'A Governor of the Asylum', with a point-by-point refutation of Best's letter of the previous week. Best had stated that the women in the cells seen by Higgins had 'straw beds'. 'The expression', commented 'A Governor of the Asylum', 'is scarcely applicable to loose straw covering the floor as in a stable.' On the question of the fire: it was, to say the least, 'an unfortunate coincidence' that all the staff save one were absent or incapacitated. 'Thus it came about that four patients were burned to death – or, as the Steward's book records it, they died.' On Best's disclaimer of responsibility, the writer retorted that Best was well paid for taking responsibility, since he received a large salary, and was permitted to take private patients in addition. The letter concluded: 'The public are convinced that if there be any prospect of a reformation of the defects and abuses which are now admitted to exist, they are chiefly indebted for it to the independent exertions and the firmness of Mr Godfrey Higgins.'

Mr Higgins' exertions continued. He pursued other cases of cruelty, some of which had been exposed at the first inquiry, but without result. One was the case of 'the Rev. Mr Skorey', an elderly cleric suffering from a mild disorder, who had frequent lucid intervals. He had been 'inhumanly kicked downstairs by the keepers, and told in the presence of his wife that he was 'no better than a dog'. To this complaint, Best replied, 'Mrs Skorey stated in evidence that she heard him knocked downstairs, which I take to be impossible . . . I mean, impossible that she could have distinguished by the ear alone whether her husband had been kicked downstairs or not.'

The male side of the asylum was not completely separated from the female side. Two female patients had become pregnant while in the asylum, one by a male patient, and one by a keeper named Backhouse. The latter openly admitted paternity, and paid regular sums to the overseers of the poor for the parish of Louth to maintain the child in the poorhouse. The keeper subsequently retired from the asylum after twenty-six years' service, received a handsome present from the Governors – and opened a private madhouse. Higgins stated that he did not think the Governors knew of Backhouse's defection, but that Dr Best certainly knew, and kept silent.[17]

The reformers then turned their attention to the records, and found that they were false in many particulars. The number of deaths for 1813 was given as eleven, but comparison with the parish registers showed that there had been twenty-four funerals. The inference was that thirteen patients whose existence in the asylum had never been recorded had died within the year. When the fire took place, it was admitted that four patients had died in the flames; but the records were so inadequate that it would have been possible for several more to have died without trace.

Higgins went through the accounts, and discovered discrepancies. 'One quarter's account was missing; of another quarter, two statements were transmitted, both apparently complete documents, but each in fact essentially differing from the other.'[18] He proved that large sums of money had been appropriated by Dr Best and his predecessor. The steward, when asked to produce the books for inspection, said lamely that he had burned them 'in a moment of irritation.'[19]

In August 1814 – nearly a year after the release of William Vickers – the Quarterly Court finally dismissed all the servants and officers of the asylum. Dr Best was either asked or permitted to resign, though this did not affect his considerable private practice.

On 28 December, the *York Herald* published his letter to the editor:

> I merely write to give you notice, that if ONE SYLLABLE shall appear, in any of your future papers in allusion to me, which may admit of an INJURIOUS or even an OFFENSIVE nature, my next communication with you will take place through my attorney.

The editor's comment on the letter was: 'It was . . . sent to intimidate me from that course which it is my duty as the editor of a Public Paper to pursue. I give it, therefore, to the world'.

At the Governors' meeting of August 1814, the Archbishop of York was absent, and Earl FitzWilliam, to whom Higgins' letter of protest had been addressed, took the chair. A new staff was appointed, and a new constitution adopted. It was laid down that two Governors were to visit the asylum each month; three ladies were to undertake the visitation of the female wards; the physician was to receive £300 a year, but was not to undertake private practice or to receive gratuities; a resident apothecary was to be appointed, whose duties would be those of superintending the issue of medicines, and also of supervising the work and the conduct of the keepers.

The scandal was over as far as York was concerned; but in 1815, it had repercussions on a national scale, when the Select Committee enquired into the Vickers case, the circumstances of the fire, the financial peculations and the destruction of the records. Godfrey Higgins gave evidence, and so – less happily – did Dr Best.

BETHLEM

The visit by six members of parliament, and the Norris case, were the first steps in a searching inquiry on conditions at Bethlem. The apothecary, John Haslam, was responsible for administering medicines and directing the control of patients, and the physician, Dr John Monro, for prescribing medicines and the form of treatment. The surgeon was Dr Bryan Crowther, who described the system at Bethlem in his book, *Practical Remarks on Insanity*:

> The curable patients at Bethlem Hospital are regularly bled about the commencement of June and the latter end of July . . . the lancet has been found a very communicative sort of instru-

ment . . . I have bled a hundred and fifty patients at one time, and have never found it requisite to adopt any other method of security against haemorrhage than that of sending the patient back to his accustomed confinement.[20]

Patients admitted to Bethlem had to be certified 'strong enough to undergo a course of treatment'. Crowther died before the Select Committee inquiry, and perhaps made a convenient scapegoat. Haslam, plainly on the defensive when he was summoned back for the third time to face a battery of questions, said that Crowther was 'for ten years . . . generally insane and mostly drunk . . . He was so insane as to have a strait waistcoat . . . he was so insane, that his hand was not obedient to his will.'[21]

Searching cross-examination by George Rose forced both Monro and Haslam into hesitation, contradiction and evasion. Haslam blamed Monro, Monro blamed Haslam, and both blamed Crowther. Monro admitted that chains were used on patients at Bethlem, but not in his private madhouse – 'They are fit only for pauper lunatics, if a gentleman was put in chains, he would not like it.' He 'seldom' went round the galleries to see the patients, but said that they were sent to him if they were physically ill. Haslam usually visited the hospital for only half an hour a day, and was sometimes absent for days at a time. There were only five keepers – three men and two women – for 150 patients.

Haslam admitted that he had known of William Norris's confinement. Norris had an unusual bone formation: the bones of his hands were smaller than his wrists, and manacles would not hold him. The device by which he had been restrained had been specially made on the order of the Governors.

Edward Wakefield, a land agent, and one of the leaders of the parliamentary reformers,[22] gave evidence that when he had first visited Bethlem, he had found a number of female patients chained to the wall by an arm or a leg, completely unclothed save for a blanket apiece. Some of these 'blanket patients' were quiet and coherent when he visited them.

One female in this side room, thus chained, was an object remarkably striking. She mentioned her married and maiden names, and stated that she had been a teacher of languages. The keepers described her as a very accomplished lady, mistress of many languages . . . the Committee can hardly imagine a human being in a more degraded and brutalizing situation.[23]

By the time the Select Committee met, the old matron had been pensioned off, and the new matron had obtained clothes for the women, freed those who were not violent, had them washed and cut their hair.

WORKHOUSES

One of the witnesses before the Select Committee was a banker named Henry Alexander, who had undertaken a self-imposed tour of forty-seven workhouses in the West Country, searching for pauper lunatics. Nine had insane inmates. One was St Peter's Bristol, where the inmates were 'comfortable' on the whole, but four patients were found in wooden cells 'like pig-styes' – dark, and lacking in ventilation and sanitation.

At Liskeard in Cornwall, he found two women confined:

In a fit place for them?
– Very far from it. Indeed, I hardly know what to term the places, they were no better than dungeons.
Were they underground?
– No; they were buildings, but they were very damp and very low. In, one of them, there was no light admitted through the door; neither light nor air . . . the whole place was very filthy.
Filled with excrement and very offensive?
– Yes.[24]

At Tavistock, where Alexander and his companions had difficulty in gaining admission, the lunatic patients had been removed from the cells, and the cells had been washed and cleaned out.

What was the state of the cells?
– I never smelt such a stench in my life . . . having entered one, I said I would go into the other; that if they could survive the night through, I could at least inspect them . . . the stench was so great I felt almost suffocated, and for hours after, if I ate anything, I still retained the same smell. I could not get rid of it; and it should be remembered that these cells had been washed out that morning, and the doors had been opened some hours previous.[25]

PRIVATE MADHOUSES

The Select Committee examined the working of the 1774 Madhouses Act, which covered only the Greater London area. They were particularly concerned with the state of the 'naval maniacs' at Hoxton and with Thomas Warburton's four madhouses, which took pauper lunatics from the parishes of Marylebone, St George's Hanover Square and St Pancras.

Mentally deranged seamen were commonly sent by the Navy to a large private madhouse kept by Sir Jonathan Miles at Hoxton. In 1814, the house contained fourteen officers and 136 seamen, together with other patients. Lengthy evidence was given by Dr John Weir, the Inspector of Naval Hospitals, who stated that although he was responsible for inspection, he had no power to effect any improvements. The mortality rate was very high, and there appeared to be no attempt at classification: clean and dirty patients, violent and peaceable, incurable and convalescent, were all thrust together without regard for their physical condition.

Sir Jonathan Miles was cross-questioned by George Rose, as chairman of the committee:

Is any medical attention particularly directed in your establishment to the cure of insanity?
– None. Our house is open to all medical gentlemen who care to visit it.
That is at the expense of the patient?
– It is . . .
Do the Government patients receive any medical treatment for the cure of their insanity?
– I cannot say that they do, exactly . . .
How many are visited by their own medical men?
– That I cannot tell without reference to my Book.
Do you suppose there are twenty?
– Yes, from twenty to thirty, probably.
Is it your opinion, then, that there are above three hundred persons in your house, who receive no attention on account of the particular complaint for which they are confined?
– Certainly. They have nothing prescribed for the cure, no doubt of that, their pay will not allow it.[26]

There were in all nearly 500 patients in the house, and the Metropolitan Commissioners had inspected it in the space of two and a half hours. Their secretary, Dr Richard Powell, admitted that on this visit, he had not checked the number of patients, and that some might have been concealed in hidden rooms or cells. He had not seen samples of the patients' food, and while he had reservations about male patients sleeping two to a bed, 'It cannot be expected that a man who pays only ten shillings a week should have a separate bed.' He considered the house 'in very excellent order'.

Dr Parry-Jones's exclusion of the metropolitan madhouses from his study becomes increasingly inexplicable as the evidence mounts. While he makes a number of references to the Select Committees of 1815–16, most of these are brief and uninformative. He mentions Warburton's houses with the comments that 'The 1815 Committee ... considered that in that year, the grounds for complaint were based upon very slender means of information',[27] and that 'the Select Committee reached no adverse conclusions regarding the conduct of Warburton himself'.[28] The evidence given on Warburton's four houses – Talbot's, the White House and Rhodes', all at Bethnal Green, and Whitmore House at Hackney, was highly contradictory, though evidence given to another Select Committee in 1827 was to reveal long-standing abuses. Parry-Jones mentions 'the revelation of many grave defects' in private madhouses in 1815–16, but gives no details.[29] He notes that keepers often defended the use of mechanical restraint after it had been abolished in public asylums because 'it is likely that financial considerations acted as a genuine brake on the introduction of the milder forms of treatment.'[30] He also notes that not all madhouse keepers were medically qualified. Many madhouses were managed by former attendants, and eight cases are mentioned in which (unqualified) women had inherited the houses from their fathers.[31]

Edward Wakefield, who had discovered William Norris at Bethlem, had visited a number of madhouses. At Miles' house at Hoxton, he had been refused admission, a keeper telling him that 'an inspection of that house would be signing my death-warrant'. At Gore House in Kensington, he was also refused admission. At Thomas Monro's house in Hackney, he was told by the former physician of Bethlem that he was very welcome to visit – if he could secure the consent of the relatives of every patient; and he was refused a list of the names of the patients.

There were a few private madhouses in which conditions were good. As an unofficial visitor, Wakefield had no power to make a thorough inspection, and had to base his opinions on what he was allowed to see. At Talfourd's Norman House at Fulham, he found fourteen ladies who appeared to be treated with the greatest kindness. They went to the local church, and were allowed out for walks – Wakefield met two who had 'just walked to Walham Green to see Louis XVIII'. London House, Hackney, also appeared to be excellently conducted. There 'One lady, who conceives herself to be Mary Queen of Scots, acts as preceptress to Mrs Fox's little children, and takes great pains in teaching them French.'[32]

While evidence of abuse had been forthcoming from other sources, the evidence of the Metropolitan Commissioners was almost entirely concerned with their own status and position.[33] Dr Powell testified that they visited all the madhouses in the area, inquiring into the administration and the condition of the patients, but not into the form of medical treatment. They considered this outside their province, despite the fact that all the Commissioners were members of the College of Physicians. The visitation lasted six days in the year; Powell himself had personally visited thirty-four houses – 'some days, perhaps two; other days, six or eight' – over an area covering all central London, and as far out as Lewisham, Stockwell, Walham Green, Enfield and Plaistow. They suspected that some houses made false returns, but did not check the number of patients returned against those actually seen in the houses. The following scrap of dialogue concerning one house is illuminating:

How many patients were there?
– Three.
Men or women?
– Women I think, but I am hardly certain.

The Commissioners had no power to refuse licences, and no power to liberate those whom they considered sane; the certificates of confinement could be signed by 'any medical man', who need not have examined the patient. No medical certificate was necessary for pauper patients. A licence was issued for each separate madhouse, but without regard to the number of patients in it. The holder of the licence was not required to be resident in the house, so that it was possible to own several houses and leave them largely in the hands of untrained keepers. No licence was needed for single lunatics, and it was possible for a madhouse proprietor to keep a number of small separate houses, each containing one patient, without inspection.

THE RESULT OF THE INQUIRIES

The Select Committee presented its evidence to Parliament. The reports were principally verbatim reports of evidence, with no attempt to sift the true from the false, or the salient points from a mass of irrelevancies. Perhaps the reformers thought that the facts spoke for themselves. Andrew Scull writes of 'the moral outrage which animated the lunacy reformers' and comments on 'the transformation of the cultural meaning of madness':

> Much of the reformers' revulsion on being exposed to conditions ... derived from this changed perspective. For them, the lunatic was no longer an animal, stripped of all remnants of humanity. On the contrary, he remained in essence a man: a man lacking in self-restraint and order, but a man for all that.[34]

The view that many people like Monro and Haslam and Warburton genuinely saw nothing wrong with treating lunatics like beasts is interesting, and accords with the evidence. As Scull points out, the change in perspective came very quickly, within a decade or two, though the unenlightened took longer to convince.

The reformers believed that changes in the law were necessary: 'the inquiries of the Committee have convinced them that there are not in the Country a set of Beings more immediately requiring the protection of the Legislature than persons in this state'; but they must have known that there was little hope of extensive legislation in the period of High Tory rule following the Napoleonic Wars. From 1815 to 1819, repeated efforts were made by Wynn and his associates to introduce new legislation, but they concentrated on a limited objective – that of reforming the private madhouses. Bills to set up an effective and powerful inspectorate were three times steered through the Commons – in 1816, 1817 and 1819. On each occasion, the Bill was rejected by the Lords after many deferments. On the last occasion, Lord Eldon made a statement which summed up the attitude of many members of the House of Lords: 'There could not be a more false humanity than an over-humanity with regard to persons afflicted with insanity.'[35]

At Bethlem, the Governors met in 1816 to consider the future of their apothecary and physician. Haslam was dismissed, and returned to private practice. His dismissal did not apparently cloud his reputation, for his biographer describes him as 'long distinguished in private practice by his prudent treatment of the insane'.[36] Dr Monro defended himself by blaming 'the crowded state of the hospital', and stated baldly, 'With respect to the merits of the mode of treatment which I have practised, consisting chiefly of evacuants, as a general rule, I know no better.'[37] He retired in 1816, and was replaced by his son, Dr Edward Thomas Monro.

The hospital had moved to new premises in 1815, and a scheme of classification had been introduced. New regulations were drawn up. A somewhat defensive publication by 'A Constant Observer' in 1823 stressed the improvements: the keepers were obliged to have physically fit patients out of bed and dressed for thirteen or fourteen hours a day, instead of leaving them in bed to save trouble; baths were 'in constant use'; the diet had been improved (though there was much use of broth and 'wholesome gruel'); the apothecary was resident; and incidents of restraint had to be recorded. 'The grand principle of this establishment', wrote A Constant Observer, 'is mildness; for it is now generally acknowledged that this mode of treating the maniac is better calculated to restore reason than harshness or severity.'[38]

'Bedlam is well-conducted', wrote Sir Andrew Halliday in 1828, 'and the patients are humanely and judiciously treated; but it still has too much of the leaven of the dark ages . . . for it ever to prove an efficient hospital.'[39]

THE SELECT COMMITEE OF 1827

By the time the matter of general lunacy reform was raised again, most of the original parliamentary reformers had disappeared from the political scene; but Lord Robert Seymour, by that time elderly and infirm, submitted a memorandum on the condition of Warburton's houses: perhaps the most outstanding piece of unfinished business.

On 13 June 1827, a Select Committee was appointed to consider the state of pauper lunatics from the metropolitan parishes. The chairman was a Dorsetshire magistrate named Robert Gordon, and the two Acts of 1828 are known as 'Gordon's Acts'. Lord Ashley, later the seventh Earl of Shaftesbury, was a member of the Select Committee. He was twenty-six years old, and had been in the House of Commons for only a matter of months. In what was to be a long career of public service, this was his first major concern, and one which was to last until his death in 1884.

Warburton had escaped definite censure in 1816; now his mad-houses were investigated again, and the so-called 'crib-room cases of Bethnal Green' provided the most startling revelation of conditions since the investigations at Bethlem and York fourteen years earlier. Evidence was given by Richard Roberts, the assistant to the overseers of St George's, Hanover Square:

A crib-room is a place where there are nothing but wooden cribs or bedsteads; cases, in fact, filled with straw and covered with a blanket, in which those unfortunate beings are placed at night; and they sleep most of them naked on the straw, covered with a blanket.'[40]

The details were supplied by John Nettle, a former patient: the unclean patients were placed in the cribs at three o'clock in the afternoon, their arms and legs secured, and left there until nine o'clock on the following morning. At the weekends, they were secured at three o'clock on Saturday afternoon, and left there until nine o'clock on Monday. Food was brought to them, and their arms were freed just sufficiently to enable them to eat it. On Monday, they were taken out into the yard, and the accumulated excrement was washed from them with a mop dipped in cold water. When Nettle was convalescent, and freed from the crib-room, he went back to examine the cribs. 'I turned the straw out of some of the cribs, and there were maggots in the bottom of them where the sick men had laid.'[41]

John Dunston, a surgeon, testified that he attended the White House every day. Warburton had stated that an apothecary lived within three or four hundred yards of the house, and had been repeatedly called in when Dunston was not available; on closer questioning, he was unable to remember the apothecary's name.

The most striking instance of evasion and falsehood was that provided by William Cordell, John Dunston's 'occasional assistant', best told in Gordon's subsequent speech in the House of Commons:

> This person was asked whether any register was kept of the patients. He replied 'Yes, we have the most perfect register you can conceive, it is an account of the treatment and condition of every patient, moral and medical . . . We can trace the illness of every patient for six or seven years, and we can find a statement of every prescription written for him, and every circumstance attending the progress of his malady. Would the House believe that there was not one word of truth in this statement? Could they believe that it was wholly false? Yet so it was.[42]

After making the statement mentioned, Cordell was again sent for by the Select Committee, and questioned for a second time:

> Are we to understand that all you have said to us is correct?
> – Yes, very probably. (A laugh).
> Is the story of the book?
> – No.
> Which are we to believe – what you have today told us, or your previous statement?
> – Take your choice. (A laugh).
> He then admitted that it was all false.[43]

A footnote to the conditions at the White House is provided by the evidence of two Commissioners who were still working under the terms of the defective Act of 1774. Dr Grant David Yates said that he understood the mode of management to be merely for confinement, not cure. Sir Alexander Frampton considered the White House to be 'excellently regulated . . . a very good house'.

> Have you ever seen any county lunatic asylum?
> – I have not.
> You have not thought it part of your duty . . . either to examine new Bedlam or to examine any lunatic asylum in order to form a comparative view of the treatment at Mr Warburton's and those other establishments near London?
> – I have not examined any of those asylums.
> How many visitations do you make to each [madhouse] in the course of a year?
> – Seldom more than one.[44]

John Hall, a Guardian of the Poor for the parish of St Marylebone, gave evidence that he had called at the White House in order
to inspect the pauper lunatics from his own parish. The parish was
paying nine or ten shillings a week for each.

> There was a little hesitation in showing us the place . . . we found
> a considerable number of very disgusting objects . . . in a very
> small room: they were sitting on benches round the room, and
> several of them were chained to the wall. The air of the room
> was highly oppressive and offensive.

These were 'the description of patients called the wet patients: they
were chiefly in petticoats; the room was exceedingly oppressive
from the excrement and the smell which existed there'.

Hall had been told by a discharged patient that the patients were
confined to the cribs at a very early hour. To check on this, he
called at the White House with Lord Robert Seymour, also a
Guardian, at about half past seven in the evening:

> Mr Jennings [the keeper] refused to let us see the patients; he
> complained of the visit at such an unseasonable hour; he said he
> hoped the legislature would protect houses from visits of that
> sort. Lord Robert looked at his watch, and it was then a quarter
> before eight. Mr Jennings was pressed three or four times by
> Lord Robert, and at last he turned round and said, 'Surely you
> would not wish to see the females in their beds at this time of
> night?', making use of the term 'night'. The answer of Lord
> Robert was, 'Show us the males'.

Jennings refused, and the Guardians were forced to withdraw. The
Marylebone paupers were subsequently removed from the White
House, and – for want of an alternative – sent to Sir Jonathan
Miles' house at Hoxton, on condition that the house should be
open to inspection day or night.[45]

The Select Committee recommended the erection of a county
asylum for the metropolis. The result was the construction of the
large Middlesex Asylum at Hanwell, which for a period absorbed
most of the insane poor from the metropolitan area.

THE ACTS OF 1828

Two new Acts of Parliament dealt respectively with private mad-houses and county asylums. The Madhouse Act removed the power of inspection from the College of Physicians, and set up a statutory authority for the metropolis. The number of Commissioners was increased to fifteen. Five of them were to be physicians, who were to be paid at the rate of £1 an hour; the others were to be unpaid. All were to be appointed by the Secretary of State for the Home Department, and were to make an annual report to him. They could recommend to him that licences should be revoked or refused. They were to visit each madhouse four times a year, and they could visit at night if malpractice had been alleged on oath. They could release any person who was in their estimation improperly confined.

Similar provisions applied to the visiting justices in the provinces. Two magistrates and a medical visitor were to visit each house four times a year, and to submit a report to the Home Department. The Act laid down a more detailed form of certification for the admission of patients; required that all houses should have regular medical attention, and that those houses containing more than 100 patients should have a resident medical officer; and required proprietors to keep detailed records which could be inspected. Records of certification, admission and death or discharge of patients were to be kept, and forwarded annually to the Commissioners or the justices.

The County Asylums Act 1828 was largely a consolidating measure, but it provided for a degree of centralization. Similar records were to be kept in county asylums, and forwarded by the justices of the peace to the Home Department. The Secretary of State acquired the power to send visitors to inspect any asylum.

So the worst abuses were at last identified, and the framework of a system to prevent their recurrence was set up. From this time on, the real initiative lay with the county asylums.

CHAPTER 4

Creating the Asylum System

At the time of the County Asylums Act 1828, there were nine county asylums in operation: Nottingham (1811), Bedford (1812) and Norfolk (1814) were followed by Lancaster (1816), Stafford (1818), the West Riding of Yorkshire (at Wakefield, 1818), Cornwall (at Bodmin, 1820), Lincoln (1820) and Gloucester (1823). The cost of these asylums was as shown in Table 4.1.

Wages and prices fluctuated during and after the Napoleonic Wars, and figures for asylums built in different years are not strictly comparable. The asylums at Nottingham, Stafford and Gloucester were joint county asylums and subscription hospitals, taking both pauper and private patients, and Lincoln was wholly a subscription hospital.

Wynn's Act of 1808 had specified that the new asylums were to

Asylum	Approx. total cost (£)	Accommodation	Capital cost per head (£)
Nottingham	21,000	80	262
Bedford	10,000	52	192
Norfolk	35,000	102	343
Lancaster	60,000	170	353
Stafford	36,000	120	300
W. Riding	55,000	250	220
Cornwall	15,000	102	147
Lincoln	12,000	50	240
Gloucester	44,000	120	367

Table 4.1 *Capital costs of asylum building, England and Wales*
Source: Halliday (1828) p. 25.

be 'in an airy and healthy situation, with a good supply of water, and which may afford a probability of the vicinity of constant medical assistance'. This posed some difficulty, because the only sites satisfying the last requirement were in large towns, which at that time were neither airy nor healthy, and which frequently had a contaminated water supply.

In Lancashire, a proposal for the erection of the new asylum near Liverpool drew strong protests from the local medical practitioners, stating that, in their opinion, the situation should be 'exceedingly retired, and quite in the country'.[1] While admitting the need for an asylum, they were not pleased at the prospect of having it built in their own immediate vicinity. Patients would be sent to the new asylum from all parts of the county, and they urged that transportation costs should be equalized as far as possible by building the asylum in a central position. Some thirty or forty doctors wrote in support, many of them advancing Chorley or Wigan as suitably 'retired positions'. The asylum was eventually constructed in the northern part of the county, about a mile from Lancaster.

In Stafford, the asylum was built next to the county gaol. The arrangement permitted of some degree of common administration between the two institutions, thus minimizing expense; but in spite of its proximity to the prison, Stafford Asylum had an excellent site, on rising ground. Though within a few minutes' walk of the town, it was enclosed in acres of park and woodland, and so was both 'retired' and 'airy'.

The Cornwall Asylum was erected at Bodmin, on a low-lying and badly-drained site which caused dissatisfaction to the Lunacy Commissioners in 1842.[2] The view was 'cheerful' and the grounds were 'extensive' according to Halliday,[3] though a French visitor some years later recorded 'les cours sont humides et sombres'.[4]

Most authorities settled the problem by building on the edge of a large town, two or three miles out into the country. In the days before suburban living became popular, the boundary between town and country was usually sufficiently distinct for an estate in the country to be within walking distance of the town. The subsequent spread of the towns meant that most of the old asylums were not physically isolated – before the end of the century, many were within the town boundaries.

Since the visiting justices had no precedents to follow in the early days, it was inevitable that they should make mistakes. Asylum

Minute Books show that a superintendent was to be appointed and paid on a capitation basis, leaving him to provide out of that sum for the complete upkeep of the establishment. The justices at Bodmin made three unsuccessful appointments before experience led them to retain control of the asylum finance, paying the Governor a salary and making separate appointments to other posts. At Stafford, the first Minute Book records how a part-time physician and a resident lay superintendent were appointed. A matron and three other senior staff were appointed separately; but the lay superintendent soon dismissed the matron, and appointed his elderly mother in her stead, assuming the post of matron to be a sinecure. The justices had to rectify this situation, and insist on a new appointment.

The fullest account of the early asylums is given in Sir Andrew Halliday's *A General View of the Present State of Lunatics and Lunatic Asylums*, published in 1828. Halliday, who had been responsible for the official census of lunatics in 1806, was a distinguished medical practitioner, but allied himself to the parliamentary reformers rather than to the asylum doctors.

The food provided in county asylums was very much better than that in gaols and workhouses. A weekly order given regularly at Stafford during this period allowed for nearly 4lb of meat, 1lb of cheese, 2 pints of milk and 2 gallons of beer for each patient and member of staff.

Patients were usually required to work in the kitchen or gardens when fit to do so. Incontinent patients slept on straw, but other patients had beds and bedding. At Bodmin, there was even a form of central heating, though the pipes were frequently in need of repair.

By 1827, the parliamentary reformers had made sufficient enquiries to be able to set out a sort of Code of Practice. This was printed as a preliminary to the Report of the Select Committee of 1827, as a guide both to what asylums should provide and what inspecting Commissioners and magistrates should be looking for. Extracts from this lengthy document demonstrate that they had remarkably high standards for the period. On accommodation:

Is the separation of the sexes complete? . . .
Are the dormitories properly ventilated? . . .
Are the courtyards airy and dry . . . do they afford some prospect over the walls? . . .

Are there complete baths for hot and cold water? . . .

On the physical care of patients:

What steps are taken to ensure the personal cleanliness of the
patients, particularly of the most unclean? . . .
How often is bathing insisted on generally? . . .
Is the practice of daily exercise . . . insisted on with all patients
able to partake of it? . . .

On occupation:

How far has manual labour been adopted with advantage, and
with what descriptions of patients? . . .
Has the active engagement of the mind to the sciences, fine arts,
literature or mechanical arts been attempted with patients of a
superior description, and what has been the result? . . .
Where graver studies would be unsuitable, has it been found
beneficial to afford patients such employments as are calculated
to engage the attention to external objects . . . such, for example,
as drawing, painting, design, models, gardening etc.? . . .
Where the mind is so diseased as to be evidently unfit for the
foregoing exercises, has benefit been experienced by furnishing
the patients in their courtyards with means of innocent amuse-
ment, from music, domestic animals, poultry, birds, flowers and
objects of a similar nature? . . .
Is it the opinion of the superintendent that a state of entire
indolence and mental inertness is decidedly prejudicial to the
patient? . . .

On moral treatment:

In the moral treatment of the patients, is it considered an object
of importance to encourage their own efforts of self-restraint . . .
by exciting and cherishing in them feelings of self-respect . . . and
generally by maintaining towards them a treatment uniformly
judicious and kind, sympathizing with them, and at the same
time diverting their minds from painful and injurious associations?

This questionnaire was apparently sent to asylum authorities,
though there was at that time no statutory power to compel them

to answer. Dr Charlesworth of the Lincoln Asylum used his own answers as the basis for a book.[5]

The influence of the Retreat is clearly to be seen in the formulation of these questions: however difficult it might be to universalize the Tukes' system, it was set as the ideal. The reformers were concerned not only with external factors – cleanliness and order – but with creating an environment in which patients could live with some personal satisfaction and dignity. Above all, they wanted to see the reduction or even the abolition of mechanical restraint, which they regarded as inhuman and anti-therapeutic.

THE NON-RESTRAINT MOVEMENT

After 1828, the county asylums, which had hitherto been few in number and widely misunderstood as to purpose, gradually emerged as the most significant factor in lunacy reform. Between 1828 and 1842, eight further asylums were constructed, in Chester, Dorset, Kent, Middlesex, Norfolk, Suffolk, Surrey and Leicester.

In the early days, the staff was usually small, and doctors and keepers tended to rely on mechanical restraint to keep order. The Act of 1808 laid down no regulations about treatment, but it provided statutory penalties against the keepers if patients escaped. The maximum penalty of £10 was heavy for a keeper on £25 a year. At Bodmin, the visiting justices in 1819 requested one of their number to apply to the Governors of Bethlem for 'patterns of the different securities necessary for patients'.[6] At Lancaster, Dr Paul Slade Knight had his own methods of restraint, including muffs and an apparatus of leather sleeves connected to a belt and leg-locks.[7] At Nottingham, the system of restraint was mild: the 'assistants and servants' were instructed to 'abstain from unnecessary acts of violence'.[8]

The non-restraint movement in the asylums started in the small Lincoln Asylum, which took only private patients. Dr Charlesworth, the visiting physician, gradually reduced the instances of restraint. Mr Gardiner Hill, the house surgeon, totally abolished restraint between 1835 and 1838.[9]

It seems evident that Charlesworth took the initiative, but Gardiner Hill succeeded with the most difficult cases which Charlesworth had hesitated to release from chains and strait jackets. The two were to spend much time and energy on the question of which

Year	No. of patients	No. restrained	Instances of restraint
Under the supervision of Dr Charlesworth, 1829–35			
1829	72	39	1727
1830	92	54	2364
1831	70	40	1004
1832	81	55	1401
1833	87	44	1109
1834	109	45	647
1835	108	28	323
Under the supervision of Mr Gardiner Hill			
1836	115	12	39
1837	130	2	3
1838	148	0	0

Table 4.2 *The abolition of restraint at the Lincoln Asylum*
Source: R. Gardiner Hill, 'The Total Abolition of Non-Restraint', in R. Hunter and I. Macalpine, *300 Years of Psychiatry*, p. 892.

should claim the merit of having introduced the system, and a lengthy controversy raged in the *Lancet* and the *Medical Circular* from 1850 to 1853. The *Lancet* referred to the *Medical Circular* as 'a scurrilous medical print' and the *Medical Circular* accused the editor of the *Lancet* of 'a career of habitual corruption'. The controversy ended with the collection of rival subscriptions. Gardiner Hill was presented with a silver tea-service, the centre-piece being an épergne inscribed with the statement that he alone was responsible for the introduction of the system of non-restraint. Dr Charlesworth had not survived the controversy, so his supporters had to content themselves with a statue in the grounds of Lincoln Asylum bearing a similar inscription.

Gardiner Hill's real achievement was that he openly abolished restraint even for suicidal and homicidal patients, and worked without the threat of restraint to reinforce discipline. He realized that it was impossible to do this without providing other means for quieting noisy or violent patients. He induced the Governors to increase the staff, and also to improve their pay, so that it would be possible to recruit relatively intelligent and well-trained nurses. He looked especially for tall, strong attendants, whose physique would deter patients from violence. He instituted a continuous night watch on the dormitories, and ensured that all patients should have plenty of exercise. All fermented liquor was banned from the asylum – unlike the practice at the Retreat, where porter was thought to have a calming influence. Attendants were permitted to hold violent patients down with their hands, or to place them in solitary confinement; however, they were not allowed to use drugs or cold baths as substitutes for mechanical restraint.

The system was not an unqualified success. To quote Gardiner Hill's account of the subsequent furore:

> Public attention was soon aroused, as indeed it might be, to the subject . . . indeed for many years I was stigmatized as one bereft of reason myself, a speculator, peculator and a practical breaker of the Sixth Commandment, by exposing the lives of the attendants to the fury of the patients.[10]

Opposition grew even among the Visiting Committee, and Gardiner Hill was eventually compelled to resign his appointment because the attendants were being encouraged to disobey him. 'Had I retained my appointment, I must have sacrificed my principles'.[11]

Dr John Conolly went to Hanwell Asylum in Middlesex in 1839. Hanwell was by far the largest asylum in the country, with 1,000 beds. Conolly had studied in Edinburgh, and practised in general medicine at Chichester and Stratford-on-Avon, becoming Mayor of Stratford. He had been appointed Professor of the Practice of Medicine in the new and struggling University of London, but relinquished this post after two years for private practice.

Sir George Thane of University College Hospital, London, subsequently alleged that Conolly 'failed in practice as a London physician', being 'essentially unscientific' – a good administrator, but a sentimental humanist unfitted for the detached and painstaking work of medical science. [12] Thane, a prominent London physician, could not understand Conolly's behaviour in deserting a prestigious post for a marginal occupation of doubtful antecedents; but Conolly's interest in the treatment of the insane was not a new factor in his life. His MD thesis, presented at Edinburgh in 1821, bore the title 'De statu mentis in Insania et Melancholia', and he had published his *Inquiry Concerning the Indications of Insanity* in 1830, the year in which he abandoned his academic post. The qualities which made him unsuitable, in Thane's eyes, for the practice of general medicine were admirably suited to the work of an administrator in a large asylum.

Before taking up his appointment at Hanwell, Conolly visited Lincoln, and undertook a thorough investigation of the methods used there, and their results. This convinced him that the system was workable on a large scale. In his book *On the Treatment of Insanity*, he described the steps he took to translate Lincoln's experience to the very different conditions at Hanwell. On 1 July 1839, he required a daily return of all patients kept under restraint, and within seven weeks from that time he had totally abolished restraint.

> The coercion chairs (forty in number) have been altogether removed from the walls . . . several patients formerly consigned to them, silent, stupid and sinking into fatuity, may now be seen cheerfully moving about the walls or airing-court; and there can be no question that they have been happily set free from a thraldom of which one constant and lamentable consequence was the acquisition of uncleanly habits. [13]

Conolly, like Gardiner Hill, realized that if the abolition of restraint was to be carried out successfully, it demanded high standards of nursing, and new ways of occupying the patients. He established classes in reading and writing for the illiterate, and in drawing, singing and geography for the literate. He advocated clinical instruction for asylum doctors, most of whom took up their appoinments with no more than a training in general medicine, and a 'place of education' for male and female keepers. The Hanwell committee refused to support his plans, on the grounds of expense.

Andrew Scull's account of Conolly[14] stresses facts which he appears to find discreditable: Conolly was born poor, married young, suffered perennially from financial problems, lacked powerful social and medical contacts in London, resigned from Hanwell after only four years, and had a financial interest in several private asylums in his later years in order to support his wife and unmarried daughters. Conolly is presented as an unabashed – and unsuccessful – medical careerist. In his determination to smash a Victorian idol, Scull appears to support some extreme examples of Victorian snobbery, and ends by siding with the parsimonious committee of visiting justices and Sir George Thane.

Conolly provides a very good example of the developing skills of the asylum doctors, which were not in medicine, but in administration and patient care. He left Hanwell after four years because his progressive ideas were consistently negated by the committee. He consistently argued that asylums should be places of last resort, and if his plans for education and training programmes were frustrated at Hanwell, they were taken up in other asylums. Conolly was doubtless ponderous (many Victorians were) and he was highly praised in his day. That is no reason for minimizing his achievements now.

A scholarly and detailed account of the progress of non-restraint in Britain and the United States is provided by Nancy Tomes.[15] As she points out, restraint was never totally abolished in English public asylums, but its use became infrequent and the Lunacy Commissioners exerted their influence against it. The Commissioners were not 'a rigid body that harshly punished the slightest deviation from the non-restraint ideal, in actuality the Commissioners neither sought nor required absolute uniformity in opinion and practice on the issue'. In the United States, 'arguing that the peculiar character of American insanity made their patients more violent, [asylum doctors] emphatically rejected the ideal of non-restraint for American institutions'.[16]

MEDICAL PUBLICATIONS ON INSANITY

Asylum doctors were beginning to publish studies on their work. They abandoned the old medical methods represented by such works as Haslam's *Observations on Insanity* (1794) and *Considerations on the Management of Insane Persons* (1817), and Bryan Crowther's *Practical Remarks on Insanity* (1811), and learned from moral management. Three works which illustrate this development are George Man Burrows' *Commentary on the Causes etc. of Insanity* (1828), Sir Andrew Halliday's *General View of Lunatics* (1828), and William Ellis's *Treatise on the Nature, Symptoms and Causes of Insanity* (1838). Ellis listed some of the factors which impeded the treatment of insanity: the quackery of some medical men, who specialized in the work because it was lucrative and unexacting; the helplessness of patients, who were unable to fight their own battles; the insistence of wealthy friends and relatives on secrecy, and their indifference to the mode of treatment, as long as the patient was kept closely confined; and above all, the general belief that insanity involved an impairment of all the faculties – 'It must be observed that patients may be insane on one subject, and perfectly sane on all others', wrote Ellis. He recommended occupation, fresh air and exercise as the best means of treatment, and commended the system at the Retreat.

Burrows kept a private asylum at Clapham, significantly also called 'The Retreat', and made a tentative approach to psychosomatic medicine, charting the interaction of mental and bodily symptoms. He deprecated the low standards and high pretensions of some sections of the medical profession, and warned them not to be led away by 'psychological disquisitions, German mystifications and Bedlam sketches . . . calculated to gratify a romantic and prurient taste'.[17]

These three studies marked the asylum doctors' move from orthodox medicine into a new field of study.

ASYLUM MANAGEMENT

The list of questions sent out by the parliamentary reformers in 1827 has one obvious omission: it said nothing about 'cures', or indeed about medical treatment. The care and treatment they wanted to see for patients was a matter of basic health care and social activity, and medical men were appointed as superintendents because they were professional men of some public standing, not because they possessed some new and exclusive technology; but once the asylums were established, the superintendents faced two dilemmas.

First, orthodox medical methods had little or nothing to offer. As Dr W.A.F. Browne, medical superintendent of the Montrose Asylum in Scotland, noted in *What Asylums Were, Are and Ought to Be* (1837), 'Medical men long acted as if nothing could be done with any chance of success in insanity. They believed that were the bowels regulated and the organic functions attended to, their duty was discharged, and the vaunted powers of medicine sufficiently vindicated'.[18] Browne says that Doctors Monro, Burrows and Ellis declared that they could cure ninety out of every hundred cases; but this applied only to recent cases 'which have not existed for more than three months, and which have been treated under the most favourable circumstances'. Browne's own more modest estimate was that 'taking all cases as they are presented, of long or short duration, simple or complicated . . . the average number cured is about one-half'.[19] The Metropolitan Commissioners in Lunacy in 1844 put the recovery rate for county asylums at only 15.4 per cent.[20]

But 'curing patients' was what doctors were expected to do, and the justification for the expensive asylum building programme. Setting up a county asylum was a considerable financial undertaking, and magistrates who had raised a county rate for the purpose expected to see results. As the asylums filled with patients, and there was never enough accommodation to meet the needs, the demand for an active policy increased.

The second dilemma for the asylum doctors was that the patients who were sent to asylums from prisons and workhouses were for the most part unpromising material, already institutionalized and often in a deteriorated condition. They wanted to be able to treat patients at an earlier stage in their illness – before their family relationships collapsed, before they lost employment, before they drifted into poverty or law-breaking.

Dr Browne also raised the problems of attendants, who were difficult to recruit and tended to be of too low a calibre. The usual proportion of keepers to patients was one to thirty, and it was impossible under such circumstances for the patients to be adequately cared for. He related a case in which a visitor enquired after a patient, and was told 'Oh, Mr D. is perfectly quiet, he has been standing on his head for the last half hour.' When keepers were few in number, they tended to remain together for company and safety rather than walking singly about the wards. They were 'the unemployed of other professions . . . if they possess physical strength and a tolerable reputation for sobriety, it is enough, and the latter quality is frequently dispensed with'.[21]

Caleb Crowther, Senior Physician to the West Riding Asylum, in his *Observations on the Management of Madhouses* (1838) discussed the problems of the appointment of superintendents to asylums. He argued that they were so well paid, and their duties so loosely defined, that they tended to mix socially with the local gentry and to neglect their duties.

The election of the superintendent was in the hands of the visiting committee of the county magistrates, mainly landed gentry who tended to appoint someone they found socially acceptable. The superintendent was usually required to be resident in the asylum, and was provided with food, light, fuel, servants and furniture. He could entertain out of the asylum funds, and received in addition a generous salary. The resident director of the Wakefield Asylum received £550 a year, plus services valued at £400 a year – a total of nearly £1,000 a year at a time when a manual worker's wage was a few shillings a week.

A perennial problem was that superintendents were frequently absent from duty when a crisis occurred. Crowther cited a case in 1833, where a patient seized a razor and committed suicide. It was stated at the inquest that the director had been away at the time, and that no orders had been given for the supervision of suicidal patients. The coroner was told that the director was 'very often from home, sometimes for weeks together ... sometimes on the Rhine, sometimes with the fox-hounds, and very often in the streets of Leeds or Wakefield'.[22]

It was still the common practice for the matron to be the wife of the superintendent. This meant that experienced female staff were controlled by a woman who combined a nominal post with marriage and the rearing of children, and who also shared the social round to which her husband's social position committed her.

When the Surrey Asylum was opened in 1841, the visiting committee was clearly aware of the kinds of issues which had been raised in the literature. They drew up rules defining the duties of the superintendent and the matron.[23] The superintendent was to be a qualified medical practitioner, to be resident in the asylum, and to absent himself only with the consent of the visiting justices. The post was to be full-time, and he was forbidden to engage in private practice. He was to visit all the patients every day; to keep case-books; and to report to the committee on every instance of the use of restraint or seclusion. His salary was £150 a year. There were no qualifications for the post of matron (women did not have qualifications in 1841), but the matron was to visit all the female wards before ten o'clock in the morning, and to be responsible for the employment and conduct of the female staff. Her salary was £80 a year.

The Surrey visiting committee also provided detailed rules for the conduct of attendants. They were to rise at 6a.m., to 'wash and comb' the patients, and to report any illness. At 8a.m. they were to serve breakfast and clean the sleeping-rooms, removing any foul straw or linen. They were to serve meals at specified times, to attend the patients at specified intervals, and were forbidden to strike or ill-treat the patients 'on pain of INSTANT DISMISSAL'.

In 1844, Sir Alexander Morison, the visiting physician, succeeded in instituting lectures for male and female attendants in which he 'endeavoured to communicate in a familiar and ... intelligible manner, the principles on which our conduct towards the insane ought to be regulated'.[24] Morison was the first to carry Conolly's ideas on training attendants into effect. Prizes were awarded to those whose conduct was judged meritorious, in order to provide them with an incentive for carrying out their duties on the new principles.

THE WORK OF THE COMMISSIONERS

The Metropolitan Commission appointed under the 1828 Madhouse Act consisted of five medical practitioners and fifteen laymen, including eleven Members or ex-Members of Parliament. Of the reformers responsible for the passing of the 1828 Act, Robert Gordon, Lord Ashley and Charles Williams-Wynn all became Commissioners. Only the medical members were to be salaried. Nicholas Hervey describes how the lay Commissioners, predominantly Evangelicals, came into conflict with the medical Commissioners, who felt that their intervention infringed professional practice. It became increasingly difficult to fill the appointments with laymen possessing the right kind of expertise.[25]

The legal profession pressed for representation, and an Act of 1832 required that at least two Commissioners must be barristers. The requirement that lay Commissioners should accompany professional Commissioners on their visits was abolished. The inspectorate was removed from the jurisdiction of the Home Office to that of the Lord Chancellor's Department. From that time onwards, the actual work of inspection was undertaken by salaried professionals, and the lay element declined.

The Commissioners faced a growing public concern about illegal detention. Some of this, like John Mitford's two pamphlets, *The Crimes and Horrors of Warburton's Private Madhouses* (1830) and *The Crimes and Horrors of Kelly House* (1830), was lurid and sensational. Richard Paternoster's *The Madhouse System* (1841) was an account said to be based on his own experience.

Paternoster, a journalist, had been confined in Finch's madhouse in London in 1838 on the representation of his father, who, he alleged, wished to defraud him of a sum of money. He was captured by violence, and deprived of any contact with the outside world. The keeper was a man who had been convicted five years earlier for homosexual offences. In Finch's house, the linen was foul, the food revolting, restraint and cold baths were used as methods of intimidation, and the answer to every complaint was 'It's your delusion'. Paternoster's friends notified the police, the Commissioners and the Press, but six full weeks elapsed before he was freed.

The Madhouse System may owe something to Paternoster's journalistic talents, but the case of Lewis Phillips illustrated clear dangers to the liberty of the subject. The story was reported to the House of Commons[26] by Thomas Duncombe, well known to the House for his championship of lost and sensational causes. Phillips was a prosperous businessman, a partner in a firm of glass and lamp manufacturers, who submitted his own account of his experiences to the House. At the suggestion of one of his patrons, he had presented himself at Buckingham Palace to try and obtain the patronage of the young Queen Victoria. He became involved in a heated argument with the guards, who were suspicious because there had been an attempt on the Queen's life a few weeks earlier. He found himself committed to one of Warburton's houses, where he remained for six months. Phillips said that the Lunacy Commissioners visited, but the patients were intimidated in advance, and one woman who did complain was severely beaten by the head attendant. He alleged that the staff of the madhouse went to extraordinary lengths to turn his brain, even introducing a woman dressed 'in paltry imitation of our Sovereign' to him on the day of the Queen's Coronation. 'Your petitioner has suffered the torture of mind and body through the acts and filthy observations and questions, too disgusting to be mentioned . . .'

Eventually, Phillips was visited by his cousins, who were his partners in the firm, and it became evident to him that they had been instrumental in securing his confinement. They offered to secure his release, arrange his passage to Antwerp and provide him with a small allowance – on condition that he signed away his interest in the family business. Phillips signed, went to Antwerp and came back within a few days, determined to have his legal rights. Dr Warburton was hastily notified, and two keepers arrived to take him back to the madhouse:

> Your petitioner, having endured so much misery, was fully
> prepared for any design that might show itself, and seeing the
> manoeuvres, immediately forced his way out of the house, crying
> 'Murder', the keepers hallooing out 'Stop, thief!'

Phillips escaped, and succeeded in indicting all the parties concerned
for conspiracy. The matter was finally settled out of court for £170.
Improved methods of certification and inspection were still an
urgent necessity.

Meanwhile, the future of lunacy reform was under threat following the appointment of the new Poor Law Commissioners in 1834.
From the passing of the Poor Law Amendment Act, the twin
watchwords were uniformity and deterrence. The Commissioners
were concerned with the problems of the able-bodied pauper who
would not work, largely ignoring the plight of those who could
not.

The number of lunatics and idiots in workhouses in 1828 was
estimated at 9,000.[27] In 1845, despite the increase in the provision
of county asylums and the growth in the practice of 'contracting
out', there were still 4,080 according to the Poor Law Commissioners, and 9,339 according to the Lunacy Commissioners.[28] A law
framed to deter the able-bodied from seeking relief was being
applied in all its stringency to people who were totally unable to
support themselves, and who were in some cases subject to coercion.

In 1838, a Select Committee on the working of the Poor Law
Amendment Act heard an Assistant Poor Law Commissioner,
Edward Gulson, attack the administration of county asylums, and
ask for power over pauper lunatics to be transferred back to the
Poor Law authorities.

> The expenses of maintaining pauper lunatics in places pointed
> out by the law for lunatic asylums is very great indeed . . . I am
> stating distinctly what I conceive to be the best for the paupers,
> and for the parish purse . . . very great jobs have been made of
> such establishments . . . a vast sum of money has been thrown
> away in the erection of some of them.[29]

Gulson thought that the Poor Law Commissioners could run
Union lunatic asylums for 'one-half or a third or a fourth of the
expense at which [the pauper lunatics] are now kept'.

The author of the proposal to bring the county asylums within the scope of the Poor Law was probably Edwin Chadwick. Gulson was his loyal adherent and close friend; but the days of Chadwick's power and prestige in Poor Law administration were over, and the proposal failed to gain support.

County asylums were certainly more expensive to operate than workhouses. A comparison of costs in 1845 shows that the cost of board and clothing alone in county asylums averaged $7s3\frac{1}{2}d$ per week, whereas the average for workhouses was $2s.7d$.[30] The real point at issue between the Poor Law authorities and the Lunacy authorities was that of custody or treatment. The Poor Law authorities wished to send to the county asylum only those patients who were dangerous or violent, and to retain those who could live in the workhouse without causing alarm or annoyance. The county asylums wanted to receive those who were treatable or curable. The issue was settled by 1842, when the Poor Law Commissioners issued a directive to Boards of Guardians:

with lunatics, the first object ought to be their cure by means of, proper medical treatment. This can only be obtained in a well-regulated asylum; and therefore the detention of any curable lunatic in a workhouse is highly objectionable on the score both of humanity and economy.[31]

This statement implied a neat division of functions, though the issues were to be fought over locally for many years; but the Metropolitan Commissioners in Lunacy were at least able to continue their work unhampered by the claims of the Poor Law Commission to control their activities.

The reports which the Metropolitan Commissioners issued between 1829 and 1842 show a constant attention to detail, and an increasingly stringent view of their duties. The Commissioners enquired as to the character and conduct of attendants and nurses; they broke with tradition in listening to patients' grievances, and investigating them; they experimented with a system of release on trial, so that the transition from the asylum to the outside world could be supervised.

The Metropolitan Commissioners were learning by experience; learning how to inspect premises, checking the records against the facts, insisting on opening every door, tasting the food, and distrusting recently cleaned seclusion rooms and easy assurances about patients' incapacities. Above all, they used their sense of smell: stench meant mismanagement, and it is notable how much attention they devoted to the problems of handling incontinence. Even so, they were not always successful in detecting abuses. Mitford's two pamphlets were probably based on events before 1828, and Paternoster was a journalist; but the Phillips case, with its evidence of intimidation before the Commissioners' visits, suggests that Dr Warburton was not the reformed character they had assumed in 1830. It also suggests that inspection was not a once-and-for-all activity: to be effective, it had to be frequently repeated.

D.J. Mellett, in *The Prerogatives of Asylumdom* provides an interesting and detailed account of the Metropolitan Commissioners' work, but complains that their reports 'indicate a self-satisfaction and optimistic faith in the bulk of licencees'. He points out that, though they assiduously amassed records, they reported few cases of 'flagrant illegality'. Though he appreciates the limitation of their powers, and their desire to secure 'a complete and general registry in lunacy', Mellett comes to the conclusion that the reports 'suggest mainly self-deception'.[32]

This is to misunderstand the conditions under which the Commissioners worked. They had to proceed very carefully, for several reasons. Some of the owners of London madhouses were distinguished medical men with family, professional and business connections with members of the House of Commons and the House of Lords. Members of both Houses had relatives in the London madhouses, and would have been alarmed at the prospect of publicity. London society was a very small circle in the 1830s. As Mellett points out, the reformers had wanted a national Commission in 1815 and 1827, but Parliament had granted the Commission only very limited powers in 1828. Commissioners knew that they were on trial, and that the House of Commons could cancel their remit if it chose. They could not afford to make enemies in high places by publishing too many revelations. Many of their activities were pursued out of the public eye. Their main aim was to spread knowledge of good practice and encourage higher standards. A sharply judgemental approach would have alienated the staff, and not improved matters for the patients. The Commissioners had to build up experience of how to inspect, and to create as few waves of opposition as possible until the time when they could ask Parliament for a wider remit.

The Commissioners' work was confined by the 1828 Madhouses Act to the private madhouses, and to the London area. In the provinces, the inspection of private madhouses must have been more cursory. The visiting justices would have varied in competence and commitment to the work, which was often unpleasant, and they would have been even more wary of making enemies, since they lived in the same locality as the madhouses they visited, and the proprietors were their – possibly wealthy – neighbours. Local magistrates did not have the experience of the parliamentary reformers. In addition to being responsible for the inspection of madhouses, they were also responsible for the financing and management of county asylums – a task for which they had no expertise, and no guidance apart from that provided by the Commissioners.

Many pauper lunatics remained in workhouses, under the deterrent Poor Law of 1834, and neither Commissioners nor justices had any power to intervene. Bethlem remained uninspected, as did lunatics in prison and single lunatics. A clause in the 1828 Madhouses Act permitting the compilation of a register of single lunatics was so hedged about with restrictions to ensure secrecy that it remained a dead letter.

'The subject of insanity has lately excited much attention', wrote Ashley in his report of 1839–40; but authority and responsibility were divided. Not until 1842 was there an opportunity to bring together all the strands in a single administration. With the events of 1842–5, lunacy reform entered a new phase.

CHAPTER 5

The National Lunacy Commission

By 1842, a new group of parliamentary reformers had grouped around Ashley. His reputation as a social reformer was well established. He was forty-one years of age; he had been a Member of Parliament for sixteen years, and a Lunacy Commissioner for fourteen. His work to improve conditions in the factories and the mines had earned public respect. He had become something of a national figure, and to the initial advantage of aristocratic connections (which counted for a good deal in Victorian England) had added those of detailed knowledge and practical experience.

On 17 March 1842, Lord Granville Somerset, one of Ashley's supporters, rose in the House of Commons to propose a Bill empowering the Metropolitan Commissioners to carry out an inspection of all asylums and madhouses in England, whatever their legal status. He pointed out the deficiencies in the existing legislation – the different systems of inspection in the metropolis and the provinces, the fact that county asylums and single lunatics were not subject to effective inspection, and the fact that Bethlem was not inspected at all.

Somerset stressed that his proposal was only the first stage in the movement to secure a national system. In the debate which followed, the scheme was subjected to a withering attack from Dr Thomas Wakley, the founding editor of the *Lancet*, who demanded the introduction of a comprehensive system at once. Wakley was particularly incensed by Somerset's proposal that the legal Commissioners should take part in the tour:

He did not suppose the noble Lord intended this proposition as an insult to the medical profession; but if it had been so intended, one of a more marked character could scarcely have been offered.[1]

Ashley rose to answer. He wished that the measure went further, but 'it would baffle the ingenuity of the Member for Finsbury [Wakley] to institute a practicable system of uniformity for all the asylums in the country'. Comprehensive legislation must wait until the House was in possession of all the facts. On the question of whether the tour should be undertaken by the legal or the medical Commissioners, he was not in favour of either professional group; he advocated lay inspection: 'A man of common-sense could give as good an opinion as any medical man he knew.' The statement did nothing to conciliate Wakley, lost him the backing of a large section of the medical profession, and hardly pleased the lawyers. The two groups were jockeying for power, but united in the intention of reducing the powers of the lay reformers.

Eventually a Bill was ordered and, after some delaying tactics by the House of Lords, became law on 5 August 1842. In its final form, the number of Commissioners was increased to between fifteen and twenty, of whom four were to be legal Commissioners and six or seven medical Commissioners. The medical and legal Commissioners were to carry out a detailed national tour of inspection of all institutions housing lunatics, with the exception of Bethlem (which remained excluded: the institution had powerful allies in Parliament), reporting especially on the use of non-restraint, the method of classification, the effect of occupation and amusements, and the condition of pauper patients.

How the asylums and madhouses which had previously been exempt from inspection by the Commissioners faced the prospect of visitation can only be guessed in most cases. At the Lancaster Asylum, a great change took place soon after the 1842 Bill was introduced. The cash book shows a sudden rush of buying: hardware, kitchen utensils, soap, candles and 'scouring liquors' were bought in large quantities. From May to September 1842, £243 was spent on blankets alone, and the former frequent indents for straw stopped completely. Evidently most of the patients had slept on straw, and were now given proper bedding for the first time.

The sudden change in policy appears to have been due less to panic on the part of the visiting justices than to a new and enlightened medical superintendent, Mr Gaskell (a surgeon). The use of mechanical restraints had been abolished in June 1841 on his orders, and the threat of inspection may have helped him to induce the justices to provide the money for a thorough overhaul of living conditions.

John Walton, in a more detailed study of the Lancaster records, notes that although the previous superintendent, Dr Paul Slade Knight, 'paid lip-service to ideals of humanity and moderation', many patients were chained, and the asylum death rate was high. 'In 1832, a cholera epidemic boosted the mortality level to 48.9 per cent, and in 1836–7, diarrhoea and sickness brought the death rate up to 26.8 per cent.'[2] Gaskell and his assistant, Dr De Vitré, introduced moral management and non-restraint, removed over 19 tons of iron bars and gates, and began a régime based on activity and good human relationships.

The Commissioners reached Lancaster in October 1842 – only two months after the passing of the Act. The Commissioners' report in the Visitors' Book expressed 'unqualified approbation', commented on the 'skill, zeal and attention' of the staff, and noted that 'the bedding is good and sufficient, and is arranged with neatness on the bedsteads during the day'.

The lay Commissioners, like Ashley and Somerset, did not take part in the tour, but the sifting of information received and the writing of the final report was largely Ashley's work. He was the acknowledged leader of the lunacy reform group. He noted in his diary:

July 2nd. – Finished at last, Report of the Commission in Lunacy. Good thing over. Sat for many days in review. God prosper it! It contains much for the alleviation of physical and moral suffering.[3]

THE REPORT OF 1844

The Report is a document in which details obtrude and the overall picture is not easily grasped. Ashley had little literary or analytical skill; but the patient piling of fact on fact provided a sound basis for the recommendations which followed.

The first part deals with county asylums, giving a mass of domestic detail on all the matters set out by the Metropolitan Commissioners in 1828 – classification, ventilation, heating, diet, cleanliness, exercise, occupation, education, leisure activities. There were apparently no outstanding abuses – the Commissioners were universally congratulatory. There were twelve county asylums which provided accommodation only for criminal and pauper lunatics, and five 'county asylums united with subscription asylums' – institutions such as those at Stafford and Nottingham where the costs of construction and maintenance had been met partly out of the county rate, and partly by public subscription. In these latter institutions, paying patients were admitted to offset the cost of maintaining paupers.

The cost of county asylums was still very high, and the Commissioners had a cautious word to say about excessive costs:

While we have no wish to advocate the erection of unsightly buildings, we think that no unnecessary costs should be incurred for architectural decoration; especially as these asylums are erected for persons who, when in health, are accustomed to dwell in cottages.[4]

Some magistrates were evidently following the example of Bethlem, and building stately homes for the poor; but stately homes were then the only large residential establishments which existed, so they had no other model. Later in the report, the Commissioners drew attention to this lack of experience:

Although county magistrates have properly the control of funds to be raised in their own districts, it can scarcely be expected that they should devote so much attention as is really necessary to make them conversant with the various points which involve the convenience, comfort and security necessary to be provided for in large asylums for the insane, and they are therefore liable to be misled as to their proper cost and construction.[5]

This emphasis on inexperience and architecture was a polite way of acknowledging Edward Gulson's opinion that 'very great jobs have been perpetrated in the erection of county asylums'. If the Commissioners wanted to keep the county asylum system clear of the rigours of the Poor Law, they had to demonstrate a concern for what would now be called cost-efficiency; and the recommendation that the design and construction of asylums should be subject to the consent and approval of a central agency made good financial sense:

> It is apparent ... that although a few of the existing county asylums are well adapted to their purpose, and a very large proportion of them are extremely well-conducted: yet some of them are quite unfit for the reception of the insane, some are placed in ineligible sites, some are deficient in the necessary means of providing out-door employment for their paupers, some are ill-contrived and defective in their internal construction, some are cheerless and confined in their yards and airing-grounds ... it appears to be deserving the attention of the legislature, whether the erection of public asylums for the insane poor may not advantageously be regulated by some independent authority ... pauper lunatics have unfortunately become so numerous throughout the whole kingdom, that the proper construction and cost of asylums for their use has ceased to be a subject which affects a few counties only, and has become a matter of national interest and importance'.[6]

Public lunatic hospitals, some of which had followed Bethlem's example in claiming exemption from the Madhouses Act, were inspected. The Commissioners commended the administration of the Retreat. They found St Luke's ill-placed, and deficient in most of the necessary amenities. They were particularly severe about the Bethel Hospital at Norwich and the Manchester Lunatic Hospital, which were found 'very ill-adapted for the reception of the insane'.[7] The same was true of St Peter's, Bristol, a pioneer establishment at the end of the seventeenth century, but now well below the standard the Commissioners set. The visiting Commissioners concluded roundly that 'the entire body of lunatics ought to be removed to more spacious premises, and to a more airy and healthy situation'.[8]

There were thirty-seven licensed madhouses in the metropolitan area. These had been within the jurisdiction of the Metropolitan Commissioners for the past fourteen years; but there were also ninety-nine houses in the provinces which were visited for the first time. The chief impression was not of widespread cruelty and neglect, but of a common evasion of the law. In many houses, the law relating to the registration of certified persons was evaded by declaring that the patient was merely suffering from 'nerves', and did not require certification. Some houses took 'low-spirited or desponding' patients as boarders. The fault may have been in the law, which made no provision for the treatment of those who were not certifiable. The licensing laws were also evaded: frequently, a proprietor would keep patients in several different houses, though he had a licence only for one. This increased the difficulties of inspection. Proprietors of private madhouses often took their duties lightly. At Cranbourne in Dorset, two Commissioners visited a certain house on three separate occasions and the proprietor was away each time, the patients being left in the care of a solitary female servant. At Belle Grove House in Newcastle, there was a repetition of an incident which the Commissioners had encountered in their first year of office: the house was being managed by a man who knew nothing at all about lunacy, because he happened to be the chief creditor of the former owner.

Previous suspicions that the local magistrates did not always take their duties seriously were confirmed: in four cases, the Commissioners found that the magistrates did not visit at all; in one, they invariably sent for the visitors' book beforehand, so that the proprietor was forewarned. Where the Commissioners found grounds for complaint, they called them to the attention of the Chairman of Quarter Sessions: in almost every case, a subsequent visit showed that no action had been taken. On the same day on which the Commissioners visited the house at West Auckland, the magistrates also visited. The Commissioners found the house 'utterly unfit'; the magistrates, only an hour or two before, had recorded 'everything in good order'.[9]

Workhouses were still under the control of the Poor Law Commissioners, and not technically included in the inquiry, since the Poor Law directive of 1842 required all lunatics to be sent to county asylums. Though it was widely known that this directive was not followed, the Commissioners avoided another clash with the Poor Law Commission. The touring Commissioners contented themselves with visiting 'such as lay in our road' – five large workhouses containing a special lunatic ward. Patients who should have been sent to county asylums within the statutory fourteen days were still being detained in the workhouses. At Redruth, patients were not sent to the asylum until they had become 'either from dirty habits or dangerous propensities, unmanageable in a workhouse or in lodgings'. At Nottingham they arrived 'in a debilitated and exhausted state',and in Surrey they 'were sent into the asylum in some cases to die'. Ashley concluded that the local Boards of Guardians were 'under some misconception as to the condition of lunatics in workhouses'.[10]

The section of the report on mechanical restraint was not Ashley's work. Ashley was a firm supporter of the non-restraint system, and had publicly praised the work done in this connection at Hanwell. He 'could not speak too highly either of the system itself, or of the manner in which it was carried out by the talented superintendent, Dr Conolly'.[11]

The report did not reflect that attitude, though the arguments for and against restraint were summarized with a show of fairness. The main arguments for absolute non-coercion were that it soothed the patient, and was thus more humane than mechanical restraint, which tended to be humiliating and degrading; that the use of restraint gave the keepers an opportunity of abusing and neglecting their patients; that the only requisite was an increase of staff, which ought not to be refused merely on the grounds of expense; and that experience showed that the general tone of the asylum improved when restraint was abolished.

The arguments in favour of 'moderate coercion' involved diametrically opposed claims: that slight restraint frequently induced tranquillity in an otherwise restless patient; that the only real alternative to restraint in the case of an excited and dangerous patient was solitary confinement, which could be even more degrading; that it was impossible for the staff, however great their devotion to duty, to exercise an unwearying surveillance; and finally, that experience showed that the best approach to the insane was that in which kindness was mingled with a show of authority.

The legal and medical Commissioners' experience at Lincoln and Hanwell led them to support the latter view: they found that the non-restraint system did not always produce the tranquillity and high moral tone claimed by its advocates. At Lincoln, they found 'unusual excitement prevailing in the disorderly ward on the female side'. At Hanwell

a violent female lunatic who had been endeavouring to bite other persons as well as herself was seized by four or five nurses, and after a violent and protracted struggle forced with great difficulty into . . . one of the cells. During this scene, there was much confusion on the ward, and the great efforts of the patient to liberate herself must have greatly exhausted her.[12]

They had seen a female patient push an elderly patient to the ground; a woman who lacerated her arm from wrist to elbow as a result of thrusting it through an unbarred window; and a male patient who had recently killed another. The Commissioners may have felt that there was some justification for the attitude of an anonymous clergyman who, while a patient in Hanwell in 1841, addressed the following lines to his Member of Parliament:

> We have in this asylum, sir,
> Some doctors of renown,
> With a plan of non-restraint
> They seem to think their own . . .
> All well-meaning men, sir,
> But troubled with a complaint
> Called the monomania
> Of total non-restraint . . . [13]

The question of the authorship of this section of the report was raised in the House of Commons by Wakley soon after its publication. He believed that 'there almost lurked about it something of a sneer at the Hanwell Lunatic asylum' and that it was obviously not Ashley's work. Wakley was also a strong supporter of non-restraint, and sarcastic about the Commissioners' conclusions:

> But, said the report, those who employ as well as those who do not employ mechanical restraint, adopt an equally mild and conciliatory method of managing their patients. The deuce they did; it was the oddest in the world. So that a man who whipped his child every morning before breakfast adopted just as mild a system of treatment as the father who endeavoured to admonish his child into the path of duty and happiness![14]

Although Ashley was present in the House at the time, he made no reply.

The recommendations of the report had two primary aims: to

secure the unification of administration over asylums and madhouses, and to extend the lunacy laws to cover all the types of
institution in which the insane were detained. The Commissioners
recommended that the provision of county asylums should be
mandatory in all counties; that record-keeping and methods of
certification should be improved; that the Lunacy authority should
have permanent power of inspection over all county asylums,
subscription hospitals, private madhouses and lunatics in workhouses; and that a central authority should be set up to approve all
sites, plans and estimates for new asylums.

THE EFFECT OF THE 1844 REPORT

Sir Robert Peel the younger, who had been a member of the Select
Committee of 1827, was now Prime Minister. Though he did not
appoint Ashley to his Cabinet, as Ashley expected (Ashley was
much offended to be offered only a minor post in the Royal
Household) he was prepared to support the Lunacy Report. Social
reform was by this time part of the Tory legislative programme, as
well as that of the Whigs.

The Lunacy Report, in spite of its turgid form, attracted much
attention. In a lengthy contribution in the *Westminster Review*, the
writer, who signed himself 'G.', found it 'highly creditable to the
Commissioners, but at the same time humiliating to us as a nation.
Our feeling of humiliation, however, ought to give way to thankful-
ness that such facts are brought to light.' He enquired of his
readers what would be their reaction if patients suffering from
acute physical ailments, such as inflammation of the lungs, were
commonly sent to workhouses, and allowed to remain there until
the disease was incurable. The link between mental and physical
illness was repeatedly stressed by reference to 'patients', 'hospitals'
and 'nurses', avoiding the derogatory and emotionally coloured
terms then still in use. With reference to such outdated official
phrases as 'order for admission', 'commitment papers' and 'keepers', 'G.' commented: 'Does not this still savour of transport to
prison rather than of removal to hospital? We recommend the total
disuse of these terms.'[15]

On the question of asylum costs, G. pointed out that their
construction was necessarily an expensive matter. If the dormitory
principle were approved as being cheaper than separate cells, it

would still be necessary to construct a number of single cells for violent and dangerous patients; and since some might be arsonists, it was essential to have the building fireproofed. When allowance was made for these considerations, he thought that the average construction cost of £200 per person for a county asylum, as against £40 per head for a workhouse, not unreasonable. He also pointed out that a comparison of maintenance costs was misleading: in workhouse accounts, the weekly cost per head was expressed in terms of food, clothing and fuel only. In county asylums, weekly costs also included staff wages and salaries and the cost of household replacements. This article was evidently influential, as it was subsequently reprinted and sold as a pamphlet.

Meanwhile, Ashley was determined to translate sentiment into action. On 23 July 1844, he brought forward in the House of Commons a motion praying that the Lunacy Report might be 'taken into consideration'. In a lengthy speech, he recapitulated the findings of the report, and ended:

> These unhappy persons are outcasts from all the social and domestic affections of private life . . . and have no refuge but in the laws. You can prevent, by the agency which you shall appoint as you have in so many cases prevented, the recurrence of frightful cruelties; you can soothe the days of the incurable, and restore many sufferers to health and usefulness . . . I trust, therefore, that I shall stand excused, though I have consumed so much of your valuable time, when you call to mind that the motion is made on behalf of the most helpless, if not the most afflicted, portion of the human race.[16]

It was unfortunate that this moving speech should have been made at an inopportune moment. Ashley appears to have known little about parliamentary tactics, and not to have realized that he had committed a blunder in bringing the matter forward at the end of a parliamentary session. He had evidently not consulted the government before acting, for the Home Secretary rose in answer, urging him not to press the motion at that stage, and promising support at a later date. Ashley agreed, and the whole matter was allowed to lapse until the following session.

Meanwhile, the press had become interested. *The Times* ran an editorial in which Ashley's inconclusive actions were criticized:

We have no wish to be severe on Lord Ashley: we have the greatest respect for his humanity, his zeal, his industry, his abilities, his piety. But he is not a political leader . . . we think that Lord Ashley only exhibited his own weakness by allowing himself to bring forward the question of the treatment of pauper lunatics at this period of the session, with the certainty of being obliged to give up the matter to the Government. The question was his own: the Home Secretary acknowledged himself unable to discuss it with him on the ground of want of acquaintance with detail. Why did not Lord Ashley keep it in his own hands?[17]

A study of *The Times* from August 1844 to June 1845, when the Lunacy Bill was finally ordered, shows that the topic of insanity was frequently featured in correspondence and items of news. 'The farce of Lord Ashley's medical and non-medical Commissioners may proceed' wrote a sceptic who signed himself 'One Who Could Say More:'

All acquainted with the subject know that it is only an expensive humbug; and if it were withdrawn altogether, there would be more real protection for the wretched inmates of these asylums, because the public would not then have the opinion that they were legally inspected, and would be more vigilant over these dens.[18]

In October, a lunatic named Big Hester escaped from confinement at Edderton, and was alleged to have devoured a girl's arm. The Law Reports gave details of a series of Chancery cases, in which the sanity of a wealthy individual was challenged by relatives in order to protect the estate. An Act of 1842 had greatly simplified the procedure for a writ *de lunatico inquirendo*, and consequently the number of cases increased at this time. Some of these cases included counter-allegations of illegal detention, such as the case of Dyce Sombre, an 'Asiatic' whose wife was evidently anxious to be rid of him, which provided several precedents in the law relating to Chancery lunatics.[19] In February 1845, allegations were made concerning the treatment of a pauper patient in the Cornwall Asylum at Bodmin, and this led to a lively and protracted correspondence on the subject of pauper lunatics in general. There were further Chancery cases in April, May and June, and on the day on which the Lunatics Bill finally passed the Commons, there was an account of a lunatic who ran amok in Pimlico, 'declaiming in the most horrible and blasphemous language'.

On 6 June 1845, the motion for the ordering of a Bill was at last brought forward. 'Sir,' said Ashley in his opening speech,

it is remarkable and very humiliating, the long and tedious process by which we have arrived at the sound practice of the treatment of the insane, which now appears to be the suggestion of common sense and ordinary humanity'.[20]

The Home Secretary seconded the motion on behalf of the government, giving it his full support and approval, and stated: 'I have the satisfaction of stating that the measures which my noble friend wishes to introduce are introduced with the Lord Chancellor's entire approbation . . . we determined to give the Bill, as a Government, our most cordial support'.

The Lunatics Bill passed the Commons on 23 July, and was returned by the Lords on 1 August with several amendments, the chief of which was a clause exempting Bethlem from all the provisions. These amendments were agreed to, and the Bill became law on 4 August. A subsidiary Bill, dealing with the erection and management of county asylums, was introduced at the same time, and after minor amendments became law on 8 August.

THE LUNATICS ACT OF 1845

The new Lunacy Commissioners – formerly the Metropolitan Commissioners in Lunacy – were named by the Act.[21] They included five laymen, three medical Commissioners and three legal Commissioners, who together constituted a permanent inspectorate. The medical and legal Commissioners were to receive a salary of £1,500 a year, and were debarred from holding any other post. In the case of death, dismissal or resignation, the Lord Chancellor was to make further appointments, maintaining the existing proportion of lay, medical and legal Commissioners. The lay Commissioners, who included Ashley and Robert Gordon, were unpaid. The chairman was to be a lay member, elected by the other Commissioners. There was a small secretariat, consisting of a secretary and two clerks.

The remit of the Commissioners was similar to that of the former Metropolitan Commissioners – inspecting, licensing and reporting; but it was extended permanently to cover all asylums, hospitals for the insane and licensed houses in England and Wales. A legal and a medical Commissioner were to visit each asylum and hospital once a year, each licensed house in the metropolis four times a year, and each licensed house in the provinces where the justices would also continue to visit – twice a year. They could visit by night, and inspect all buildings and outhouses. They were to enquire about any patient under restraint, and to inspect all the prescribed records. They could discharge patients after making two visits at an interval of seven days (apart from criminal or Chancery cases).

The Commissioners retained their licensing function in the metropolitan area. Licensing in the provinces remained in the hands of the magistrates, but a copy of every provincial licence was to be sent to the Commissioners for their information.

The reporting function of the Commissioners formed a permanent link with the Lord Chancellor's office. They were to report once every six months to furnish routine particulars of the number of visits undertaken and the establishments visited, and annually in June to supply details of visits in the preceding year.

New forms of certification were laid down: that for private patients required a statement of the medical and social history of the patient, signed by the petitioner, together with two detailed medical statements to the effect that the person concerned was 'an insane person or an idiot or a person of unsound mind', and safeguards to prevent collusion between the parties concerned. The form of petition for a pauper patient had to be signed by a justice of the peace or officiating clergyman of the parish, and also by the relieving officer or overseer. This took the same prescribed form, and required the same detailed statements.

All institutions for the treatment of the insane were now required to keep an admission book, in which the name of the patient had to be recorded within two days of reception, and the diagnosis within seven; a book in which to enter the cause of the patient's removal from the institution, whether by death, discharge, transfer or escape; a medical visitation book to include 'details of restraint, seclusion, medical treatment, injuries and acts of violence'; a medical case-book; a visitors' book which was to contain the reports of those who made an official or unofficial inspection; and a patients' book, in which visitors or Commissioners might make observations on the condition of individual patients.

In addition, the proprietor or superintendent was made legally responsible for forwarding notice of each individual reception, death, discharge, escape or transfer to the Commissioners within seven days of the occurrence and if the institution was outside the metropolitan area, also to the justices. Thus there were five different sets of documents to deal with, and five sets of records to be kept, in addition to the certification documents.

REFORM OR BUREAUCRATIC CONTROL?

The Act was regarded as a humane and progressive move by Parliament, press and commentators. The *Annual Register* for 1844 called it 'One of the minor, but not the least valuable fruits of the session'. In a small country with some 17 or 18 million inhabitants, central planning and administration made it possible to disseminate knowledge on such issues as architecture, building, finance and patient care, and to insist on national standards from Cornwall to the Scottish border. The Commissioners' power to inspect and remedy abuses was a notable step forward in human rights.

Though there was opposition, it came largely from private mad-house keepers who still resisted inspection, and from local magistrates who resented not being left to their own devices. In Parliament, the only opposition came from those who thought that the provisions did not go far enough.

Ashley, in the light of his experience in the metropolitan area, believed implicitly in the value of documentation as a safeguard against irregular practice. With hindsight, it is possible to see that the insistence on record-keeping led to a deadening bureaucracy. Unnecessary complication of paper-work tends to defeat its own ends, for when the law becomes so complex that it may be transgressed unwittingly, deliberate evasion is easily explained away.

It is also possible to see that the system which was appropriate for the period in which it was set up was soon to be swamped by sheer numbers. The unprecedented increase in the population in the second half of the nineteenth century meant that any fixed stock of accommodation – for schools, for prisons, for hospitals – was full to overflowing before the buildings had been completed, and centralized administrations became unwieldy and unresponsive to changing needs.

But Ashley and his colleagues did not have the benefit of hindsight. The reform grew out of necessity, and was designed to save patients from the even more centralized and much less humane Poor Law. If the ruthless logic of Benthamism was carried into practice, it was not in the asylums, but in the work of the Poor Law Commissioners who wanted to take them over and run them more cheaply.

Modern objections to the establishment of the Lunacy Commission on the grounds that it represented 'state control' and 'medical domination'[22] seem to ignore the social and economic context in which it was set up. David Mellett, who has a good chapter on pauper lunatics[23] comes to the conclusion that

> 'the institutional care and control of the insane was often a function of group values only tenuously related to scientific or medical considerations. Especially it was bound up with a series of social and economic factors, partly because county asylums and other institutions . . . were financed publicly; partly because the majority of patients came from low class backgrounds, and the cost . . . had to be met out of the local rates'.[24]

One cannot ignore the poverty and social distress of many of the patients who came to the asylums; the cruelty and neglect of some of the large private madhouses; and the sheer inefficiency and penny-pinching of many of the people – madhouse proprietors and local justices – who were responsible for lunatics before the national Lunacy Commission began its work. A powerful central body could insist on adequate financing and raise standards. There is no other way in which this could have been achieved.

Ashley and his colleagues had worked long and hard for this moment of success. They were not to know how their creation would develop in the next thirty or forty years, or how much opposition it would attract. They solved the problems of lunacy reform in one generation, only to be faced with new situations and unexpected problems in the next.

CHAPTER 6

The Triumph of Legalism

In 1841, the asylum doctors formed their own professional organization, the Association of Medical Officers of Asylums for the
Insane. In 1853, Dr J.C. Bucknill, medical superintendent of the
Devon County Asylum, founded the *Asylum Journal*. A year later,
this publication became the *Asylum Journal of Mental Science*, and
in 1859, the word 'asylum' was dropped from the title. In 1865, the
Association changed its name to the shorter, but scarcely less
cumbrous, one of the Medico-Psychological Association. The subject of study was variously described as 'medical psychology' and
'physiological psychology'. Behind this play with words was an
attempt to find verbal formulae which would describe a new
professional group whose concerns were very different from those
of other medical practitioners.

Yet the asylum doctors were becoming increasingly conscious of
their status as members of the medical profession. The Medical
Registration Act of 1858 gave medical practitioners a much improved status, practically outlawed quackery and reorganized medical education. The General Medical Council was set up, with
power to fix examination standards, and to make registration as a
'qualified medical practitioner' dependent on reaching these standards. The asylum doctors wanted to be associated with these
desirable developments; but they were conscious that their work
was only marginally 'medical', and that there were non-medical
groups who made claims to expertise – in particular, senior asylum
nurses, who often knew the patients better than the doctors did,
and the lay Commissioners in London. To defend themselves

against these claimants, they drew closer to medicine, which was the source of their prestige and their exclusivity. In 1858, the *Journal* carried a sustained attack on the non-medical members of the Lunacy Commission by Dr J.E. Huxley, medical superintendent of the Kent Asylum, who claimed that they were 'pronouncing judgements on a medical matter without medical knowledge'.[1]

There was, however, little or no specialist medical knowledge available for the treatment of insanity. Patients came into the asylum, often dirty, flea-bitten, physically debilitated and suffering from malnutrition. When they were clean and well fed, some recovered, and some did not; but the specialist skills which the asylum doctors possessed were derived from the practice of moral management and non-restraint, not from medicine. As medical science made advances in other fields, these 'non-medical' skills were increasingly discounted.

In the event, the main challenge to the asylum doctors in the second half of the nineteenth century did not come from the lay Commissioners or the nurses. It came from the lawyers. While medicine was still engaged in throwing off the shackles of a long association with barbering and charlatanism, lawyers had been organized for centuries. Restrictive, powerful and prestigious, the legal profession had become aware of the growing status of the asylum doctors, and (somewhat belatedly) of the importance of the liberty of the subject issue. Pressure from the Lord Chancellor's Department had resulted in that department taking over the supervision of the Metropolitan Commission in Lunacy in 1832, and in the appointment of barristers to the Commission. From 1845, medical and legal Commissioners were of equal numbers. Asylum visits were undertaken by a barrister and a medical practitioner working together, and the lay Commissioners were restricted to working in London.

Legal interest in lunacy law was focused on the protection of the sane against illegal detention rather than on the care and treatment of the insane. While the medical profession stressed the importance of early treatment, the legal profession piled safeguard on safeguard to prevent it. While the asylum doctors wanted to overcome the stigma attached to treatment, the lawyers increased the stigma by their determination to draw a firm line of demarcation between the sane and the insane. The legal lobby was strengthened by two factors: the development of the first libertarian pressure group, and some alarmist reportage in the press. The Alleged Lunatics' Friend Society was founded in 1845 by Luke James Hansard, son of the original printer to the House of Commons, 'for the protection of the British subject from unjust confinement on the grounds of mental derangement, and for the redress of persons so confined'. By 1851, ten Members of Parliament were vice-presidents.

The Society's Annual Report of 1851 complained that 'the alleged lunatic may be confined, cut off from all communication with his friends, and placed in circumstances most calculated to render him insane for thirteen weeks or more before the quarterly visit of the magistrates or Commissioners can afford him any opportunity of appeal'. It admitted that the Commissioners acted with 'praiseworthy vigour' in pursuance of their duties, but quoted Ashley himself as saying that the system of inspection was still 'both irregular and imperfect'. The Society was not on good terms with Ashley, who found its activities embarrassing. Its members visited asylums and investigated individual cases, taking the view that any patient who was not obviously deranged at the time of the visit should be released immediately.[2]

Even with their new status, the asylum doctors were under constant attack. In 1859, an article by Dr Bucknill in the *Journal of Mental Science* complained of the activities of the press:

the mob of newspaper writers in the dullest season have suddenly started game, upon which they could all run, and like a scratch pack, they have opened their sweet melodious voices on the poor mad-doctor; and a scratch pack it was indeed, with every intonation of threatening cry, from the noble bay of the hound, to the small yap of the cur. It is a wonderful thing, this newspaper press of ours, the fifth estate as it is called, the bulwark of right, the palladium of liberty . . . the fountain of the pure waters of truth, but alas, sometimes also the sewers of calumnious false-hood . . .'[3]

Dr Bucknill was afraid that any legislative action resulting from publicity in the press would be 'a sop to the Cerberus of public opinion'.

THE SELECT COMMITTEE OF 1859

Public agitation concerning the lunacy laws continued. There were rumours of ill-treatment at Hanwell, complaints from released patients, and a constant flow of indignant letters and articles in the national newspapers. Among those vilified was Daniel Hack Tuke, great-grandson of William Tuke of the Retreat, and a consultant physician of some standing. He wrote:

> The author himself did not escape animadversion, and was represented in a newspaper as a brutal mad-doctor using a whip upon an unfortunate patient. The charge was the offspring of a bewildered editor who was obliged to acknowledge that he had been the victim of his own imagination.[4]

The second Derby administration, in which Spencer Walpole was Home Secretary, appointed a Select Committee of the House of Commons in February 1859. Both Walpole and his Liberal predecessor in office, Sir George Grey, were members of this Committee, which continued to sit during the next Liberal administration. The reform of the lunacy laws was not a party issue.

Shaftesbury (Ashley had succeeded to the earldom in 1851) gave clear and lengthy evidence on the working of the 1845 Act before this Committee, which took up three separate hearings. He thought that the law was defective, but for a series of rather unexpected reasons. The authority of the Commissioners was too limited: they had no jurisdiction over Scotland, and none over patients taken abroad – he considered foreign asylums 'wonderfully inferior to our own'. He thought that the greatest single cause of insanity was alcoholism, and that the most effective measure of prevention was the formation of temperance societies.

Shaftesbury considered that the quality of the nursing and medical staff was one of the most important factors in the development of lunacy treatment. Most urgent was the problem of recruiting male and female nurses of the right type. Wages were low – in many hospitals, no more than twelve guineas a year – 'the wages of a housemaid'. The hours were very long, and the work was exacting. There was no great shortage of female nurses, because 'the tendency of woman's nature is to nurse', and few other professions were open to women. Good male attendants were far more difficult to recruit. Commissioner W.G. Campbell, another witness, said of male asylum attendants, 'They are all of too low a class. They are an uneducated class.' He considered that there was truth in the assertion that they frequently used force against their patients when they could do so undetected by authority. The development of professional standards could, he thought, best be assured by the institution of formal qualifications and a higher wage-scale.

Shaftesbury urged the importance of 'a school for students of lunacy'. At this time, only St Luke's Hospital in London received medical students and gave them systematic instruction, since Conolly's attempts to set up a similar school at Hanwell had failed; but Shaftesbury had not modified his low opinion of the medical component in the work of asylum doctors. He pointed out that even a trained and qualified medical man often knew no more about lunacy than a layman, and based his judgement of a patient's condition not on his medical knowledge, but on his general experience of human behaviour.

Public asylums had now been provided for almost every county in England and Wales, some by joint contracting arrangements between two counties, made possible by an amending Act of 1853. The larger and more populous counties, such as Lancashire and Middlesex, had built more than one. Bethlem had finally been brought under the supervision of the Commissioners in 1853, and private asylums (no longer called madhouses) were decreasing in number. Shaftesbury thought that the association of the profit motive with the care of patients was unfortunate, since the proprietor of a private asylum was likely to be inclined to keep his paying patients as long as possible. The county asylum was now the normal channel of treatment for both fee-paying patients and pauper lunatics.

There were still many chronic patients in workhouses. Mr Andrew Doyle, an inspector of the Poor Law Board, stated that of 126,000 workhouse inmates, 6,947 were known to be insane. Doyle denied knowledge of any cruelty against pauper lunatics in workhouses, but with hesitation and little conviction.

The Commissioners had no idea how many single patients existed – 'and we have spent years trying to learn it'. The Lord Chancellor kept a list, but there was no assurance that this was accurate or up-to-date, and they were not allowed to see it, though they could ask for specific information from it; and they could only visit a single lunatic with the Lord Chancellor's permission.

The tenor of Shaftesbury's evidence,[5] and that of the other Commissioners, was in direct contrast to that given by the chairman and secretary of the Alleged Lunatics Friend Society. The chairman, Admiral Saumarez, was a surgeon's son and a peer's nephew, with a distinguished naval record. The secretary, Gilbert Bolden, was a solicitor. Both were at pains to placate Shaftesbury by paying tribute to the work done by the Commissioners, but they made great play of Shaftesbury's admission that the system of inspection was not yet perfect, and of Commissioner Campbell's opinion that attendants still used violence against patients. They were determined that every possible safeguard against illegal detention should be devised, even if this might sometimes delay or hamper treatment. They complained that the Commissioners would not give them the power to visit alleged lunatics, and asked that any justice of the peace should be empowered to grant them the right to make visits.

The most controversial of the Committee's recommendations was one suggested by Gilbert Bolden, which was to form a point of debate and bitter recrimination for the next thirty years: this was the proposal to introduce a magistrate's certificate in private cases, as for pauper patients.[6] Shaftesbury opposed this with all the force at his command, and was successful in preventing it from becoming law during his life-time, though the proposal was to be revived after his death in 1885.

THE SELECT COMMITTEE OF 1877

In 1877, the public preoccupation with the dangers of illegal detention surged up again. One of the reasons was the popularity of Charles Reade's novel, *Hard Cash*, first published in 1863.

Reade later defended himself against the charge of being 'a sensation novelist', claiming that the novel was the result of 'long, severe, systematic labour, from a multitude of volumes, journals, pamphlets, reports, blue-books, manuscript narratives, letters and people whom I have sought out'. This was probably true; but he set the book in the post-1845 period (the details of admission and discharge procedures are those laid down in the 1845 Act) and neglected to say that most of his sources were drawn from the scandals and revelations of the earlier part of the century, which the 1845 Act had been framed to prevent.

The book tells the story of a young man, Alfred Hardie, wrongfully confined at the instance of his father, who wishes to gain control of his fortune. Alfred is captured by violence, beaten, intimidated and drugged, and subjected to the unwelcome attentions of the matron. When at length he manages to convince a visiting magistrate of his sanity the process of regaining his freedom involves lengthy correspondence and legal delays. The story has strong echoes of Richard Paternoster's account in *The Madhouse System* (1838). The similarities are too strong to be merely coincidental; but some of Reade's material comes from even earlier sources.

In one scene, Alfred tells the visiting magistrate that instruments of restraint are hidden in a locked room:

> Baker had not the key; no more had Cooper. The latter was sent for it: he returned, saying that the key was mislaid.
> 'That I expected,' said Alfred. 'Send for the kitchen poker, sir. I'll soon unlock it.'
> 'Fetch the kitchen poker,' said Vane.
> Cooper went for it, and came back with the key instead.[7]

This is very similar to a passage in the evidence of Godfrey Higgins, fifty years earlier, when he came upon a locked door in the York Asylum. At another point in the narrative, Alfred is made to say, 'one or two gentlemanly madmen . . . have complained to me that the attendants wash them too much like hansom cabs; strip them naked and mop them on the flagstones'. This echoes the evidence given on the notorious 'crib-room cases of Bethnal Green' by an ex-patient, John Nettle, to the Select Committee of 1827.

Reade had certainly studied the available literature, and to that extent he could claim that his account was 'based on fact'. But most of his information related to cases of abuse – not normal practice – discovered and rectified many years before *Hard Cash* was written. He took the framework of the law as it was in his own day, and fitted into it sensational cases from the past. Reade is said by his biographer to have been vague about dates,[8] but it was clearly to his advantage to be so if he wanted to write a 'sensation novel'. By 1863, events were much less sensational, but many readers must have taken the book for an account of contemporary abuses.

On 12 February 1877, a Select Committee of the House of

Commons was appointed under the chairmanship of Thomas Dill-wyn to inquire into the operations of lunacy law 'so far as regards security afforded for it against violations of personal liberty'. Both Dillwyn and his associate Stephen Cave showed in their questions a remarkable lack of knowledge of any issues except those relating to illegal confinement.

'Do you consider', asked Cave of Shaftesbury, 'that the facility with which patients are admitted to asylums is not too great at the present day?'

Shaftesbury's retort was 'No, certainly not ... we stated so in 1859, and we state it still more emphatically now'.[9]

His patience was wearing thin. At the age of seventy-six, he was nervous and depressed, uncertain of how long his failing powers would enable him to carry on his public work. On 11 March 1877, shortly before he was called to give evidence before the Select Committee, he noted in his diary: 'My hour of trial is near; cannot, I should think, be delayed beyond the coming week. Half a century, all but one week, has been devoted to this cause of the lunatics, and ... the state now, as compared with the state then, would baffle description.'[10] Now he undertook the laborious task of educating the Select Committee.

The *Journal of Mental Science*, reporting his evidence, stated that 'His lordship spoke with a thorough mastery of every lunacy question about which he was asked.'[11] Shaftesbury himself was in one of his self-doubting moods. 'Beyond the circle of my own Commissioners and the lunatics I visit', runs an entry in his diary, 'not a soul ... has any notion of the years of toil and care that, under God, I have bestowed on this melancholy and awful question.'[12]

The Select Committee was apparently won over. The report stated that 'allegations of mala fides or serious abuse were not substantiated':

> The Committee cannot help observing here, that the jealousy with which the treatment of lunatics is watched at the present day, and the comparatively trifling nature of the abuses alleged, present a remarkable contrast to the horrible cruelty ... apathy ... and indifference of half a century earlier.[13]

On the vexed question of a magistrate's order, the Committee did not 'attach any special importance to the order emanating from a magistrate'.[14] They felt it was permissible for voluntary boarders to continue to be allowed in small licensed houses, provided that the Lunacy Commissioners were informed within twenty-four hours of reception. 'Nervous' cases had been admitted to licensed houses without formality since 1862.

THE LANCET COMMISSION OF 1877

In the same year in which the Select Committee made its report, the *Lancet* sponsored a fact-finding commission on *The Care and Cure of the Insane* under the direction of Dr Mortimer Granville. Dr Granville personally visited a number of asylums, both public and private, in London and the Home Counties, and produced a voluminous report. This expressed his belief that, after a period of activity in which the worst abuses of the madhouse system had been remedied, asylums were marking time, and in some cases regressing from the standards of 1845. At Hanwell, he found that Conolly's work had 'languished':

> There was no open retrogression at Hanwell, but it is difficult to believe that there was any progress. Things went on very much in the humdrum way which might have been expected to follow a period of energetic reform.[15]

At Wandsworth (the Surrey Asylum) he noted with approval the 'judicious practice' employed by the medical officers, of visiting the wards unexpectedley by day and night. 'Everywhere attendants, we are convinced, maltreat, abuse and terrify patients when the backs of the medical officers are turned. Humanity is only to be secured by watching officials.' At Dartford, the staircases were 'cramped and draughty', the patients' clothing 'worn and dirty', the corridors 'meagre', the lavatories 'very defective'. Bethlem and St Luke's were doing outstanding work, but both were 'singularly ill-adapted for the residence of large bodies of patients'. Though Bethlem was well endowed, St Luke's was 'starved and crippled in its work in a fashion that reflects dishonour on our great City firms and the wealthy classes of the metropolis'.

Lack of the personal touch, lack of money – these were the real evils of the system. The remedy was to be found in a radical change of attitude:

Patients labouring under mental derangement should be removable to a public or private asylum as to a hospital for ordinary diseases, *without certificate* . . . the power of signing certificates of lunacy [i.e. for paupers] should be withdrawn from . . . magistrates.[16]

Despite the work of the Lunacy Commissioners, the report of the Select Committee and the *Lancet* report, the constant allegations of illegal detention continued. The columns of *The Times* exhibit all the old fear and prejudice against the insane. On 5 April 1877, a leading article commented that 'if lunacy continues to increase as at present, the insane will be in the majority, and freeing themselves, will put the sane in asylums'. This bogey of the supposed increase of insanity, though officially denied, occurs again and again. On 23 May, there was a letter signed 'A Lunatic's Victim' which deplored the tendency of the present laws 'to protect the liberty of the lunatic at the expense of the lives, liberty and comfort of the sane'. Two days later came a complaint from an attendant: 'I have been cut down with a hatchet once, and shut up for three hours in the strong room of a private asylum with a patient suffering from delirium tremens, who stood 6ft 2 ins, hanging at my throat . . . and all for £25 a year.'

THE CASE OF MRS GEORGIANA WELDON

These two public prejudices – fear of the insane and fear of illegal detention – reached a new height in 1884, through the much-publicized case of Mrs Weldon[17], an eccentric lady of considerable means and some social position. Her husband, who held the position of Windsor Herald, deserted her in 1875, leaving her with a house and £1,000 a year. She was a spiritualist, and was said by a specialist in mental disorder to 'have peculiar ideas on the education of young children and the simplification of ladies' dress'.

Mr Weldon, as the petitioning relative, requested Dr Forbes Winslow[18] to take Mrs Weldon into his private asylum at Hammersmith. The ensuing proceedings were almost farcical. Dr Winslow and an attendant went to the house. Mrs Weldon bolted the door. A former mental patient who was secretary of the Alleged Lunatics' Friend Society appeared, presumably through the back entrance.

As Dr Winslow and his attendant forced an entry, Mrs Weldon escaped disguised as a nun.

Here were all the ingredients of a popular *cause celèbre*: the society background, the wealthy and beautiful lady under threat of duress, the dramatic escape in disguise. An interesting legal point arose from the fact that the events took place at a time when a married woman's property might legally belong to her husband. The marital home in which Mrs Weldon took refuge against Dr Winslow therefore legally belonged to Mr Weldon, who had consented to Dr Winslow's entry; and any damages Mrs Weldon received would have become her husband's property. The passing of the Married Woman's Property Act in 1882 changed the situation, and Mrs Weldon, secure in the possession of her own fortune and her own house, commenced legal action. It is surprising that feminist writers have so far shown little interest in the Weldon case, which has many interesting ramifications.[19]

With the support of the Lunacy Laws Amendment Association and the editor of *The Spiritualist*, Mrs Weldon started a series of law-suits. She sued Dr Forbes Winslow for alleged libel, assault, wrongful arrest, false imprisonment (in that she was under duress in her own house before she made her escape) and trespass. She sued her husband for the restitution of conjugal rights; she sued the editors of *Figaro* and the *Daily Chronicle* for alleged libel; she sued the two doctors who signed the medical certificates. She hired the Covent Garden Opera House for a meeting on her own behalf, at which she distributed copies of one of her own pamphlets, and sang from a box at the side of the stage. She subsequently disagreed with the management over the cost of the hall, and sued an impresario called Rivière, and the composer Gounod, who shared his business interests, for breach of contract. Specialists in mental disorder disagreed in court over whether she was eccentric but sane, or incoherent and deluded.

There never was a clear judgement in the Weldon cases. There were trials, re-trials and appeals. For months, the legal columns of *The Times* were filled with accounts of Mrs Weldon's protests and eccentricities. In the end, she won some of her cases – in particular those against Dr Forbes Winslow and the two certifying doctors.

Discussions on the principle of the liberty of the subject degenerated into squabbles on minor legal issues; but the Weldon cases brought the question of the lunacy laws into public discussion in an atmosphere of heated debate and partisanship following Baron Huddleston's celebrated 'crossing sweeper judgement', in which he stated at the end of Mrs. Weldon's first trial:

> It is somewhat startling – it is positively shocking – that if a pauper, or as Mrs Weldon put it, a crossing-sweeper, should make a statement, and then that two medical men, who had never had a day's practice in their lives, should for a small sum of money grant their certificates, a person may be lodged in a private lunatic asylum, and that this order, and the statement, and these certificates, are a perfect answer to any action.[20]

Baron Huddleston was one of the last of the old Barons of the Exchequer. His statement is remarkable for the extent to which popular outcry had skewed legal judgement. No patient could be confined to a private asylum on the representations of a crossing-sweeper unless he or she happened to be a member of a crossing-sweeper's family; and the number of wealthy crossing-sweepers able to send their relatives to private asylums must have been relatively small.

The asylum doctors were the villains of the piece. A spokesman for the asylum doctors (probably Daniel Hack Tuke, then the editor) wrote in the *Journal of Mental Science*: 'It is very easy to talk glibly about the liberty of the subject, and so difficult to guard against the licence into which that too often degenerates.' He continued with a reference to 'the crude views which are entertained upon this subject in some quarters . . . we think it right that we may be credited with ordinary honesty and integrity'. The doctors were only too well aware of the weight of public sentiment which was mounting against them. The commentary sounded a sombre note:

> Of one thing we are sure, and that is that troublous times are before those entrusted with the care of the insane. Already we know of several threatened proceedings by former patients . . . Lunacy law will be amended, or probably re-made, and the foundations will be laid at the cost of some martyrs.[21]

TIGHTENING THE LAW

Following the publicity of the Weldon cases, there was a strong movement for the revision of the lunacy laws, which brought together successive Lords Chancellor and the legal profession working for the same ends as the Lunacy Laws Amendment Society and a variety of patients with real or fancied grudges. Shaftesbury's pleas and Granville's recommendations for early treatment and easier methods of admission and discharge were swept aside.

Shaftesbury was now a very old man, in his eighties. He noted in his diary 'the sensible decline of mental application and vigour'. His diary shows an almost incredible pressure of work. He was afraid that 'body and mind are falling to pieces.'[22] His days were overloaded, and he suffered mental and nervous exhaustion. He wrote: 'I cannot bear to leave the world with all the misery in it.' Shaftesbury and Selborne had been opposed on many issues; there is an acrimonious correspondence between them in *The Times* about Church matters (Selborne was a High Churchman, Shaftesbury an Evangelical) as early as 1842. In 1883, Selborne had introduced a Lunacy Bill into the House of Lords. This was withdrawn owing to lack of support at the time; but on 5 May 1884 (six weeks after the 'crossing-sweeper judgement'), Lord Milltown, an Irish peer and a barrister put forward a motion that 'in the opinion of this House, the existing state of the lunacy laws is unsatisfactory, and constitutes a serious danger to the liberty of the subject'. He described the state of the lunacy laws as 'intolerable . . . a damning blot . . . [on] the Statute Book'.[23]

The Weldon case had never come to the direct attention of the Lunacy Commissioners, since they would only have been officially notified of Mrs. Weldon's detention after her reception into Dr Winslow's asylum. Since she 'escaped', this never occurred; but Mrs Weldon had subpoenaed the Commissioners in her case against one of the certifying doctors, and commented later that 'Lord Shaftesbury . . . seemed not to care much for the judge's opinions'.[24]

Milltown's motion was carried – to Shaftesbury's great distress. A long correspondence between Shaftesbury and Selborne then ensued, but there was no possibility of compromise between them. In 1885, Selborne introduced a Lunacy Amendment Bill in the Lords, and Shaftesbury tendered his resignation from the chairmanship of the Lunacy Commission.

In June, the Bill was shelved, and Shaftesbury was persuaded to remain in office. The shelving of the Bill may have been due to genuine pressure of parliamentary business; to the obstruction of the Irish MPs, who at this time were blocking all legislation in the House of Commons; to the public respect in which Shaftesbury was held; or to a combination of all three. Shaftesbury did not have long to live, and died on 1 October.

In the session 1885–6, political conditions were unsettled. In the following session, two Bills were introduced in the House of Lords by the then Lord Chancellor, Lord Halsbury, who paid tribute to the work done by his predecessors in office, Lord Selborne and Lord Herschell. The first Bill was a consolidating measure. The second was the Lunacy Acts Amendment Bill, which included a number of points raised by the Dillwyn Committee ten years before, and introduced again in an amended form the highly controversial clause requiring a magistrate's order in non-pauper cases. The Lunacy Commissioners opposed the clause, but Lord Halsbury thought that 'no alteration of the law would be satisfactory that did not make further provision for the liberty of the subject'.[25]

Both Bills were passed by the Lords and sent to the Commons; but the Lunacy Acts Amendment Bill was withdrawn by the Solicitor-General after the first reading. No reason was given, and both Bills lapsed. In February 1888, the Lunacy Acts Amendment Bill appeared once more in the Lords – this time containing the provisions of both the previous Bills. The Lord Chancellor summarized the intentions of the new Bill as follows:

1. The introduction of a judicial authority for ordering the detention of any person as a lunatic.
2. The provision that all orders of detention should cease to have effect unless renewed at the stated time. This placed the onus of continued detention on the medical profession, rather than leaving the question of discharge to their initiative.
3. Protection to medical men and others 'against vexatious actions where they have acted in good faith'. This clause conciliated the Medico-Psychological Association following the widespread alarm caused by the case of *Weldon* v. *Winslow*.
4. Restrictions on the opening of new private asylums. Shaftesbury had written to Lord Milltown only six months before his death

to say that he had not changed 'by one hair's-breadth' his opinion of 'the dangers which beset all private asylums, and of the necessity of placing the whole care of lunacy on a public basis'.

5. Consolidating clauses.[26]

The Lord Chancellor was saying to the Medico-Psychological Association 'If you want legal protection, you must take the magistrates clause' and to the Lunacy Commissioners 'If you want to reduce the number of private asylums, you must take the magistrate's clause.'

The Bill lapsed in the Commons in that session; but the Lord Chancellor reintroduced it in the Lords in February 1889, and after some reference back to the Lords, the Commons also passed it. It received the Royal Assent on 26 August. A Consolidating Act, the Lunacy Act 1890, was finally passed in the following session.

THE LUNACY ACT 1890

The final form of the Act was an extremely long and intricate document, expressing few general principles, and providing in detail for almost every known contingency. Nothing was left to chance, and very little to future development. The following summary gives only the main provisions.

Administration

1. Central: the Lord Chancellor continued to be responsible for the appointment of the Lunacy Commissioners, and to receive their reports. The Lunacy Commissioners and their secretariat continued to exercise powers of visitation and inspection over all institutions, and all lunatics except Chancery lunatics (who were dealt with by the Judge in Lunacy and the Masters in Lunacy, also responsible to the Lord Chancellor).

2. Local: the local authority responsible for public asylums was now not the magistrates in Quarter Sessions, but the county or county borough council – new authorities constituted under the Local Government Act 1888. They were to build and maintain asylums either singly or jointly, and to appoint Visiting Committees of not fewer than seven members.

Admission

There were four methods of admission to an asylum or licensed house: –

1. By reception order on petition (for private cases). The petitioner, a near relative or other person stating his connection with the patient, had to make a statement before a magistrate, and to undertake to visit the patient, in person or by proxy, every six months. Two medical certificates were necessary in addition to the magistrate's order. The order was to remain in force for the period of one year, and was then renewable for periods of two years, three years and successive periods of five years, on the report of the medical officer of the asylum.
2. By urgency order (for private cases). In emergency, a relative's petition and one medical certificate could hold a patient for up to seven days. At the end of that time, a reception order had to be completed, or the patient discharged.
3. By summary reception order (for pauper cases). The Poor Law Relieving Officer or the police were responsible for notifying a magistrate. One medical certificate was necessary in addition to the justice's order. A summary reception order had a duration of fourteen days.
4. By inquisition (a form applying only to Chancery lunatics). In an uncontested case, the Judge in Lunacy could direct the Masters in Lunacy to take evidence. If they considered the patient to be of unsound mind, a 'committee of the person' could be appointed to administer the estate. If the alleged lunatic wished to contest the case, he could request a trial by jury, which often meant protracted litigation.

These methods of admission had grown out of existing legislation. The procedure for reception on petition had developed from the Madhouses Act of 1828, the summary reception order had emerged out of the eighteenth-century Vagrancy Acts, and the procedure for Chancery lunatics went back to the Praerogativa Regis of Edward II.

There were detailed regulations to prevent collusion between the parties responsible for the process of certification. Prohibited relationships were spelled out at length: there was no attempt to frame a general principle of non-collusion.

Care and treatment

A complicated system of documentation and inspection was laid down. This was an elaboration of the system evolved by Shaftesbury and his colleagues for the 1845 Act. The Lunacy Commissioners were to send two of their number – a barrister and a medical practitioner – to every public asylum at least twice a year; to every licensed house in the metropolis four times a year, with two additional visits by a single Commissioner; to licensed houses outside the metropolitan area twice a year; to registered hospitals (i.e. subscription hospitals not run for profit) once a year. The Commissioners were to visit without previous notice, at any hour of the day or night as they saw fit. They were to make detailed enquiries concerning the structure of the building, the classification, occupation and recreation of the patients, the physical condition and diet of pauper patients, the admission, discharge and visitation of all the patients, and the use or non-use of mechanical restraint. They were to submit a report giving the number of visits made and the number of patients seen to the Lord Chancellor every six months, and were to make a detailed report, to be laid before Parliament, once a year.

In public asylums, two members of the visiting committees were to visit every two months, and to lay an annual report before the local authority. In licensed houses and registered hospitals, the justices' visitors were to inspect as follows: two, one of whom was to be a medical practitioner, twice a year; one, twice a year.

Restraint: restraint by instruments and appliances was only to be used for the purposes of surgical or medical treatment, or to prevent the patient from injuring himself or his fellow-patients. A medical certificate was necessary for each instance of restraint, and a report book was to be kept. A copy of the records was to be sent to the Commissioners once a quarter.

Correspondence and interviews

All letters written by private patients to certain persons in authority, including the Lord Chancellor, a Judge in Lunacy, a Secretary of State, a Lunacy Commissioner or a Chancery Visitor were to be forwarded unopened. The Commissioners could direct that notices explaining this right should be placed in an asylum, and could choose the actual site of the notice, to ensure that it would be seen by all private patients. Pauper patients possessed the same right of having letters to persons in authority forwarded unopened, but there was no obligation on the Commissioners to ensure that they were aware of this right.

Discharge

1. Absence on trial: any two visitors of an asylum were empowered to consent to the absence of a patient on trial for as long as they thought fit. During the period of trial, an allowance not exceeding the cost of his board in the asylum might be made to a pauper lunatic. In the case of a private patient, the written consent of the person on whose petition the original reception order was made was required.
2. Boarding out: pauper lunatics might be boarded out with a relative or friend if the visiting committee and the Guardians of the Poor Law Union agreed. An allowance was payable as for a patient on trial.
3. Full discharge: a private patient might be discharged on the direction of the person who signed the petition for a reception order. A pauper patient might be discharged on the direction of the Poor Law authority. In either case, the medical officer of the asylum possessed a right of veto, and could issue a barring certificate if he considered that the patient was 'dangerous and unfit to be at large'.

    Two Commissioners, one legal and one medical, might discharge a patient after giving seven days' notice of their intention to do so. Any three members of the visiting committee could order a discharge, or two with the consent of the medical officer; or, in the case of a pauper, any two visitors, if a friend or relative was willing to be responsible for the patient.
4. Escape: any patient escaping from an institution might be recaptured within seven days. After the expiry of that period, fresh proceedings for certification were necessary.

Single lunatics

The procedure for visitation and inspection of single lunatics received for profit continued as under the 1845 Act. For the first time, single lunatics confined in their own homes, or in charitable institutions, could be visited by the Lunacy Commissioners. They might pass on their findings to the Lord Chancellor, who could have the patient removed from custody, or transferred to an asylum.

Penalties and misdemeanours

Misdemeanours were spelled out in detail, and ranged from obstructing a Commissioner in the course of his duty to conniving at a patient's escape. A schedule of heavy penalties was appended.

The very length of this Act singles it out from all previous attempts at legislation, and it bears the heavy impress of the legal mind. Every safeguard which could possibly be devised against illegal confinement is there. Dillwyn's suspicions, Mrs Weldon's accusations, Shaftesbury's doubts, Hack Tuke's fears, Milltown's wrath and the determination of three successive Lords Chancellor helped to shape it. From the legal point of view, it was very nearly perfect. From the medical and social viewpoint, it was to hamper the progress of the mental health movement for nearly seventy years.

CHAPTER 7

Stagnation

Lunacy law is regarded by politicians as a minor subject, but a contentious one. Few subjects place them more at the mercy of extremist groups and sudden surges of popular agitation. Once a major change in the law has survived the parliamentary process, they are often reluctant to tinker with it. The 1890 Lunacy Act was to remain in force until 1959. Though later Acts made it possible for increasing numbers of patients to be admitted in other ways, successive governments avoided the issue of replacing a piece of legislation which had consumed so much parliamentary time and raised so many parliamentary hackles.

The 1890 Act was a reflection of legal determination to take control of a process which concerned the liberty of the subject – a desire to draw a firm legal boundary between the sane majority and the insane minority. Lunatics were to be consigned to the asylum by a magistrate in a process analogous to conviction for a criminal offence. The Act was also a reflection of popular fear and distaste for asylums and their patients. It was already out of date in 1890, because the asylum doctors were moving towards a more humane system in which patients could be admitted and discharged without the stigmatization of legal procedure.

The barrier of certification and the emphasis on custodialism which resulted from the 1890 Lunacy Act contributed to the decline in standards of care and treatment. Asylums could only take certified patients; and patients could not be certified until their condition had reached a stage where it was obvious to a lay authority – the justice of the peace. Because certification involved the restriction of liberty by a judicial authority, patients resisted it, and relatives were often reluctant to invoke it. Being certified was equivalent to being given a prison sentence – with the added problems that detention was indeterminate, and the status of 'pauper lunatic' carried social penalties, like not being able to vote or to make a will. Patients' chances of making a successful return to normal living were very much reduced: in Goffman's terms, they suffered from 'spoiled identity', because the stigma would follow them after discharge, making it difficult for them to marry or find employment if the facts were known.

Because certification was a necessary preliminary to treatment for those who could not afford private care, most medical practitioners tried to avoid sending patients to asylums, except as a last resort; and medical students who wanted to specialize in psychiatry often avoided a sphere where most of the work was routine, and where there was little opportunity for the improvement of skills.

Some lawyers, predictably, take a different view of the 1890 Act. Dr Clive Unsworth regards it as a sound piece of legislation, on the grounds that 'legalism' is the proper use of law to regulate human affairs.[1] In this view, what cannot be dealt with by law is not of (legal) interest; but there are two kinds of law: prescriptive law, which specifies what people are not allowed to do, on pain of sanction enforced by the courts, and enabling law, which gives other agencies, such as administrative tribunals and hospital authorities, a degree of discretion. For most lawyers, the criminal law is the dominant paradigm, following the principle that whatever is not forbidden is allowed,[2] and giving ultimate authority to the courts. This was the model followed in the 1890 Act. Prescriptive law could forbid illegal detention, forbid brutality to patients, require the completion of documents; but it could not (and cannot) cure patients, manage an asylum or a hospital, ensure that patients are treated with humanity, or improve staff morale. It could damage all these useful activities by a negative approach which encouraged the observance of the letter of the law at the expense of the spirit which originally inspired legislation.

The title of the previous chapter, 'The triumph of legalism', describes an approach to lunacy law in which the preoccupations of the legal profession with illegal detention took precedence over the concern of the Lunacy Commission and the asylum doctors for patient care. By the 1880s, illegal detention was a minor issue: the

Lunacy Commissioners had devoted much time and trouble to identifying and remedying abuses. When such cases did occur, they were usually in the private asylums, which were being phased out. One of the strengths of a public asylum system is that the authorities do not have the same incentive to retain patients in confinement as they do in profit-making institutions. The lawyers' concentration on the issue of illegal detention came fifty years too late, and distorted the work of the asylums by increasing the stigma of admission and making them places of last resort.

From the point of view of asylum management, the 1890 Act was a disaster. It also hampered research and development in psychiatry. When new theories of the aetiology of mental illness were formulated, and new techniques for treatment tried, they developed outside the asylums. Psychoanalysis and psychotherapy were to develop in the universities, the consulting rooms and the out-patient clinics – but not in the asylums, where staff morale was low, and custodialism cramped the possibilities of care and treatment.

THE 'INCREASE IN INSANITY'

The report of the Select Committee of 1859 indicated that, even at that date, there was considerable concern about the increase in the numbers of lunatics in asylums. The total number of patients known to the Lunacy Commissioners had increased from 20,611 in 1844 to 35,982 in 1858. There were theories in plenty on the reasons for this phenomenon. Dr Browne of Montrose thought in 1837, against all evidence, that insanity was caused by wealth, and that the apparently high rates of insanity in the United States were caused by 'the luxurious social habits to which the good fortune of our transatlantic brethren has exposed them'.[3] Shaftesbury and the Lunacy Commissioners attributed the increase to three factors: the rise in the general population; the greater availability of asylum accommodation; and their own industry in discovering previously unnotified cases. Shaftesbury, in evidence to the 1859 Select Committee, stated that he thought that the numbers were reasonable when these factors were taken into account, and that the true incidence of insanity might be decreasing.[4]

By the early years of the twentieth century, the asylum system was to grow into a bureaucratic monster of a kind which Shaftesbury and his colleagues certainly could not have imagined; and Shaftesbury's arguments were not sufficient to account for the dimensions of the increase.

In the half century between 1859 and 1909, the general population roughly doubled, but the number of persons of unsound mind in institutions quadrupled (Table 7.1). The need for asylum beds had been badly under-estimated in the early days: in 1806, Bedfordshire reported that there were no lunatics within its boundaries, yet the county magistrates found no difficulty in filling an asylum in 1814. New asylums were frequently overcrowded before they were officially opened. The industry of the Commissioners seemed to lead to a situation where the more accommodation there was, the more lunatics came forward to fill it.

Despite an energetic asylum building programme in the second half of the nineteenth century, asylums increased in size. It was always cheaper to pack more patients into existing accommodation than to provide for the construction costs and staffing costs of starting afresh.

THE GRANT-IN-AID OF PAUPER LUNATICS

In 1874, the Lunacy Commissioners finally won their battle on behalf of pauper lunatics in workhouses. The Government agreed to a grant-in-aid from the Consolidated Fund of 4s. per head for each pauper lunatic removed to an asylum. This gave an incentive to Boards of Guardians to get their pauper lunatics out of the workhouse, because it took some of the costs off the rates. The Lunacy Commissioners and the asylum doctors welcomed the move, because they thought it would end the practice of sending deteriorated chronic patients to the asylum, while keeping young and acute patients in the workhouse; but central funding led inevitably to a tightening of central control over the work of the Commissioners, and the transfers, primarily of yet more chronic and deteriorated patients, put new pressure on asylum accommodation. The Commissioners, in their Annual Report of 1875, welcomed the decision, but began to have misgivings: they noted that the grant-in-aid scheme might mean 'the transfer to asylums of chronic cases . . . thus rendering necessary . . . a still larger outlay than heretofore in providing additional asylum accommodation'.[5] They were right: the operation of the grant-in-aid was to be a

Year (1 Jan.)	Known persons of unsound mind (000s)	Increase on previous year	Number per thousand population
1859	31.4	–	1.60
1864	38.7	+ 7.3	1.93
1869	46.7	+ 8.0	2.17
1874	54.3	+ 7.6	2.36
1879	61.6	+ 7.3	2.44
1884	69.9	+ 8.3	2.77
1889	75.6	+ 5.7	2.66
1894	83.0	+ 7.4	2.79
1899	95.6	+ 12.6	3.03
1904	117.2	+ 21.6	3.49
1909	128.2	+ 11.0	3.66

Table 7.1 *Known persons of unsound mind, England and Wales, 1859–1909*
Sources: 54th Report of the Lunacy Commissioners, 1909, Appendix A; Census Returns, England and Wales.

Year	No. of county and city asylums	Total patients	Average no. per asylum
1827	9	1,046	116
1850	24	7,140	297
1860	41	15,845	386
1870	50	27,109	542
1880	61	40,088	657
1890	66	52,937	802
1900	77	74,004	961
1910	91	97,580	1,072
1920	94	93,648	966
1930	98	119,659	1,221

Table 7.2 *The size of county asylums, England and Wales 1827–1930*
Sources: Annual Reports of the Lunacy Commissioners to 1910; Annual Reports of the Board of Control for 1920 and 1930.

major factor in converting the asylums into huge custodial institutions (Table 7.2). The asylum doctors' dream of taking 'early and curable' cases was no nearer fruition.

The operation of the grant-in-aid also accelerated another trend: the increasing proportion of female patients. Dr Browne thought women more prone to insanity than men, on account of 'the peculiarities of their constitution, the delicacy of frame and susceptibility of mind by which the sex is distinguished'.[6] and quoted figures from France, Italy and Scotland to support his contention.

	Class of patients	*Male* *No.*	*(%)*	*Female* *No.*	*(%)*
Licensed asylums	private	6,918	(56.7)	5,288	(43.4)
County asylums	private	819	(56.5)	630	(43.5)
Charitable asylums	private	2,391	(55.8)	1,894	(44.2)
Licensed asylums	pauper	5,350	(49.9)	5,374	(50.1)
County asylums	pauper	9,403	(51.5)	8,835	(48.4)
Charitable asylums	pauper	2,106	(56.0)	1,653	(44.0)
All patients		26,987	(53.3)	23,674	(46.7)

Table 7.3 *Proportions of male and female patients admitted to asylums, England and Wales, 1844*
Source: *1844 Report*, Table 15, p. 152.
Note: Bethlem and St Luke's are excluded from the figures for charitable asylums.

Until the middle of the nineteenth century, there was a predominance of male patients in asylums, because physical violence was the primary indicator of a need for containment. Elaine Showalter points out that Dr John Thurnam's *Observations and Essays on the Statistics in Lunacy* (1845) suggested that male asylum patients outnumbered women by about 30 per cent, and comments that 'the domestication of insanity and its assimilation by the Victorian institution coincided with its feminization'.[7] The Metropolitan Commissioners' figures for 1844 show a less extreme picture, but still indicate an excess of males over females in all sectors except that of pauper accommodation in licensed asylums (Table 7.3).

By 1872, out of 58,640 certified lunatics in England and Wales, 31,822 (54.3 per cent) were women. Dr Showalter suggests that the grant-in-aid increased the proportion of women sent from workhouses to county asylums, because women were more likely to be reduced to poverty than men: the death or desertion of a male breadwinner left women carrying enormous social burdens in child care, with few opportunities for self-support. Also, Victorian social norms were applied more strictly to women than to men:

By the 1890s, the predominance of women had spread to include all classes of patients and all types of institutions: female paupers and female private patients were in the majority in licensed houses, registered hospitals, and the county asylums. The only remaining institutions with a majority of male patients were asylums for the criminally insane, military hospitals and idiot schools'.[8]

It is also likely that the grant-in-aid increased the proportion of old people in asylums; and again women would predominate, since women have a longer expectation of life than men. The first (noncontributory) old age pension was not introduced until 1908. The workhouse was the only recourse for those who could not maintain themselves, and chronic malnutrition must often have led to mental confusion.

ASYLUM SIZE AND ASYLUM MANAGEMENT

The original asylums were small institutions in which it was possible to preserve some of the values of face-to-face relationships, and size was recognized as an important factor in asylum management. The Retreat had only thirty beds when it opened. The Select Committee report of 1807 specified that county asylums should not exceed 300 beds.[9] Nottingham Asylum was built for 80. Of the first nine asylums, built by 1827, the average size was 116 beds; but the asylum populations grew rapidly. At Lancaster, the asylum was originally constructed in 1816 for 170 patients, and by 1852 it accommodated 600.

John Walton describes how the growth in numbers put 'severe pressure on attempts to treat patients as individuals' and how moral treatment 'was vulnerable, in the long run, to the combined pressures of increased scale, cheeseparing economies, overworked medical superintendence, ageing patient populations and untrained, unsupervised nursing staff'.[10] So the asylums fell prey to 'the perils of a mechanical routine, of the reduction of patients and attendants to cogs in an almost self-regulating machine'. At Lancaster, despite the energetic efforts of Gaskell and De Vitré and their successors, despite the introduction of training for attendants and activity programmes for the patients, there were 'revelations of violence and petty tyranny' on the wards.

The work of the attendants was 'arduous' and 'exhausting'. They were responsible for all aspects of caring for patients: exercise, amusements, employment, dressings and poultices, fomentations, and the care of the incontinent. At the West Riding Asylum at Wakefield, they averaged about seventy hours per week on duty, often with split shifts, so that they might only have four hours' sleep in twenty. Their rates of pay were low. Between 1860 and 1880, 91 out of 567 attendants were dismissed for reasons varying from 'dishonesty' and 'cruelty' to being drunk on duty. The asylum doctors were generally not keen on training for attendants, but the nurses took the blame when things went wrong on the ward. 'When the medical men found that the asylum system, with its institutional pressure and its authoritarian structure, could not be run without violent mishap, it was the nurses and attendants who carried the can'.[11]

A network of asylums was created around London by the London County Council after it was set up in 1888.[12] The LCC did not bear the full responsibility for metropolitan lunatics, as the Metropolitan Asylums Board managed 'huge, barrack-like institutions' for chronic patients; but the LCC Asylums Committee took over Hanwell, Colney Hatch, Banstead and Cane Hill – all big institutions – and the numbers kept rising. Temporary units of corrugated iron were added. (One at Colney Hatch was lined with matchwood: in 1903 it caught fire and 51 patients were killed). The demand for new large institutions 'nurtured a specialist field within nineteenth century architecture' – no longer stately homes for the poor, but institutions of 'drab functionality and grim solidity'. The Asylums Committee 'kept up a meticulous system of monitoring'. There were standard weekly menus, with the size of the portions specified. Ward staff wore military-style blue uniforms, with the inevitable bunches of keys. Patients were engaged in routine manual work for the asylum. As David Cochrane notes, there were 'elaborate programmes of entertainment' including cricket, football, fêtes, a cinematograph, weekly dances and walking parties; but 'the stark reality of incarceration overshadowed this image of social richness'.[13]

The point about architecture is an important one: asylums built between 1845 and the First World War illustrate vividly in their physical structure the changes which took place in asylum régimes. High walls and long drives kept patients away from the outside world. Long straight corridors made for easy surveillance. At Rainhill Hospital, near Liverpool, built in 1851, the main corridor was one-third of a mile long. A ward was a complex – usually day room, dining-room and dormitory – in which sixty or more patients might be grouped together behind stout double-locked doors.

'Refractory' patients stayed there. Of those who were considered fit to join working parties, the men worked on the farms and gardens, or cleaned the long corridors, while the women went to the laundries, the kitchens and the sewing-rooms. Their work was organized for the maintenance of the institution, not for their benefit. Many asylums found it easier to get inmates to contribute to the smooth running of the institution than to decant them into the outside world. Patients moved from place to place in groups, 'counted in' and 'counted out' of the wards by nurses who could not remember their faces.

Some of the London County Council asylums were built for 2,000 patients, and accepted more. It was always easier and cheaper to add another ward or wing to an existing institution than to build afresh somewhere else. Dr Mortimer Granville, in the report of the *Lancet* Commission, had noted the trend to large asylums in 1877. By that date, the number of patients in Hanwell had risen from the original 1,000 to nearly 2,000:

> The treatment is humane, but it necessarily lacks individuality, and that special character which arises from dealing with a limited number of cases directly . . . it is only in a small asylum that this potent remedy, the sane will working quietly, patiently and directly, can be brought to bear on individual cases.[14]

THE CARE OF THE 'FEEBLE-MINDED'

The asylum system had grown up taking a heterogeneous population, including patients diagnosed as 'idiots'and 'imbeciles'. The movement to provide separate accommodation and an educational régime for these patients[15] started with the foundation of an 'asylum for idiots' in London in 1847. This moved to Redhill in Surrey, and became the Earlswood Asylum, which in 1881 had 561 inmates. A similar institution, Starcross, was founded in Exeter in 1864, and the Northern Counties Asylum for Idiots and Imbeciles at Lancaster in 1868. A permissive Idiots Act in 1886, promoted by Lord Shaftesbury and the Charity Organization Society, stated specifically that the terms 'idiot' and 'imbecile' did not include lunatics. Yet the 1890 Lunacy Act stated equally specifically, ' "Lunatic" means an idiot or person of unsound mind.' Since at that time only a few specialized institutions had been built, and there were still thousands of people in lunatic asylums who were classified as 'idiots' or 'imbeciles', it may have seemed advisable to recognize the situation rather than to embark on yet another major building programme.

In 1904, a Royal Commission on the Care of the Feeble-Minded was appointed under the chairmanship of the Earl of Radnor. The term 'feeble-minded' had no settled meaning, and the discussions of the Royal Commission ranged over the many aspects of what was termed 'social degeneracy'. Early in its deliberations, the Radnor Commission seriously considered the possibility of including mental illness, criminality, illegitimacy, alcoholism and pauperism in the definition of 'feeble-mindedness' as well as mental deficiency.[16] Members were much influenced by the 'eugenic school' – a movement which was powered by the developing science of genetics. Sir Francis Galton, a half-cousin of Charles Darwin who shared many of his evolutionary ideas, founded the journal *Biometrika*, in 1901, and set up a eugenics laboratory at University College, London.[17] Galton's books *Hereditary Genius* (1869) and *Natural Inheritance* (1889) were based on the assumption that, just as Mendel's Law applied to the transmission of physical characteristics, so qualities of ability and character were inherited. Eye colour, hair colour, height and build were all affected by heredity. Similarly, musical or mathematical ability could be inherited, as could the qualities necessary for great statesmen. Conversely, it was argued that 'social degeneracy' would be transmitted from generation to generation: criminality, habitual pauperism and other socially undesirable traits could be passed on from one generation to the next.

The 'scientific' study of family inheritance originated in the United States, and was based on some highly judgemental studies of doubtful validity. An influential piece of research was Robert L.Dugdale's study of the Juke family:[18] this began with five mentally defective sisters, one of whom was known as 'Margaret the mother of criminals'. Their descendants by the early 1870s numbered 540 persons, and these, together with 169 people connected with them by marriage or cohabitation, made up the data-set. Among them were 128 prostitutes, 142 habitual paupers on outdoor relief, 64 workhouse inmates, and 76 habitual criminals. A later study of the Jukes was undertaken in 1915 by Arthur H. Estabrook of the Eugenics Record Office, who concluded that 'over half the offspring either is mentally defective or has anti-social traits'.[19]

Another case given much prominence was that of 'Martin Kallikak senior', published by Goddard in 1912. 'Kallikak' was a pseudonym, made up of the Greek words *kallos* and *kakos*, signifying the noble and ignoble (literally the rich and poor) elements in the family. Kallikak had an illegitimate son by a (presumably) feeble-minded girl. This son, Martin Kallikak junior, had in four generations 480 descendants, of whom 143 were classified as feeble-minded, 36 as illegitimate, 24 as alcoholics and 33 as sexually immoral. Kallikak senior later married a 'normal' girl, by whom he had 496 descendants. Of these, all except three were classified as 'normal'. The three failures were merely charted as 'somewhat degenerate'.[20]

Even Galton never claimed that his propositions could be demonstrated with quite this clarity. The value-judgements inherent in the social labelling on which the arguments rested stand out very clearly today, as do the fallacies inherent in retrospective diagnosis of a single line of descent over four generations; but the Juke and Kallikak cases fuelled the movement for the 'eugenic idea', and at least one member of the Radnor Commission was trying to draw up similar studies based on English case-material.[21] The Commission received a great deal of evidence, much of it contradictory, and final recommendations were restricted to mental deficiency. They were impressed by the development of intelligence testing (another of Galton's interests) and by the work of an American, J.McKeen Cattell, who evolved the first systematic tests of perception and the association of ideas. Cattell published his first study in 1896.[22] In 1898, Binet published his Etude Experimentale. The Binet-Simon tests, which are still used in a revised form, were first published in 1905, while the Commission was deliberating. Intelligence tests made it possible to assign a 'mental age' to individuals by establishing norms for each age-group. While later studies have introduced many reservations about the appropriateness of intelligence testing for people with learning difficulties,[23] the impact of Binet's work at the time was very marked.

The Radnor Commission decided to restrict their recommendations to 'mental defectives', and to build on the foundation of the permissive Idiots Act of 1886. The fact that a Royal Commission on the Poor Laws was set up in 1905 may also have helped to narrow their view of their remit, since that Commission took on the wider issues concerned with poverty.

One popular preoccupation in the early years of this century was with the fear of a 'declining national stock'. General Booth's *In Darkest England*[24] introduced the concept of the 'submerged tenth' of the population, and there were fears that this proportion would grow. Mental defectives were thought to be totally lacking in sexual restraint, and very prolific. One witness before the Radnor Commission, the General Inspector to the Local Government Board, stated that every Board of Guardians was familiar with the problem of the mentally defective girl who came to the workhouse, perhaps five or six times, to bear her illegitimate children. The children were 'nearly always defective'. Mental defectives, he told the Commission, tended to be imitative and highly suggestible. They were often sexually exploited, or led into crime by unscrupulous acquaintances.

The Commission considered sterilization, but rejected it on the grounds that the main criterion for action should be the protection and happiness of the defective rather than the 'purification of the race'. There were no effective methods of birth control: the only possible answers were guardianship or 'permanent segregation'. 'Mental deficiency colonies' – a reflection of Britain's imperial heritage at the time – were seen as a move away from the institutionalization of the asylum system.[25]

The Radnor Commission's recommendations were embodied in the Mental Deficiency Act of 1913. Colonies were run on educational lines by the mental deficiency committee of a local authority, usually with a headmaster. They were not classified as a health responsibility, or placed under medical direction, until the passing of the National Health Service Act of 1946. Lunatic asylums gradually began to transfer out patients who were 'subject to be dealt with' under the Mental Deficiency Act, but as late as the 1950s there were still many patients in mental hospitals whose primary condition was mental handicap rather than mental illness.

THE BOARD OF CONTROL

Under the terms of the Mental Deficiency Act, the Lunacy Commission was replaced by the Board of Control. This body continued to deal with both mental illness and mental deficiency, but the two systems became increasingly separate.

The Board of Control consisted of not more than fifteen

members, of whom twelve were salaried members. Four were legal Commissioners, and four medical Commissioners. In a move away from legal control, major responsibility for the oversight of the Board was transferred back from the Lord Chancellor's Department to the Home Office. Responsibility included the general power to make regulations determining the Board's work, the supervision and regulation of the activities of local authorities, the right to appoint the Chairman of the Board, and the right to appoint and fix the salaries of the Board's secretary and inspectors.

THE FIRST WORLD WAR

When war broke out in 1914, there were 140,466 'notified insane persons' distributed among ninety-seven county and county borough asylums. London had ten asylums, of which eight had more than two thousand beds. In all areas, there was overcrowding. This became worse in 1915, when nine of the larger asylums were transferred to the War Office as emergency military hospitals. The remaining mental hospitals became crowded with displaced patients. Standards of care suffered from lack of space and lack of staff, and the tuberculosis rates rose alarmingly.[26]

War-time conditions reduced standards of staffing and accommodation in asylums to very low levels. By 1915, 42 per cent of asylum medical staff had volunteered, and been accepted, for military service. Many of these men were killed in action. Their places were taken by retired or physically unfit medical practitioners, many with no previous experience of asylum work.

The Board of Control had no figures on the number of nursing staff who left for active service, but they believed that it was considerably higher than the figure quoted for medical staff. In war-time conditions, it was often impossible to replace mental nurses, even by untrained workers.

During the war years, the number of 'notified insane persons' went down. The figure for 1915 showed an increase of 2,411 on the previous year, but by 1916 there was a reduction of 3,278. The reduction continued year by year until about 1920, when there was a return to the pre-war increase rate of two thousand to three thousand a year.[27] Professor F.A.E. Crew of the University of Edinburgh was to argue after the Second World War that war produced group solidarity and prevented mental breakdown[28]; but it is likely that the comparatively few doctors left to the civilian population were more than ever reluctant to certify patients when asylum conditions were so poor. The war years probably marked the lowest point in the history of the overcrowded and stagnating asylums.

CHAPTER 8

Into The Community

After the end of the First World War, conditions in the mental hospitals, as they were now increasingly being called, began to improve again. Staff were demobilized, war hospitals closed down and their premises were returned. Outstanding among these was the Maudsley Hospital, which had been completed during the war, was used for the treatment of 'shell-shock' cases, and from 1923 was employed for its original purpose as a civilian hospital. Dr Henry Maudsley, the 'aristocrat's alienist'[1] and a son-in-law of John Conolly, had backed the movement for a centre which would give expression to new ideas on the treatment of mental illness. Maudsley, whose private practice was extensive, was a very wealthy man. In 1907, he offered £30,000 to the London County Council for a new asylum, on a series of conditions: it was to deal exclusively with early and acute cases; it was to have an out-patient department; it was to take 75 to 100 patients, 50 to 75 of them pauper patients, and the rest fee-paying; it was to make provision for teaching and research; it was to be in a central position in London, and within three or four miles of Trafalgar Square; it was to be recognized as a school of the University of London; and it was to be managed and maintained by the London County Council. Later, he contributed further sums, and on his death left a bequest of £10,000 for research.

The new hospital was completed in 1915, in which year it was exempted from the terms of the 1890 Act and allowed to take patients without certification. In 1924, the Maudsley became a teaching school of the University of London. In 1948, on the setting up of the National Health Service, it was administratively united with Bethlem, England's oldest mental hospital, to form the only postgraduate school in the teaching of psychiatry.[2]

In 1918, the Board of Control drafted a report[3] for the Government Reconstruction Committee, making recommendations for the future:

1. Treatment for limited periods should be possible in mental hospitals without certification. A Bill 'to facilitate the early treatment of mental disorder of recent origin' was introduced into the House of Commons by Cecil Harmsworth in 1915, but the timing was unsuitable, and it was withdrawn for lack of support. Now that staffing and accommodation were improving, the proposal was renewed.

2. The development of units for psychiatric diagnosis and treatment in general hospitals. Psychiatry was drawing closer to general medicine, largely because of a growing interest in psychosomatic conditions.

3. Senior posts in mental hospitals should be restricted to medical practitioners with a postgraduate diploma. A Diploma in Psychological Medicine, or Diploma in Mental Diseases, had been instituted in three universities, Edinburgh, Durham and London, in 1911. By 1918, courses were also organized by the Royal College of Physicians and the Universities of Leeds and Cambridge.

4. Out-patient clinics, which the Board considered 'inseparably connected with the improvement of methods of dealing with incipient insanity' should be supported and extended. These clinics had been developed in several city centres during the war, and had excited considerable interest as a means of early treatment and reducing mental hospital populations.

5. The Board should be empowered to make grants for after-care work by voluntary societies. This referred to the work of the Mental After-Care Association, formed in 1879, when the Chaplain of the Middlesex Asylum at Colney Hatch published two papers in the *Journal of Mental Science* on the subject.[4] He stressed the need for some form of care for discharged patients. Lord Shaftesbury accepted the presidency of the new association, expressing the conviction that 'The After-Care Association was required to supply a real want. It was a seed plot from which in

time good results would spring'.[5] The work of the MACA was at first on a comparatively small scale, but in 1919 it was recognized and considerably increased when the London County Council authorized the Association to deal with patients discharged on trial, making payments up to the full cost of maintenance. This pioneer work was repeatedly commended by the Board of Control.

These recommendations were the essence of the developments which were to take place in the 1930s; but any plans for immediate improvement had to be shelved in 1921, when the Geddes Axe severely curtailed expenditure in all government departments.

One major sign of change was the setting up of the Ministry of Health in 1919. This new department of state took over the functions of the Local Government Board, including Poor Law and housing policy, and in 1920 took over the powers given to the Home Office by the Mental Deficiency Act of 1913.[6] The Board of Control welcomed the change as 'an important step' towards bringing its work 'into a proper and desirable relation with the central health authority'.[7]

THE PRESTWICH INQUIRY

One of the powers transferred to the Ministry of Health was the power to hold a public inquiry. In 1922, an inquiry was held in connection with the allegations against Prestwich Hospital made by Dr Montague Lomax in *The Experiences of an Asylum Doctor*.[8]

Dr Lomax stated that the patients were poorly fed and poorly clothed; that they were closely confined, though a number of them would have benefited from parole, with no detriment to the community; that the nurses were mostly unqualified, unsuited to the nature of their work and had, in a number of specific cases, treated the patients with open cruelty. It was a picture of a drab institutional life where, as a result of ignorance and neglect, abuses were still practised.

A spate of newspaper articles and speeches followed the book's publication, and a small high-level departmental committee was set up to investigate under the chairmanship of Sir Cyril Cobb. Dr Lomax found the members hostile, and refused to give evidence. He was also facing considerable hostility from the medical press.

The final report[9] of the Cobb Committee largely discounted his evidence. The Committee pointed out that Lomax had served in Prestwich during the war, when conditions were admittedly poor; and that he had no special qualifications in psychiatry, so that he might have misconstrued certain measures of policy. At the same time, they agreed that conditions at Prestwich were still poor; that there was a great lack of trained staff, and that some unsuitable untrained staff had been recruited in order to keep the institution running at all. It was seldom possible to allow patients out of the building, because nurses could not be freed from other duties to accompany them. They agreed that patients were poorly and uniformly clothed, and that the diet was monotonous and unappetizing.

How far did these conditions apply to other mental hospitals? The Cobb Committee was hampered in finding out: as a departmental committee, it had no power to hear witnesses on oath, or to protect them against subsequent victimization. The Asylum Workers' Union refused to allow its members to give evidence for this reason. The Committee confined itself to two general issues – the construction of mental hospitals, and the recruitment of staff. They recommended that future mental hospitals should have not more than a thousand beds, and should be constructed on the villa-system, with a number of small, separate units spread round the grounds. This would restore face-to-face relationships, and make it possible to designate separate reception and convalescent wards.

There was still a lack of suitable nursing staff, both male and female. Examinations for mental nurses had been set up on a national scale by the Medico-Psychological Association in 1891. In 1919, the Nurses' Registration Act set up the General Nursing Council, which refused to recognize the examinations of other bodies such as the MPA, and set up its own Mental Nursing Certificate two years later. The theoretical standard was higher than that of the MPA examination; but too few mental nurses had the ability or the will to take either.

Dr T.W. Harding has two interesting pieces of evidence on the Lomax case[10]: one is a long confidential minute written by Percy (later Sir Percy) Barter, a senior civil servant in the Ministry of Health, supporting Lomax's views. The confidential minute effectively ties Lomax's account of asylum conditions to the subsequent reforms.

At the time, Lomax was largely opposed by his medical colleagues. The *Lancet* and the *British Medical Journal* cast doubt on his competence, pointing out that, though in his early fifties, he was only a temporary assistant medical officer, and had held only short-term and junior asylum appointments. Dr Harding's other major piece of evidence consists of extracts from Lomax's casenotes, which give a convincing picture of a humane and conscientious doctor with a respect for patients' rights.

THE ROYAL COMMISSION OF 1924–6

Montague Lomax had asked for a Royal Commission. In 1924, the Macmillan Commission was appointed by the Home Secretary to inquire into 'the existing law and administrative machinery in England and Wales in connection with the certification, detention and care of persons who are, or are alleged to be of unsound mind' and also into 'the extent to which provision is or should be made ... for the treatment without certification of persons suffering from mental disorder'. The Commission listened to Lomax with respect on the evils of the old mental hospital system. Their secretary, a civil servant in the new Ministry of Health, was Percy Barter, who had previously supported Lomax's views, and who was later to become Chairman of the reorganized Board of Control in 1930. His influence on the humanization of the mental hospital system was to continue through to the 1950s.

The Chairman of the Royal Commission, Hugh Pattison (later Lord) Macmillan, was the Lord Advocate for Scotland. The majority of the members had legal qualifications – including the two medical members, Sir Humphrey Rolleston, President of the Royal College of Physicians, and Sir David Drummond, Professor of Medicine in the University of Durham. There were no psychiatrist members. It appears that every possible step was taken to ensure that the proposals would carry the support of the legal lobby.

The Macmillan Commission set out to receive evidence on the existing system from those who operated it – the Board of Control, government departments, voluntary agencies, relieving officers, magistrates, psychiatrists and others; and also to receive evidence on the shortcomings of the existing system. There is some evidence of the Commission's impatience with the National Society for

Lunacy Reform, which brought forward a number of ex-patients who wished to give evidence. After the first day's public hearing, the Commission decided that the atmosphere was 'one of recrimination and controversy', and directed that future hearings of this kind should be held in camera. 'We do not find', they recorded, 'that the evidence received from this source made any constructive contribution to the main purpose of our Inquiry.'[11] They received over 360 letters from individual patients. 'Some of these', they noted, 'were unintelligible.' Almost all the evidence came from official sources. In the past, agencies representing patients had often been clamorous, and time-wasting; but this kind of agitation was an outlet for a genuine public anxiety, and might have been allowed a greater measure of attention. In the event, the Commission's main interest was in re-stating the principles laid down by the Board of Control in 1918, and in proposing a new and flexible system.

Principles of Care and Treatment

1. *The interaction of mental and physical illness.* Mental illness was defined as 'the inability of the patient to maintain his social equilibrium'. This was 'essentially a public health problem, to be dealt with on public health lines'. It should be a community service, based on the treatment of patients in their own homes, and with a strong preventive element. The statement on the interaction of mental and physical illness has become a classic, and is here quoted in full:

It has become increasingly evident that there is no clear line of demarcation between mental and physical illness. The distinction as commonly drawn is based on a difference of symptoms. In ordinary parlance, a disease is described as mental if its symptoms manifest themselves predominantly in derangement of conduct, and as physical if its symptoms manifest themselves predominantly in derangement of bodily function. A mental illness may have physical concomitants: probably it always has, though they may be difficult of detection. A physical illness, on the other hand, may have, and probably always has, mental concomitants. And there are many cases in which it is a question whether the physical or the mental symptoms predominate.[12]

For many people in the medical profession, this was thinking of a new kind. Insanity had been treated as a borderline subject, a sort of poor relation of general medicine. The Macmillan Commission's intention was to change the conceptualization of general medicine as well as that of psychological medicine.[13] Psychiatry was not to be a specialism of medicine: it was to form a system of treatment as extensive and as prestigious as that of general medicine. The Macmillan Commission took the view that there were probably as many different kinds of mental illness as of physical illness, and there was a great deal of research to be done. In the future, the healing of mind and body would be interactive and complementary. As the understanding of psychosomatic conditions grew, they expected that the psychological component in much (or all) physical illness would be recognized as well as the somatic component in mental illness. The link with the general hospital was to work to the increased understanding of both parties.

2. *Terminology*. A medical terminology was adopted – 'hospital', 'nurse', 'patient' and so on – because that was less stigmatizing, and more acceptable to patients and their relatives, than the older terminology of 'asylum, 'attendant' and 'lunatic'.

3. *Voluntary Treatment*. 'The keynote of the past', said the Commission, 'has been detention. The keynote of the future should be prevention and treatment'.[14] The 1890 Act represented one solution to the problem of how to deal with those whose behaviour conflicted with that of the society in which they lived. It was the solution of compulsion, hedged in with 'anxious provisions' and 'bristling with precautions against illegal detention'.[15] The other solution was voluntary treatment. It had been granted a grudging and very limited approval in 1862 and 1890 by the provision that voluntary boarders could be accepted in private asylums. It had been pressed for strongly by the Board of Control in 1918. The Maudsley Hospital was the only public hospital where psychiatric in-patient treatment could be given without certification. In other mental hospitals, the old dilemma remained. In order to get treatment, patients had to be certifiable; and in order to be certifiable, they had to be left untreated until they reached the point of social breakdown. This was 'contrary to the accepted canons of preventive medicine'.

The Commission thought that in future, legal intervention should be confined to three functions: protecting the patient against neglect or ill-treatment; ensuring that personal liberty was infringed only as long as necessary in the patient's or the public interest; and making provision for proper treatment.[16]

4. *Class Distinction*. 'The present legal status of the great bulk of insane persons in this country', noted the Commission, 'is that of paupers'. They recommended the abolition of the old connection with the Poor Law, and the abolition of all legal distinctions between private and pauper patients – 'the justification for which has largely disappeared under modern social conditions'.[17]

5. *After-care*: 'The transition from asylum life to the everyday world is a stage of peculiar difficulty for the recovered patient. The home and family life to which he returns may be unsuitable or unsympathetic; employment may be hard to obtain, and friends may be unable or unwilling to help'.[18]

Recommendations

To meet criticisms that the Board was 'inaccessible' because its members were constantly away on visitations, a smaller Board was recommended, to consist of a lay chairman, a legal member, a medical member and a woman. Visitation would be carried out by fifteen Assistant Commissioners, while the Board remained in London.

On admission to mental hospital, it was recommended that 'The lunacy code should be recast with a view to securing that the treatment of mental disorder should approximate as nearly to the treatment of physical ailments as is consistent with the special safeguards which are indispensable when the liberty of the subject is infringed'.[19] Certification should be a last resort, not a preliminary to treatment. Voluntary patients should be able to enter mental hospitals without legal formality, and to discharge themselves. There should be no distinction in the method of certification for private and public patients.

Local authorities should be encouraged to establish out-patient clinics, to provide observation beds in general hospitals, and to finance after-care work.

The future size of mental hospitals should not exceed a thousand beds, and new mental hospitals should be constructed on the villa-system. Nurses should be graded – the best receiving double training in both mental and general nursing, the average nurse being trained in mental nursing, and those who could not reach the required standard of theoretical work forming a separate grade. Entertainment and employment for patients should be developed, and a special officer should be appointed for patients' activities. Voluntary visitors should be encouraged to act as friends of patients; and closer links should be developed between mental hospitals and general practitioners.

HUMANIZING THE MENTAL HOSPITALS

In the 1920s, while the Macmillan Commission was sitting, and its report was being discussed, the Board of Control's Annual Reports show that conditions in mental hospitals were improving. In some hospitals, patients were allowed to wear their own clothes, instead of drab and depressing asylum garments. Small articles previously regarded as unnecessary for 'paupers', such as nail-brushes and writing-paper, were being supplied. The comparatively new invention of the cinema had beneficial effects. (In 1931, the Board was to deplore the introduction of the talking film, on the grounds that silent films of good quality were becoming increasingly difficult to obtain, and that talking films were too expensive and too complicated to be used in mental hospitals. Fortunately, the technological difficulties were soon overcome). Occupational therapy was being introduced in some hospitals, on a pattern developed in the Netherlands. The Board stressed repeatedly that patients must not be left to 'deteriorate in wearisome idleness', and that occupation and interest were part of the treatment.

The topics of pre-care, after-care and research were constantly stressed. 'The successful treatment of mental disorders on modern lines' the Board noted in 1928,'is prejudiced by the inability to make adequate provision for the patient except during the relatively acute phase.' Out-patient clinic work was on the increase, but social care was slow to develop. The development of training in psychiatric social work was a hopeful sign: in 1928, the Commonwealth Fund of America provided grants for four British social workers to train in the United States, and the first British course was set up at the London School of Economics in 1929.[20]

Major changes occurred in relation to the Poor Law and local government under the Local Government Act of 1929. In a long overdue reform, Boards of Guardians were at last abolished, and Public Assistance Committees of the local authority took their place. 'Paupers' became 'rate-aided persons', and the links between the health services and the new public assistance services were strengthened.

THE MENTAL TREATMENT ACT OF 1930

The Government was nervous about the controversy which legislation concerned with mental illness could provoke. Experience of parliamentary reactions to Lunacy Bills in the 1880s suggested that the passage of the Mental Treatment Bill would be difficult, and so it proved. Since the major opposition was expected to come from the House of Lords, the Government took the precaution of having it introduced in that House by Earl Russell, a barrister who had been a member of the Macmillan Commission. Both peers and members of the House of Commons showed a tendency to embark on long and irrelevant anecdotes on the subject of mental illness, and the quality of debate was distinctly patchy;[21] but the main speakers were well briefed, and the Bill was passed without major changes. It did not repeal the 1890 Act, but provided another system to parallel it and, it was hoped, in time to render it out of date.

The Mental Treatment Act made provision for voluntary treatment in mental hospitals; reorganized the Board of Control on the lines proposed by the Macmillan Commission; gave an official blessing to the funding of psychiatric out-patient clinics and observation wards; and abolished an outmoded terminology. 'Asylum' was replaced by 'mental hospital' or simply 'hospital', and 'lunatic' by 'person of unsound mind', except in certain specific legal contexts (the law continued to refer to 'criminal lunatics'). Since the Local Government Act of 1929 had ended the use of 'pauper', a 'pauper lunatic' became, by virtue of two Acts of Parliament, a 'rate-aided person of unsound mind'.

Certification procedures continued as laid down in the 1890 Act; but two new categories for patient admissions were introduced – 'voluntary' and 'temporary'. A voluntary patient was one who had the power of volition, and made a written application for treatment. Such patients could discharge themselves at seventy two hours' notice. Temporary patients were defined as persons 'suffering from mental illness and likely to benefit by temporary treatment, but for the time being incapable of expressing [themselves] as willing or unwilling to receive such treatment'. The initial duration of a temporary order, six months, might be extended for two further periods of three months with the consent of the Board of Control.

A PERIOD OF EXPERIMENT AND REFORM

The early 1930s were in many ways an unpropitious time for social reform. There was a severe economic depression. Unemployment was rising rapidly: between 1929 and 1931, it almost doubled. Unemployment benefit was first frozen, and then cut,[22] and there were many people living near starvation level. As voluntary admission became more common, some mental hospitals had difficulty in distinguishing applicants who were in need of treatment from those whose primary need was a bed and a square meal. The confusion between poverty and mental illness had returned in a new context.

But the depression meant that mental hospitals were better staffed. Other kinds of employment were hard to find, and there was a considerable influx of new recruits, particularly men, into mental nursing. Many of them came from the depressed areas – among them, small tradesmen, miners and craftsmen. The hospital authorities usually required that they should be physically fit, play football or cricket, or play a musical instrument. Although some went back to other employment when the years of crisis were over, a surprising number remained to make good trained mental nurses.

Out-patient clinics developed rapidly. Many of them were in general hospitals, which meant that patients came forward more readily, and medical students were introduced to psychiatric practice. From all aspects the increasing links between general and mental hospitals were seen as being of advantage to both.

The use of voluntary procedures for admission rose steadily after a patchy start. By 1938, voluntary patients accounted for 35.2 per cent of all admissions, and 15 per cent of hospitals were admitting more than half their patients with voluntary status.[23] The reconstituted Board of Control waged a vigorous battle for better conditions for all patients in mental hospitals, rather than simply for voluntary patients, to avoid creating an additional stigma against those who were certified. The distinction was not one of social status, degree of illness or need, but simply one of volition.

The Board's Annual Reports in the 1930s show a new capacity for independent assessment, and occasionally for stinging rebuke. A note on the provision of mental hospital libraries runs: 'Because patients are allowed to read anything, it must not be assumed that they will be content with any rubbish produced by past piety or present ineptitude . . . A generation accustomed to Edgar Wallace will not, even in dementia, take kindly to Victorian sentimentality, or the "life and remains" of eminent divines.'[24] It was suggested that the Red Cross or the county library might supply suitable books, and that clubs and hotels might be induced to supply magazines.

Women patients had a champion – probably Dame Ellen Pinsent, one of the reformers of the mental handicap services, who was now the woman Senior Commissioner of the Board. 'Only advanced dementia', runs a passage in the 1932 Report, 'would reconcile the average woman to the type of garment still worn in some hospitals.' Two years later came the comment: 'A good hair cut and shampoo have a real tonic value . . . the woman who is content to wear her hair untrimmed and a frock like a sack certainly is not normal.' This recognition of the therapeutic value of clothes and hairdressing was new to many hospitals, where committees were apt to consider such things as unjustifiable luxuries.

Food was important: patients needed to be reassured by familiar dishes ('a generation accustomed to fish and chips cannot be expected to eat steamed cod with anything but reluctance').[25] Entertainments and recreation were encouraged. By 1934, almost all hospitals had a programme of activities covering the whole year. There were cinema shows and sports such as cricket, football and hockey. Some hospitals organized dancing classes. Most had regular dances for men and women patients, and were beginning to break down the rigid segregation of the sexes.

The question of open and closed wards figures prominently in the Board's reports in the 1930s. The admission of voluntary patients indicated that some wards at least should be left unlocked, and the patients should be free to come and go independently. At first, this roused many tensions. Nursing and medical staff were accustomed to walk the hospital to the accompaniment of jangling keys, and for a nurse to lose his or her keys was the quickest way to be 'sent down the drive' – that is, dismissed; but it was found that, except among very disturbed patients, opening the doors and granting 'parole' had a tranquillizing influence. The Board of Control endorsed the parole system, which usually had four grades: 'hospital parole' was leave to go in and out of the ward; 'ground parole' was leave to go anywhere in the hospital and its grounds; 'outside parole' was leave to go anywhere in the neighbourhood for the day; and 'weekend parole' was a period at home on trial before final discharge.[26]

Professional training improved: the Diploma in Psychological Medicine became the recognized psychiatric qualification for a medical practitioner; the GNC and the RMPA (the Medico-Psychological Association had become 'Royal' in 1926) continued to develop nurse training; and several universities ran courses for social workers. The specialist psychiatric social workers trained at the London School of Economics tended to go into child guidance work and adult psychiatric clinics, but a number of basic-trained social workers found their way into mental hospitals.

Two new mental hospitals were built in this period: Bethlem and Runwell. The first Bethlem, in Bishopsgate, was left for a site on Moorfields in 1676. This second hospital was the 'Bedlam' of the eighteenth century. The third, in Southwark, was occupied in 1815. When the Southwark site became overcrowded, and the limited space unsuitable for new methods of treatment and activity programmes, the Governors issued an appeal, and £50,000 was suscribed for new buildings set in a park at Beckenham, Kent. This was completed in 1930. Bethlem remained a charitable foundation until 1948, when it was united with the Maudsley Hospital.

Runwell was a completely new hospital – the first to be constructed since the First World War. It was built for a thousand patients on the villa-system, with small units housing twenty or twenty-five patients scattered over a wide area of parkland. There was a resocialization programme, and group therapy was practised. A separate research wing was built and equipped. As a symbol of the new attitude to mental illness which the hospital represented, a swimming pool was built in front of the main entrance.

Bethlem and Runwell embodied the most advanced thinking of the 1930s. They differed as much from the grim Victorian institutions as the 1930 Act differed from the 1890 Act, and for the same reasons. They were to be the last of their kind. Apart from small satellite units, there has been no new mental hospital building since.

THE FEVERSHAM REPORT

There were three major voluntary associations working with mentally ill people by 1939: the Mental After-Care Association, founded
in 1879, which helped patients discharged from mental hospitals;
the National Council for Mental Hygiene, founded in 1918, which
concentrated on educational and preventive work, and had an
international network of contacts; and the Child Guidance Council,
founded in 1927. The Central Association for Mental Welfare,
founded in 1896 as the National Association for the Care of the
Feeble-Minded, provided services for mentally handicapped people
and their families. These organizations had grown up piece-meal,
as voluntary associations often do. They had been created in
response to different needs. In some areas, notably in London and
the Home Counties, their work overlapped. In others, there was no
provision at all. Sometimes a single society would be found carrying
an overwhelming burden of work for which its small staff and
slender budget were wholly inadequate.

A Ministry of Health committee set up to review the voluntary
services under the chairmanship of Lord Feversham[27] swiftly came
to the obvious conclusion: whatever the cost in personal loyalty,
the associations should amalgamate to form a national Mental
Health Association. Three of them amalgamated on the outbreak
of war to form a Mental Health Emergency Committee. (The
Mental After-Care Association refused to join, and continued its
separate activities for many years on a diminishing scale). In 1939,
the Emergency Committee became the Provisional National Council for Mental Health, and in 1946 it became the National Association for Mental Health, now known as MIND.

The Feversham Committee, which included high-level representatives of the voluntary associations and the British Medical Association, took the opportunity to review the state of the mental health
services. Its members were unanimous in considering the effects of
the 1890 Lunacy Act highly damaging. They stressed the need for a
full-scale review of existing legislation to meet the new developments in the treatment of psychoneurosis. The Committee concluded that the 1930 Mental Treatment Act had done much to
improve the situation, but its implications were not yet fully recognized throughout the country. Out-patient clinics were generally ill-
equipped, under-staffed, often had inadequately trained personnel,

and were too few in number. Clinic work required a multiprofessional team including a psychologist and a psychiatric social worker, with adequate secretarial backing.

The increase in voluntary admissions to hospital was encouraging, but the stigma on hospital treatment remained, and there was a need for a programme of mental health education to improve public knowledge and understanding. Many local authorities, when asked if they carried out mental health education, had replied that the subject was 'taboo', and that there was 'no demand'. To the Feversham Committee, the fact that the subject was taboo was precisely the reason for promoting educational work.

How was this to be done? Some local authorities had pointed out that, while general health education could be undertaken at a popular level by posters and slogans on the lines of 'Coughs and Sneezes Spread Diseases', such methods were inappropriate for mental health work. The Feversham Committee thought that more subtle approaches might be used. In some mental hospitals, the staff had set themselves the task of integrating the hospital with the local community. Lectures and informal talks were given to local groups – Rotary, church groups, youth clubs and others. Tours of the hospital were arranged for teachers, magistrates, social workers, local councillors, students. There was a general letter to relatives, to be given to them on the patient's admission, which gave them information about the hospital's work and changing attitudes to mental illness. A hospital Open Day enabled people in the locality to see the work for themselves. The new national voluntary association was to undertake educational work of all kinds, at a variety of levels.

1939 proved not to be a good year in which to plan for the future; but, though most of the Feversham Committee's recommendations could not be carried out in war-time, they had a considerable influence in the early post-war years.

CHAPTER 9

A New Service For A New Age

Up to the outbreak of war in 1939, the development of mental health services outside the hospitals was patchy and sporadic. Where medical, nursing and social work staff were well qualified and enthusiastic, an efficient service had been provided; but where the old ideas about mental illness were still current, there was apathy and indifference. There was no effective central authority – for while the Board of Control was doing its best to bring mental hospitals in line with modern practice, those institutions no longer represented the whole range of treatment. The community services – out-patient clinics, domiciliary visits by social workers, occupation centres, industrial centres were of increasing importance; but though the Ministry of Health exercised a certain control over the activities of local health authorities, it was largely a financial control. The Ministry appears to have taken little positive action to encourage the development of services outside the hospitals. The initiative lay with the energetic local authorities: the apathetic were allowed to rest in peace.

THE SECOND WORLD WAR

War brought a crop of fresh problems. As in the 1914–18 war, many doctors were called up for service with the Forces, and about half the mental hospital accommodation was taken over for emergency purposes – for military hospitals, air-raid casualty centres or general hospital accommodation in areas to which city populations were evacuated. Out-patient clinics collapsed for want of trained staff, or staff of any kind. Though the work was a reserved occupation, many nurses, male and female, left to join the Forces. Those mental hospitals which continued in operation faced acute shortages of clothing, food and heating, with an unprecedented degree of overcrowding and under-staffing. This meant the return of the locked door, of inactivity, of isolation; and again the tuberculosis rate soared. The hospitals which had built small separate units in the grounds for voluntary patients soon had to devote them to tubercular patients. In the time of the Second World War, tuberculosis was still a killer, and isolation was a necessity.

At the same time, mental health issues acquired a new and wider significance. The war of 1914–18 had been fought in France and Belgium. This time, the civilian population was involved. As gasmasks were issued to adults and children (there were special gastents for babies), air-raid shelters were set up in back gardens, and trenches were dug in public parks, there was considerable apprehension that there might be mass panic and widespread mental breakdown.

In October 1938, when war was recognized as inevitable, a committee of psychiatrists from the London teaching hospitals was set up to consider the implications for the mental health services. Their advice to Government was that three to four million acute psychiatric cases could be expected within six months of the outbreak of hostilities.[1] However, there was a lively correspondence in the *Lancet* in the autumn of 1939 in which most writers took a less alarmist view. Some stressed the importance of 'organization and preparedness'. The Ministry of Health was reported as having explained to the press how psychiatric casualties would be treated in the event of the outbreak of hostilities:

> The arrangements are that these cases will be treated at first-aid posts, and given a sedative, and if they are in a fit state, will go home. 'Bad cases' would go to one of the casualty hospitals.[2]

Fortunately, in view of these limited preparations, war did not produce the mass hysteria which had been feared; but it did produce some remarkable new initiatives in mental health provision. Perhaps the most striking of these was the appointment of Dr J.R. Rees as Director of the Army Psychiatric Services. Dr Rees was the Director of the Tavistock Clinic, Britain's most avant-garde psychoanalytic clinic, founded in 1920. A number of senior staff from 'Tavi' went with him, including Dr Ronald Hargreaves, later Chief of the Mental Health Section of the World Health Organization, Dr John Bowlby, best known as the author of *Child Care and the Growth of Love*, Dr T.F. Main, later Director of the Cassell Hospital, and the psychologist Dr W.R. Bion. This specialized group of unorthodox research workers found themselves in uniform, with commissioned ranks up to that of brigadier, and unexpected scope for developing their work. From their collaboration were to come many of the ideas which shaped psychiatry and social psychology in the 1950s and 1960s.[3]

While the war was in progress, and even when its outcome seemed doubtful, plans for social reconstruction were actively discussed. The Beveridge Plan for social security, published in 1942, rested on three assumptions: children's allowances, full employment and a National Health Service.[4] The key question in relation to mental health was whether mental hospitals were to be included in the centralized NHS scheme, or left with the county authorities. In April 1943, the Minister of Health, Ernest Brown, ruled that the new scheme would only apply to physical illness, and that services for mental illness would be excluded;[5]but this decision was short-lived. Mental hospitals were included in the scheme set out by the White Paper of 1944, which quoted the Macmillan Commission on the interaction of mind and body.[6]

The Future Organization of the Psychiatric Services, published in June 1945, was the result of deliberations between representatives of the Royal Medico-Psychological Association, the British Medical Association and the Royal College of Physicians. The report was based on the premise that 'the argument for treating psychiatry in all essential respects like any other branch of medicine' was 'strong and conclusive':

> there is everything to be said for making the administrative structure of psychiatry exactly the same in principle and even in major detail as that of other branches of medicine.[7]

The advantages of this policy seemed clear. Psychiatry would have parity of esteem with other medical specialisms. The artificial divorce between the treatment of the mind and the treatment of the body would be ended, and the gap between the treatment of the psychoses (largely in county mental hospitals) and the treatment of the neuroses (largely in voluntary hospitals and private practice) would be bridged. The stigma which still attached to the old asylums would be reduced or even eliminated. But the report marks a significant shift from the findings of the Macmillan Commission. Mental health work (increasingly involving other professions as well as medicine) was not to form a separate service with its own rationale and organizational imperatives. Only the medical element was recognized, and this was to be assimilated into the structure of general medicine. The status of psychiatry within medicine was improved – and so were the salaries of psychiatrists, which had previously lagged behind those of other medical specialists. The Medical Qualifications Act of 1858 was the first landmark in the medicalization of mental health care: the National Health Service Act was the second.

THE NATIONAL HEALTH SERVICE ACT, 1946

The main body of the Act contained few specific references to mental health. The Minister of Health now became the central authority for all health services, and county mental hospitals were transferred, like other hospitals, to the new Regional Hospital Boards. Some RHBs set up separate Hospital Management Committees for mental hospitals, while some experimented with mixed groups to serve the varying health needs of given populations.

Local authorities lost their hospitals, including county mental hospitals, but acquired rather vague powers under section 28 of the Act. This read:

A local health authority, with the approval of the Minister, may, and to such extent as the Minister may direct, shall ... make arrangements for the purpose of the prevention of illness, the care of persons suffering from illness or mental defectiveness, or the after-care of such persons ...

This convoluted clause gave the local authorities permissive powers, with a hint of future mandatory action.

Nearly two years of questioning and debate lay between the passing of the Act and the Appointed Day. On 5 July 1948, the National Assistance Act, the National Insurance Act and the

National Health Service Act came into force simultaneously, with meshing provisions.

There were many administrative problems. From a mental health perspective, the chief difficulty was that the mental hospitals were in the wrong places. Local government was still organized in counties and county boroughs, and there was no direct administrative relationship between local authority boundaries and those of hospital catchment areas. The mental hospitals were often in county areas, while the bulk of their population came from nearby county boroughs. It is no accident that the mental health services which became well known for hospital/local authority integration were sited in or near county boroughs with roughly the same catchment area: in Nottingham, Oldham, Portsmouth, York, Worthing and Bristol, personal contacts and regular case conferences made it possible to develop a high degree of continuity of care, whether the patient was in or out of hospital.

Not all local authorities understood that their powers and duties stretched beyond the mandatory responsibility of transferring certified patients from the community into hospital – the task of the 'Duly Authorized Officer' under the 1890 Lunacy Act. One Medical Officer of Health of a sizeable county borough was heard to query, 'What the hell is after-care?'

The local Health Committee now took over the statutory duties formerly carried out by Public Assistance Committees, and was required to appoint a Mental Health Sub-Committee. Many Duly Authorized Officers (DAOs) became Mental Welfare Officers (MWOs), serving the sub-committees; but although some Mental Health sub-committees developed positive programmes of their own, in other areas it was the practice for the Mental Health sub-committee to meet five minutes before the main Health Committee: the MWOs would recite the lists of certified patients transferred to hospital while the Health Committee members hung up their hats and coats.[8]

MENTAL HOSPITALS AFTER THE WAR

In the early post-war years, mental hospitals, which often reached a maximum of 2,500 or 3,000 beds, had a distinctive culture of their own. They were no longer extended households, or landed estates, but acquired an mixture of the ethos of a public school and a holiday camp. Perhaps the new model also owed something to the organization of an Army, Navy or RAF base, because many staff and patients had spent six or seven years in the Forces.

Most large hospitals had an Education Department, with a staff of several teachers who would tackle anything from literacy classes to discussion groups. Some had an Art teacher or even an Art Department, where staff would encourage patients to find expression through painting and drawing, and there were some remarkable mental hospital murals completed by art classes as a group exercise. The Council for Music in Hospitals sent musicians in full evening dress to play Bach and Mozart to the patients. Perhaps more popular were the concert parties, complete with red-nosed comedian who would lead a sing-song, and the brass bands. There were whist drives and beetle drives and outings to the seaside. There were films twice a week. There were gymnastic sessions and physical work-outs and dancing lessons.

Sport played a considerable part in mental hospital life, particularly cricket and football for the men. Each hospital would have its own first team, composed of younger staff and patients. The cricket team would be provided with flannels, and caps and blazers bearing the hospital crest. The football team would have its own distinctive 'rig'. Away matches (usually with other mental hospitals or mental handicap hospitals) were occasions of great excitement. The team would be cheered off as the coach went down the long drive, and greeted with enthusiasm or commiseration on its return. Some long-stay patients could recite the scores from matches with this hospital or that over ten or twenty years.

The hospital would have its own institutional celebrations: Christmas, with a long series of ward parties; Sports Day, when patients and staff would join in races and other events, the Committee wives' hats would rival Ascot, and much merriment would be caused by the sight of doctors (junior doctors) battling with pillows on a greasy pole, or dipping their heads into a tub full of water for floating apples. There was an element of role-reversal in this, but it did not extend to the senior staff, who kept their dignity.

The position of the medical superintendent was still one of great prestige and great authority. The nursing staff would tell stories of the imposing medical superintendents of earlier days: one made his daily rounds in a frock coat and a top hat, another wore plimsolls to creep round the wards at night. Some medical superintendents ate alone in state, their food separately prepared and served, rather than joining the medical staff. At least one hospital had a corridor 250 yards long, built specifically so that the medical superintendent could move from his house to his office in privacy, without having to encounter staff or patients on the way. Dr Walter Maclay, the last Senior Commissioner of the Board of Control before its abolition in 1959, had a joke about an admission certificate for a patient which ran on the following lines: 'This patient is arrogant, overbearing, and suffers from delusions of grandeur. He thinks he is a medical superintendent. In fact, he behaves just like a medical superintendent.'

Despite much genuine kindness and good will, patients still occupied the lowest rank in the mental hospital culture. It was common to hear a staff member say to another, 'Don't do that – get a patient to do it for you.' Patients provided the labour which made the whole enterprise possible at low cost, working in farms and gardens and kitchens and laundry, sweeping the vast wards and the endless corridors. In return, the hospital gave isolated and friendless people a certain sense of belonging, and could literally provide care from the cradle to the grave. If a woman patient had a baby, there would often be an arrangement with the local Registrar of Births, Deaths and Marriages that the address recorded on the birth certificate was not 'X-shire County Mental Hospital', but some innocuous substitute like '4, London Road'. If a patient died without relatives, the hospital had its own sad little cemetery, and would take charge of the funeral. Discharged patients were encouraged to come back, like old boys and old girls of a school, to see the staff and their former comrades.

The medical superintendent and his staff took a pride in the proportion of voluntary patients admitted: this was taken as an indication that the old prejudices associated with certification were being overcome, and that patients came willingly for treatment. The prevailing philosophy was that many people had been deterred from seeking early treatment by the stigma of 'being taken to the asylum', and that an increase in numbers indicated an active and successful mental health policy.

After the implementation of the National Health Service Act (1946), a programme of physical upgrading was undertaken by the Regional Hospital Boards. Standards of equipment and furnishing in many mental hospitals were well below those acceptable in general hospitals. New medical equipment was provided, new kitchens were installed, some distressing Edwardian furniture was removed, and experimental colour schemes replaced the drab greys and dirty cream of the pre-war era. There was a vogue for 'colour therapy': pillar-box red and bright yellow for depressed patients, dove-grey and pale blue for manic patients; but the improvements were in the nature of minor works, and could not make much impact on the old Victorian buildings, which became increasingly expensive to maintain and heat, and were manifestly unsuitable for the post-war era. The main problems were the increasing numbers of patients, and the enduring and immutable nature of the architecture.[9]

THE PARLIAMENTARY DEBATE OF 15 FEBRUARY 1954

At the beginning of 1954, there had been no major consolidation of the law relating to mental illness for sixty-four years. The Lunacy Act of 1890, though to some extent by-passed, was still in force. It was over a quarter of a century since the Macmillan Commission had recommended sweeping changes, but the majority of its recommendations had not been implemented. After the initial upheavals of 1948, the whole system settled down again for over five years; then, in the winter of 1953/4, it flared into life.

Afterwards, commentators were to talk of the 'three revolutions' – pharmacological, social or administrative, and legal – which dated from that same winter. The curtain-raiser was a parliamentary debate – the first on mental health for twenty-four years.

The debate was initiated on a Private Member's Bill by Kenneth Robinson, then Labour Member of Parliament for St Pancras North, and subsequently Minister of Health. The terms of the motion set the tone for the debate:

That this House, while recognising the advances made in recent years in the treatment of mental patients, expresses its concern at the serious overcrowding of mental hospitals and mental deficiency hospitals, and at the acute shortage of nursing and junior medical staff in the Mental Health Service; and calls upon HM Government and the hospital authorities to make adequate provision for the modernization and development of this essential service.[10]

Mr Robinson directed attention to four main shortages: shortage of beds, shortage of suitable buildings, shortage of staff, and shortage of money. Sometimes patients had to sleep in beds placed end to end in the corridors, or crammed together in the wards no more than nine inches apart – and still there were not enough beds. A small number of short-stay beds had a rapid turnover of patients; in the rest, chronic patients lived out their institutional lives over many years. Despite advances in treatment, there was no evidence that the rate of chronicity was dropping. Since the population was ageing, it was likely to increase.

Most of the accommodation which existed was unsuitable, since the hospitals had been designed to meet concepts of treatment now long outmoded. 'The Victorians could not build other than solidly, and there the buildings stand, grim, almost indestructible, and they constitute the majority of our mental hospital accommodation.' Out of a total of forty million pounds spent on capital expenditure in the first five years of the Health Service, only 16 per cent had been spent on mental and mental deficiency hospitals. The Minister had, as a somewhat belated gesture, set aside a million pounds for them in the coming year, 'but he knows, and we all know, that this is a drop in the ocean. We want many, many millions, and we want them urgently'.[11]

The junior minister, Patricia Hornsby-Smith, agreed in reply that the existing buildings were 'an appalling legacy', and that replacing them was 'not a question of a few million pounds, . . . [but] a question of thousands of millions over many years'.[12]

It was from this daunting financial prospect that the three revolutions offered deliverance. The psychotropic drugs, including the phenothiazines, first developed in a Paris pharmaceutical house in 1953, began to be used in the treatment of many forms of mental illness; mental hospitals began the 'open door movement' which was in time to reduce their numbers and bring their work closer to that of the community services; and a Royal Commission was appointed, thus starting a movement for the reform of the law.

From the point of view of therapy or of public policy, the coincidence of these three movements was fortunate, since each reinforced the other, and hospital authorities had begun, of necessity, to judge their work by the number of patients they could discharge rather than by the numbers they could induce to come forward for treatment; but the fact that all three movements operated in the same time-period made it impossible to trace cause and effect in any one movement with any confidence. Tooth and Brooke were later to call 1954–9 'the key years . . . the years of therapeutic flux'.[13]

THE PHARMACOLOGICAL REVOLUTION

The psychotropic drugs, such as tranquillizers, sedatives and euphoriants or anti-depressants, control mood-swings. Chlorpromazine (Largactil) was the first in general use, enabling patients under stress to relax, though remaining fully conscious. It could be used to relieve the more distressing symptoms of mental illness, while leaving the patient accessible to other forms of therapy.

The new drugs were soon being widely prescribed. Within the mental hospitals, they created a totally different atmosphere. There was no longer any justification for 'refractory' wards, for wired-in airing courts, for strong-arm tactics on the part of staff. The more distressing sights of mental hospital wards – patients erupting into fits of violence, fighting off imaginary enemies, cowering in corners, or actively hallucinating, simply ceased to exist. Some patients were able to go home sooner; some did not need to enter hospital at all, since their symptoms could be controlled and their illness treated while they remained at home. The emphasis began to shift from talk of 'pre-care' and 'after-care' to talk of 'alternative care'.

In the early days, the new drugs were prescribed very freely, and there was much optimism among psychiatrists. Only gradually was it realized that the phenothiazines alleviated, but did not cure. The symptoms were suppressed, but there were often marked side-effects, and the causes remained untouched. By 1961, Professor Morris Carstairs noted in *The Practitioner* that 'Few would claim that our current wonder drugs exercise anything more than a palliative influence on psychiatric disorders. The big change has been rather one of public opinion'.[14]

THE SOCIAL REVOLUTION

In September 1953 – pre-dating the development of the new pharmacology by a matter of weeks – the World Health Organization published a report which offered a new model for the development of mental health services, and offered the prospect of a reduction in hospital beds. The 'classical' system in which the mental hospital, virtually a closed system, dominated the services was contrasted with the 'modern' system, in which a variety of services operated as 'tools' in the hands of the community, and the hospital became one such tool at the disposal of the medico-social team. Among the other tools listed were day hospitals, out-patient clinics, mental health education directed to community leaders, hostels, and therapeutic social clubs. The balance of power would shift from the medical staff of the hospital to the medico-social team in the community, which would operate a flexible range of services adapted to patients' needs.[15]

As we have seen, even in the second half of the nineteenth century, British mental hospitals had outside working parties, patient outings and unlocked wards, while parole systems set up in the 1930s had given patients a degree of freedom of movement. Now, as the open door movement developed, wards which had previously been kept locked were unlocked, and soon some hospitals had no locked wards at all. Unsightly airing courts were dismantled, and used for gardens or car parks. Industrial therapy units were built, where patients could work for a normal, if rather low, wage instead of working to maintain the hospital. This was unpopular with occupational therapists, who pointed out that many of the industrial tasks were boring and repetitive: for example, a patient with a diagnosis of schizophrenia who spent hours fitting the spokes on umbrellas, or assembling the components of electric plugs, might become even more isolated; but industrial work was generally popular with patients, because it enabled them to earn money, and to feel that they were in something approaching normal employment. Much of the work the hospitals could obtain was of a dull and repetitive nature – the only work the trade unions were prepared to let them have on contract.

Therapeutic community systems grew out of war-time experience in dealing with refugees and Forces personnel. Dr T.F. Main (one of the 'Tavi' brigadiers) found it impossible to help Forces patients in a clinic setting where he was bound by traditional stereotypes of interaction (other ranks do not usually converse easily with brigadiers), and he used human relations theory in a call for the abandonment of formal roles and a new sincerity in relationships:

The doctor . . . no longer owns 'his' patients. Patients . . . are no longer his captive children . . . but have sincere adult roles to play, and are free to reach for responsibilities and opinions concerning the community of which they are a part.[16]

In the hands of Dr Maxwell Jones,[17] this belief became an ideology in which the whole life of the hospital community was structured for therapeutic potential. Formal roles – doctor, nurse, patient – were abandoned. Through group meetings, tensions were ventilated, communication was established, defences were broken down, and problems worked through. The main theoretical input was from social psychology, notably from the work of Bion[18] and Foulkes.[19] There was much discussion of 'collapsing the authority pyramid' and 'acting out' and 'reality confrontation'. The system had both theoretical and practical problems [20], and many of the therapeutic communities of the 1960s lost their psychodynamic nature as patients capable of participating stayed for shorter and shorter periods. The real community life was not within a closed environment, but outside it. The lasting achievements of the therapeutic community movement were less in the few units which maintained highly psychodynamic systems, than in the many which were led to examine their rules and regulations, and to substitute flexible and relaxed programmes for rigid and unimaginative ones.

The barriers between the hospital and the outside world were crumbling: day hospitals offered a new setting for care, and there was much excitement at the discovery of a mode of treatment which was said to be 'cheaper and better for the patient'.[21] Day hospitals could be attached to mental hospitals or general hospitals, and many offered a full range of hospital facilities to patients who had supportive home backgrounds and lived within travelling distance. On the in-patient wards, 'shift systems' were introduced, enabling double use to be made of patient facilities: some patients came by day or by night only; some were in hospital from Monday to Friday, others at weekends.[22] This idea had only a limited success: patients did not slot neatly into pre-arranged schedules, some found the constant shuttling back and forth disorienting, and staff found their work-load heavier; but it helped to reduce the barriers between the hospital population and the outside world.

Some hospitals developed patient social clubs, and clubs for ex-patients,[23] and these were well-attended. (People were much more clubbable in the 1950s, and the clubs were held to reduce stigma, not to perpetuate it). Many patients were willing to attend, to meet

others, and to have an informal chat with doctor, nurse or social worker. Clubs were often run enthusiastically by staff-patient committees.

These developments in the British mental health services had no parallel in the United States, where isolated state mental hospitals of ten or even fifteen thousand patients were common, some surrounded by barbed wire; where nearly all patients were compulsorily detained; and where the patient population was racially heterogeneous (which could cause problems in communication, not only between black and white, but with Hispanic and other minority groups, who often spoke no English). It is important to recognize that popular portrayals of the mental hospital in films – for example, in *The Snake Pit* and later in *One Flew Over the Cuckoo's Nest*, which have become classics – are based on American experience, and not on the much smaller, less restricted and more dynamic British mental hospitals.

Three parties of American psychiatrists, visiting Britain in the mid-1950s under the auspices of the Milbank Memorial Fund, were astonished at the 'British experiment', and the extent to which the hospitals they visited relied on voluntary status and patients' co-operation rather than on restraint and compulsion. They praised the open door system, the developing hospital-community relations, and the way in which the majority of patients were not subject to 'judicial commitment'. A New York psychiatrist reported:

> My trip to England did not teach me new methods of psychiatric treatment, but accomplished something far more significant: it changed my attitude toward the function of the mental hospital, and the needs of the mentally ill. The progress we so admired in England, which is culminating in the open door and community-oriented psychiatry, arose from the attitude that mentally ill patients were still responsible people who were competent to control their own behavior except for brief periods ... We discovered that the mental hospital was not the exclusive site for psychiatric treatment, but served as a centre for community-based mental health programs which included consultation with family doctors, clinic treatments, and day care ...[24]

Another participant concluded:

> Those of us who have had a good 'take' from the British vaccine

underwent a revolutionary upheaval, and emerged with a whole
new set of concepts about our patients, about our institutions,
about our professional roles, and we see almost every detail from
a radically different point of view.[25]

THE LEGISLATIVE REVOLUTION

The Royal Commission on Mental Illness and Mental Deficiency
met from 1954 to 1957 against a background of change. Many of
them, like the chairman, Lord Percy, who had served on the
Macmillan Commission of 1924–6, and Dr T.P. Rees, who had
pioneered the open door system at Warlingham Park Hospital, had
a long acquaintance with the mental health services – which was
not necessarily an asset when established assumptions were
being challenged. The rather complicated terms of reference of the
Commission instructed them to inquire into the existing law and
administrative machinery affecting 'persons who are or who are
alleged to be suffering from mental illness or defect', and 'the
extent to which it is now, or should be made, statutorily possible
for such persons to be treated as voluntary patients without
certification'.

The Commission was thus limited to legal and administrative
issues, with a clear directive to the effect that they were to consider
ways of reducing the existing formalities of admission and discharge. Though they took evidence which ranged over a much
wider area, they were primarily concerned with the state of the law.
It is notable that their members included only two jurists: the
chairman, Lord Percy, was a diplomat. The Royal Commission
asked a number of witnesses where the stigma of mental illness lay
– was it in the nature of the illness, the nature of treatment, the
out-dated buildings, or the fact of certification? The consensus of
opinion was that the stigma lay in what a legal member of the
Commission called 'the heaviness of procedure'[26] – that, is, in the
magistrate's order which equated the deprivation of liberty for the
purposes of treatment with the deprivation of liberty for the purposes of punishment.

Their conclusions involved a total repudiation of the principles
of 1890, and its replacement by a flexible system in which patients
could receive treatment without stigma.

The main recommendations were based on a memorandum submitted and oral evidence given by the Chairman of the Board of

Control, and the Senior Medical Commissioner to the Board. Their proposals were sweeping, including the abolition of many special legal formalities connected with mental illness, the absorption of the mental health services into the general pattern of the National Health Service, the abolition of the Board of Control itself, and the extension of local authority powers and duties.[27] Other witnesses supported these proposals. There were few dissentients and no minority reports, and the Royal Commission proceeded unanimously to recommendations which were accepted by Government and embodied in a major new parliamentary Bill.

When the Bill was considered by the House of Commons at its second reading, the Minister of Health, Derek Walker-Smith, pointed out that it was very long, containing 146 clauses and eight schedules; but it replaced in comparatively simple form a mass of legislation, repealing fifteen entire Acts and parts of thirty-seven others. He referred to an editorial in *The Times*, which had called the existing laws on mental health 'a jungle':

> They are certainly complex, difficult, and in many respects out of date. Consequently, in replacing the mosaic – to use a politer term – of the law and procedure produced by our fathers and forefathers, with a single contemporary design, we are making a clean sweep.[28]

Advances in medical and social skills and a change in public attitudes 'as rapid as it is welcome' had rendered the existing laws out of date.

'One of the main principles we are seeking to pursue', said the Minister, 'is the re-orientation of the mental health services away from institutional care towards care in the community.' The Royal Commission had recommended that there should be a specific grant for capital development by local authorities. The Minister admitted that this had not been found possible, and added that the annual grant to mental health services would in future be part of the local authority block grant, which made it impossible for central Government to restrict expenditure to specific services; but the mental health services of local authorities were expanding rapidly, and he was optimistic about the future.

Though the provisions of the Bill spelled out the sorts of service local authorities should provide, it in fact added nothing to their powers and duties under section 28 of the National Health Service Act 1946. In debate, Members of Parliament pressed for detailed local authority planning and mandatory requirements for the provision of services. The Minister agreed, stating in the House:

> I propose to issue a direction under section 28 of the National Health Service Act very soon after the Royal Assent is given to the Bill, so as to impose a duty on local authorities to provide these mental health services.[29]

In the Lords, the Bill was introduced by Lord Hailsham. His powerful legal talents were devoted, not to legal definition, but to the support of a Bill designed to minimise the legal elements in mental treatment. He described the Bill as 'the first fundamental revision of the English mental health laws since 1845', and made no specific mention of the 1890 Act.[30]

THE MENTAL HEALTH ACT 1959

1. The Act repealed all previous lunacy, mental treatment and mental deficiency legislation, and provided a single code for all types of mental disorder.
2. 'Mental disorder' was defined as 'mental illness, arrested or incomplete development of mind, psychopathic disorder, and any other disorder or disability of mind'.
3. The Board of Control was abolished, existing officers being transferred to the Ministry of Health. The Board's functions of inspection and review were transferred to local health authorities.
4. Local health authority mental health services provided under section 28 of the National Health Service Act 1946 might include the provision of residential accommodation, centres for training and occupation, the appointment of mental welfare officers, the exercise of the functions of guardianship and 'the provision of any ancillary or supplementary services'.
5. Mental Health Review Tribunals, organized on a regional basis, took over the 'watchdog' functions of the Board of Control in individual cases of compulsory detention. They were to consist of legal members, medical members, and 'members having such experience in administration, such knowledge of the social serv-

ices, or such other qualifications and experience as the Lord Chancellor considers suitable', to be appointed by joint consultation between the Lord Chancellor and the Minister of Health. The chairman of the Tribunal, and the chairman of any particular panel, was always to be a legal member. Tribunals were given the power to discharge patients from compulsory detention or from guardianship.

6. Patients could be admitted to any hospital or mental nursing home without formalities of any kind, and without liability to detention. This clause, which is phrased negatively ('Nothing in this Act shall be construed as preventing . . .') replaced the previous arrangements for voluntary treatment in the Mental Treatment Act 1930. Since the patient's volition was no longer required, this clause made it possible for patients who had no power of volition to be admitted informally, provided that they did not positively object.

7. Compulsory admission was of three kinds: an observation order, requiring two medical certificates, and lasting 28 days; a treatment order, requiring two medical certificates, and with a duration of one year for the first three consecutive occasions, and then two years at a time; and an emergency order, requiring an application from a mental welfare officer or relative, and one medical certificate, lasting only three days (but renewable in the form of an observation order or a treatment order). These clauses conformed to existing practice, except that a magistrate's order was no longer required for admission for treatment.

8. Informal patients could discharge themselves at any time. Compulsorily detained patients would be discharged when an order lapsed without renewal. They could also be discharged by the responsible medical officer, by the managers of the hospital or nursing home, by a Mental Health Review Tribunal after application and hearing, or by the nearest relative after giving seventy two hours' notice, provided that the responsible medical officer did not issue a barring certificate.

The effects of the Act

For the reasons outlined by the Minister, the 1959 Act was a considerable legislative advance. It freed the mental hospitals and most of their patients from separate designation, and greatly reduced stigmatizing procedures; but the commitment to provide local authority mental health services did not have the force which had been hoped for. A ministerial review of these services was carried out. Local authorities supplied information on the services they provided, and those they hoped to develop; but shortly after the Act came into force, the earmarking of financial items in the Rate Support Grant for particular services was abolished. Thereafter, local authorities received a block grant, and – within budgetary limits – had considerable freedom in how they allocated it. While this development was generally welcomed by the local authority associations, and had many advantages in other respects, it led to increased disparity in provision. Some local authorities regarded mental health as a high priority, or had the money to spare for it; others, through lack of interest or the decision that there were more urgent needs, did little more than meet their statutory obligations.

But there were other forces at work which were destined to bring even more radical changes to the mental health services – and to obliterate many of the gains of the 1950s.

CHAPTER 10

The Ideologies of Destruction

After the passing of the 1959 Act, it would have been reasonable to expect a period of consolidation and cautious experimentation; but within two years, the whole scene changed. In 1961, a new Minister of Health, Enoch Powell, announced a policy of abolishing mental hospitals, and cutting psychiatric beds by half, with little promise of improvement in community services. Opposition to this draconian policy was muted by three new theoretical analyses from abroad, all published in the same year, and all opposed to mental hospitals, though for very different reasons.

THE POWELL POLICY

It had become the tradition for the Minister of Health to make the inaugural speech at the Annual Conference of the National Association for Mental Health, and to use the occasion for a review of developments or an announcement of new policy. Most of the two thousand delegates who gathered at Church House, Westminster in March 1961 probably expected a congratulatory statement on the working of the 1959 Mental Health Act, which had been introduced by the same Conservative Government less than three years earlier; but Enoch Powell had his own very strong convictions about the need to reduce public sector spending on the National Health Service.[1] At that time (before his rivers-of-blood speech and his defection to the Ulster Unionists) Powell was rated a very sound Conservative politician, and regarded as a future Prime Minister. The delegates found themselves listening to a startling new policy announcement:

I have intimated to the hospital authorities who will be producing the constituent elements of the national hospital plan that in fifteen years' time, there may well be needed not more than half as many places in hospitals for mental illness as there are today. Expressed in numerical terms, this would represent a redundancy of no fewer than 75,000 hospital beds. Even so, if I err, I would rather err on the side of under-estimating the provision which ought to be required ... if we are to have the courage of our ambitions, we ought to pitch the estimate lower still, as low as we dare, perhaps lower.[2]

The Minister hoped that most of the patients receiving psychiatric treatment in hospital in fifteen years' time would not be in 'great isolated institutions or clumps of institutions', but in wards or wings of general hospitals. The mental hospital was to go. He continued:

Now look and see what are the implications of these bold words. They imply nothing less than the elimination of by far the greater part of this country's mental hospitals as they stand today. This is a colossal undertaking, not so much in the physical provision which it involves as in the sheer inertia of mind and matter which requires to be overcome. There they stand, isolated, majestic, imperious, brooded over by the gigantic water-tower and chimney combined, rising unmistakable and daunting out of the countryside – the asylums which our forefathers built with such immense solidity. Do not for a moment underestimate their power of resistance to our assault. Let me describe some of the defences which we have to storm.[3]

Later, Mr Powell made references to 'erring on the side of ruthlessness', to 'doomed institutions', and to 'setting the torch to the funeral pyre'.

His audience, composed in the main of senior psychiatrists and administrators, had not expected this policy change, which was introduced without consultation. Their main task in the preceding few years had been to try to get money and technical support from a reluctant Ministry to improve the hospitals. Now they found themselves described as 'the defences we have to storm' by a Minister who had not only avoided their assault, but was attacking them from the rear.

Year	In-patients (000s)	In-patients per thousand population
1914	138.1	3.8
1919	116.7	3.1
1924	130.3	3.4
1929	141.1	3.6
1934	150.3	3.7
1939	–	–
1944	–	–
1949	144.7	3.3
1954	151.4	3.4
1959	133.2	2.9

Table 10.1 *Mental illness: resident population of mental hospitals and other institutions, England and Wales, 1914–59*
Source: Annual Reports of the Board of Control. Figures include patients in general hospitals and mental nursing homes as well as mental hospitals.
Note: No figures available for war years 1939 and 1944.

Three weeks later, a Ministry circular gave a more detailed view of the new policy. As a result of a statistical analysis undertaken by the General Register Office, a sixteen-year projection had been undertaken on the need for beds by mentally ill patients. This indicated 'a large and progressive decline' in requirements. Though all the variables could not be controlled or taken into account, it seemed likely that the need for beds would drop from over 150,000 to about 80,000. Regional Hospital Boards were asked, as a matter of urgency, to review their mental hospital accommodation and to make plans for redundancy:

> to ensure that no more money than is necessary is spent on the upgrading or reconditioning of mental hospitals which in ten to fifteen years are not going to be required for some different purpose ... for the large, isolated and unsatisfactory buildings, closure will nearly always be the right answer.[4]

The technical report on the statistical projection was published in the *Lancet*.[5] The authors were Geoffrey Tooth, a Principal Medical Officer in the Ministry of Health, and Eileen Brooke, a statistician in the General Register Office. Dr Tooth and Miss Brooke had taken the figures for resident populations in mental hospitals from 1954 to 1959, and found a 'small but steady reduction' which they attributed to three factors: the extension of out-patient treatment, more active in-patient treatment, and the rehabilitation of long-stay patients. All these factors were likely to have an increased effect in the future. There were 'trends which might have the reverse effect' – the ageing of the population, the possibility of a hard core of patients difficult to discharge, the uncertainty of public tolerance, or an adverse economic climate which would make it difficult for mentally ill people to be self-supporting.

Bed-requirements for a standard population of a million people were extrapolated from the 1954–9 trend. The paper ended: 'It seems unlikely that trends of this magnitude based on national figures are no more than temporary phenomena; though many factors may modify the rate of change, the direction seems well-established.' This was a more modest claim than that put forward either by the Minister or in the circular.

REACTIONS TO THE NEW POLICY

Even on the day of the Minister's first announcement, the Conference Report shows that reactions were both violent and mixed. Dr Stanley Smith of Lancaster Moor Hospital, among others, spoke with enthusiasm of 'the pharmaceutical age', and concluded his speech: 'Let us be frank: we believe that the days of the large purely mental hospital are over. Let us welcome the change, not bury our heads.'

Other delegates to the Conference pointed to the social achievements of British psychiatry, and feared that the mental hospitals would be left to decline and disintegrate. Dr D.H. Clark of Fulbourn Hospital, Cambridge, which had a record of experiments in social therapy, hoped 'that the comments made at the Conference would go back to the Minister'. He continued:

That the mental hospitals were finished and had nothing further to contribute had been said before over the past twenty years. He would like to remind everyone of the revolution which had taken place in British psychiatry during the past decade which had originated in the mental hospitals, and that it was the hospitals which had led the world by their work in getting patients back into the community. He was particularly worried about two implications arising from the speech: did it mean that there was to be no further upgrading in mental hospitals? Was a running down process intended? That must not happen. Squalid conditions still endured in many psychiatric hospitals.

Mrs. Bessie Braddock, a redoubtable Labour MP who had been on the House of Commons committee which scrutinized the Mental Health Bill at the report stage, was particularly disturbed that the new policy was being introduced without any consultation:

> This was not the proper place for much comment, but she could promise there would be a lot in Another Place. Although she had been constantly in touch on questions of integration, and the health service generally, she had not known that a new policy of pulling down all the old mental hospitals . . . had been established.

On the second day of the Conference, the principal speaker was Professor Richard Titmuss of the London School of Economics, who cast considerable doubt on the government's intention of providing an adequate community service to replace the hospitals:

> If English social history is any guide, confusion has often been the mother of complacency . . . What some hope will exist is suddenly thought by many to exist. All kinds of wild and unlovely weeds are changed by statutory magic and comforting appellation, into the most attractive and domesticated flowers . . .[6]

So the 'ever-lasting cottage-garden trailer, "community care"' joined 'that exotic hot-house climbing rose "the Welfare State" with its lovely hues of tender pink and blushing red, rampant all over the place, often preventing people from "standing on their own feet"'. Community care was in fact limited to 'a few brave ventures scattered up and down the country from Worthing to Nottingham'. The pace of discharge from hospitals had been accelerated, but the community services were not available to meet the patients' needs when they came out. It was probable that the amount of money spent per head on the mentally ill in the community had actually decreased in the past decade; and less money was spent on them than on the treatment of fowl pest.

Professor Titmuss ended by asking for three acts of policy as an assurance that the Government 'really meant business': a specific earmarked grant to local authorities for mental health services in the following financial year; new central government grants for the training of social workers; and a Royal Commission on the training of doctors. There was no official reply, and only the third of these proposals was met (by the appointment of the Todd Commission of 1965–8, of which Professor Titmuss was a member).

Opinion in the mental health field was similarly mixed. Dr A.A. Baker, who was later to become Director of the Hospitals Advisory Service had a paper on 'Pulling Down the Old Mental Hospital' published within three weeks of the official announcement. He forecast that mental hospitals would continue to empty, and that long-stay populations would gradually disappear.[7] This started a lengthy correspondence in the medical journals, one group of doctors contending that the run-down of mental hospital beds was the only progressive policy, while another held that the impact of pharmacotherapy was relatively limited, and that the community services were unlikely to be able to meet the demands thrust upon them. On the whole, the first group was optimistic, politically Right-wing and inclined to the organic school of psychiatry, which most easily assimilated to the ethos of general medicine. The second tended to be pessimistic, politically Left-wing, and inclined to psychotherapy or social psychiatry.

A number of commentators were critical of the statistical projection on which the forecast was based. Rehin and Martin described it as 'the arbitrary application of a not very sophisticated numerical formula'.[8] Dr Alan Norton made a simple mathematical point when he questioned whether, if the decline took place, it could be expected to be linear: a curve would produce a different answer, and a slower rate of change.[9] Jones and Sidebotham listed twelve objections to the circular and the Tooth–Brooke paper, most of which have stood the test of time.[10] Although resident populations had begun to decline, admission rates had continued to increase, so that the work of mental hospitals was becoming more intensive.[11]

THE IDEOLOGICAL ATTACK

Though many of the points made against the Powell policy were to be borne out by subsequent events, Enoch Powell's determination to abolish the mental hospital received unexpected support from both the far Left and the far Right. In 1961, the academic world was stirred by two major studies originating in the United States, and one from France. These were so different in kind from each other, and so different from the rationale of the Powell policy, that it seems likely that they all arose independently. Erving Goffman, an anthropologist, worked in the US National Institute of Mental Health, and subsequently became a Professor of Sociology. The publication of *Asylums*[12] was to have a profound effect on institutional care in many different types of agency. Michel Foucault, who trained in clinical psychology, held a Chair in the Collège de France. His analysis percolated slowly in the English-speaking world, because it was written in very lofty academic French, and was not translated as *Madness and Civilization* until 1972.[13] Dr Thomas Szasz, a Hungarian-born American, was a New York psychiatrist who produced in *The Myth of Mental Illness*[14] the first of many books on the failings of his own profession. The new analyses came across the Atlantic and, more slowly, across the English Channel, and Britain was caught in the cross-fire.

This was the point at which the study of the mental health services acquired an international dimension: until 1961, British experience had taken its own path, and drew respect from practitioners in many other countries. Only Sweden and the Netherlands had a comparable record of advance in social care and treatment. Now the increased speed of communication, and the comparative ease and cheapness of international travel, meant that ideas spread swiftly from country to country; and theoretical blasts from the United States and France, where conditions in many mental hospitals deserved the fierce criticism they attracted, were used to buttress Britain's finance-led policy of abolishing a more advanced service.

The impact of the ideas generated at this time is still so great that it is necessary to recall that they originated in another era. The year 1961 is already 'history'. It was the year in which John Fitzgerald Kennedy became President of the United States. Ronald Reagan was a film actor who did not even rate a mention in *Who's Who in America*. Harold Macmillan was the British Prime Minister, and Margaret Thatcher was a young back-bencher in the House of Commons. Nobody had heard of AIDS or the micro-chip, and the Cold War with the Soviet bloc was still at its height. The population of British mental hospitals was over 130,000, and that of mental hospitals in the United States was over half a million.

Goffman and the total institution

Erving Goffman used a period of eighteen months' field work in St Elizabeth's Hospital, Washington, D.C. as the basis for a stream of new concepts about the pathology of institutional life. The book was not primarily about mental hospitals: it was a cross-service analysis of many kinds of institution, ranging from concentration camps, prisons and military bases through to old people's homes, boarding schools and monasteries. Much of his material was drawn from secondary sources. One of Goffman's great strengths was in pin-pointing and naming common institutional practices. Like a botanist in a forest of strange plants, he identified, classified and listed. He defined his field carefully:

> Every institution captures something of the time and interest of its members, and provides something of a world for them: in brief, every institution has encompassing tendencies. When we review the different institutions in our Western society, we find some that are encompassing to a degree discontinuously greater than the ones next in line. Their encompassing or total character is symbolized by the barrier to social intercourse with the outside and to departure that is often built right into the physical plant, such as locked doors, high walls, barbed wire, cliffs, forests or moors. These establishments I am calling *total institutions*, and it is their general characteristics I want to explore.[15]

Not all institutions were total institutions; but the description of institutional practices, if strained at times by the width of the analytical framework, created resonances in many different settings.

Goffman charted the 'mortification of the self', in which the individual's identity was systematically stripped away by admission procedures, with the 'ritual bath' as the symbolic point in his shaping and coding to the new identity of inmate: 'the individual is likely to be stripped of his normal appearance, and of the equipment and services by which he maintains it, thus suffering a personal defacement'.[16]

The inmate in an institution was liable to be subjected to 'indignities of speech and action', 'defilements of the body' and even physical attack. It is notable that most of Goffman's examples of these processes are drawn from the more openly assaultive worlds

of prisons and the Armed Forces rather than from mental hospitals.
However, his approach is Kafkaesque: a nameless, archetypal individual is threatened by a nameless, archetypal organization which
has the power not only to imprison, but to force the imprisoned to
accept its authority. In *The Castle*, Kafka's 'K' dies 'like a dog', the
prisoner of the mind and will of the State.

The Western world was
haunted by the knowledge that there were still many totalitarian
régimes in which this was possible – in the Soviet bloc, in China, in
Viet Nam, in South America; but Goffman moved the analysis to a
more domestic level: even in the so-called democratic countries of
the West, pockets of institutional oppression could be identified.

In the mental hospital world, Goffman classified shock treatment
and psychosurgery as physical assault, and regarded psychotherapy
as a more insidious form of attack, collapsing the patient's defences
back on himself. He described very poignantly the 'betrayal funnel',
through which the mental patient often passed, from the first
contact with a family physician as a free individual to the ultimate
loss of freedom, while the admitting relative went back to a life
'incredibly thick with privileges'. He noted the 'piston effect', by
which, in a society without hope, any small change in care or
treatment might be hailed as a great advance. He detailed the
'sense of dead and heavy-hanging time' among inmates who are
'exiled from living'; the group activities which were invented to
counter it (lectures, art classes, field games and dances); the constant invasions of personal privacy:

Every total institution can be seen as a kind of dead sea in which
little islands of vivid, encapturing activity appear. Such activity
can help the individual withstand the psychological stress usually
engendered by assaults on the self. Yet it is precisely in the
insufficiency of these activities that an important deprivational
effect of total institutions can be found. In civil society, an
individual pushed to the wall in one of his social roles usually
has an opportunity to crawl into some protected place ... At a
time when these resting points are most needed, they may be
most difficult to obtain.[17]

Goffman turned a deadly analytical eye on the staff culture – the
official Sports Day, the house magazine, the annual party, the
Christmas celebration, the institutional theatrical, the official visits

– and described how, in a system of 'binary management', staff and patients formed different cultures, and restrictions of contact helped to maintain 'antagonistic stereotypes':

> Two different social and cultural worlds develop, jogging along-side each other with points of official contact, but little mutual penetration. Significantly, the institutional plant and name come to be identified by both staff and inmates as somehow belonging to the staff, so that when either grouping refers to the views or interests of 'the institution', they are referring . . . to the views and concerns of staff.[18]

The inmates developed their own 'lingo' which some staff in the lower echelons might speak, reverting to standard speech in address-ing authority. Inmates lived an 'under-life' in a world of 'make-dos' and 'secondary adjustments', scavenging for food and cigar-ettes and magazines, 'stashing' their possessions in illicit storage places, running their own illegal exchange systems. 'When existence is cut to the bone, we learn what people do to flesh out their lives'.[19]

Goffman argued that institutional life was essentially abnormal: the normal way to live was to have separate environments for work, domestic life and leisure. Inmates of a residential institution were unable to live effectively, because all these activities were collapsed into a single existence under 'an overall rational plan'.

> There is an incompatibility, then, between total institutions and the basic work-payment structure of our society. Total institu-tions are also incompatible with another crucial element in our society, the family. Family life is sometimes contrasted with solitary living, but in fact the more pertinent contrast is with batch living, for those who eat and sleep at work, with a group of fellow workers, can hardly sustain a meaningful domestic exist-ence.[20]

Above all, he insisted that mental patients were forced to undergo an experience which was positively anti-therapeutic, their lives cramped and warped by institutional structures which in reality served the needs of relatives, police, judges and psychiatrists.

All this was presented with a vividness and a clarity which attracted a wide readership. Goffman became something of a cult figure among a new generation of sociologists, though, like many cult figures, he was more talked about than read. Though he qualified what he had to say very carefully, the qualifications were often forgotten in the widespread condemnation of mental hospitals which followed. It is notable that he showed no interest at all in mental health reform movements. Though he held a research grant from the US National Institute of Mental Health (NIMH) from 1954 to 1957, he does not even mention the high-powered American Joint Commission for Mental Health, appointed in 1955, which produced its report *Action for Mental Health* in the same year in which he published *Asylums*. He had an office in NIMH, and the whole organization must have been buzzing with its findings.

It is entirely possible that Goffman simply decided to ignore the reform movement. He may well have believed that plans and policy statements at federal level would not make much difference to the 'underlife' of institutions where compulsorily detained patients fought for cigarette ends and scavenged in the trash cans. As a deviance theorist, Goffman had little time for the official perspective, even when officials were trying to change the system.

Goffman had no enduring interest in mental hospitals, and moved on to become one of the leading exponents of social interaction theory.[21] He never claimed that all the features he described were to be found in any one real-life institution: simply that there was a cluster of factors which tended to occur when groups of stigmatized people were cut off from the outside world. The 'total institution' was an abstraction, a Weberian ideal type (like 'bureaucracy'). It was not intended to be a straight description of reality.

Goffman drew his empirical evidence, as he was entitled to do, given his theoretical framework, from an extreme case: St Elizabeth's Hospital, Washington, D.C., where he did his field work in the relatively uncommitted role of a remedial gymnast, was an atypical mental hospital, even by American standards. Some at least of its inmates were violently disturbed people, drawn to the city by the proximity of the President, Congress and the Pentagon, and classified as security risks, and the régime was known to be dominated by locked doors and jangling keys. But there was enough truth about most institutions in his analysis for many of his points to strike home. His work contained some disturbing shafts of insight and, ironically, was more readily received in Britain than in many parts of the United States.

Despite the book's title, much of what he had to say was not directed at mental hospitals in particular, and he never claimed that all institutions were alike. The identification of common features was the first step. Readers were promised a second volume which analysed the differences; but when Goffman died in 1982, the second volume remained unwritten.

Foucault and the study of Unreason

Foucault, the most Parisian of Frenchmen, exerted a massive influence on sociological thought through an analysis deliberately based on emotive images rather than on logical argument. He is one of the fathers of the deconstructionist movement, in which nothing is taken to mean what it says, most historical events (except the ones he selects as relevant to his theme) are dismissed as merely superficial phenomena, and every event, every statement, must be subjected to scrutiny for hidden meanings and underlying realities. Peter Laslett described *Madness and Civilization* as 'puzzling', 'enlightening', 'baffling', 'muddling' and 'stimulating'.[22] Foucault's thought cannot be logically assessed, because it does not proceed by logic, and indeed rejects a logical approach.

The brilliant images of the empty lazar houses and the Ship of Fools in the opening chapter dazzle and bemuse the reader. We are told that the lazar houses which once gave shelter to lepers stood empty for three hundred years before they were filled with lunatics; that Ships of Fools commonly sailed the inland rivers of Western Europe, dumping their pathetic cargoes of society's rejects. Reason says that the small mediaeval lazar houses must have fallen into decay long before asylums were thought of; and that no ship's captain was likely to have set sail with a passenger list composed of known lunatics: these are literary and artistic images, not statements of fact.[23]

Images apart, Foucault is distinctly, perhaps deliberately, obscure:

madness is the false punishment of a false solution, but by its own virtue it brings to light the real problem, which can then be truly resolved. It conceals beneath error the secret enterprise of truth ... Madness has ceased to be – at the limits of the world,

of man and death – an eschatological figure: the darkness has
dispersed on which the eyes of madness were fixed, and out of
which the forms of the impossible were born.[24]

Such gnomic statements are either very profound or complete
nonsense. Even reading *Madness and Civilization* in the original
French, and substituting 'folly' for 'madness' (a better translation)
is not greatly illuminating. References to Gilles de Rais, Hierony-
mus Bosch, one of the Brueghels (it is not clear which), Cervantes,
Goya, Van Gogh, and the Marquis de Sade, with a variety of
classical and mythological allusions, build up the atmosphere, but
do not clarify the facts. Most commentators have played safe, and
accorded Foucault a nervous respect.

Folie et déraison (*Madness and Civilization*) was Foucault's doctoral thesis. He was originally a philosopher, trained in a rigid
Hegelian framework, and he took a Diploma in Psychopathology,
spending three years observing practice in mental hospitals and
clinics. He wrote a book on the subject, *Maladie mentale et person-
nalité*, which shows signs of his mental tensions at the time, mixing
orthodox psychopathology with Marxist revolt. Foucault's transla-
tor, Alan Sheridan, comments that it shows 'a distinct sense of self-
mutilation' and adds: 'It was only a matter of time before the
straitjacket would snap, and its wearer take his revenge.'[25]

After that, he taught for some years in Sweden, Warsaw and
Hamburg before returning to Paris with his doctoral thesis. He had
initial difficulties in getting the thesis accepted by the Sorbonne,
because it crossed so many different fields, but it was finally
classified as 'History of Science', and accepted. By 1970, he had
advanced to such academic eminence that he was offered a Chair
at the prestigious Collège de France, and allowed to choose his
own title. He chose 'Professor of the History of Systems of
Thought'. In 1977, he published *Surveiller et punir*, translated as
Discipline and Punish.[26]

In charting the History of Systems of Thought, Foucault uses
the synchronic approach – that is, he treats 'thought' as a phenomenon that exists independently of historical or geographical context.
This makes it possible to sweep together events and ideas from
different periods and different cultures, and to claim that there are
similarities which have not previously been identified. Unlike Goffman, he does not even acknowledge that differences exist.

Basically, Foucault's theme is simple: capitalism is the source of oppression, and the régime must be overthrown. There is no such thing as altruism. Social reform is only the new face of oppression and repression.

In his chapter on 'The Birth of the Asylum', Foucault confuses Pinel's *traitement moral* (treatment through the emotions) with the very different system of moral treatment practised at the Retreat. There are many references to 'Pinel and Tuke', 'Tuke and Pinel', which imply that the movements initiated in Paris and York were similar, or even identical. The only basis for this is Foucault's assertion that it is so. In fact, Pinel was a medical man. His biographer Dr Semelaigne describes in detail how he ordered the chains to be struck off his patients at the height of the French Revolution on the politically inspired orders of the Assemblée Nationale: it was a symbolic enactment of Rousseau's 'Man is born free, but is everywhere in chains'.[27] Tuke was a York grocer with a Quaker conscience. Foucault has selected three facts as relevant to his assertion: both Tuke and Pinel removed chains, they acted in the same year, and 'traitement moral' sounds like 'moral treatment'. He ignores as irrelevant the facts that they were working in different countries which were then at war, that there was no contact between them; that Pinel acted under political orders and Tuke in accordance with the principles of a religious social reform movement; that Pinel was a medical man and Tuke distrusted and opposed medical methods; and that the Salpétriére and Bicêtre, two large and gloomy mediaeval hospitals in Paris, bore (and still bear) little resemblance to the small and homely York Retreat.

One of the concluding sections of *Madness and Civilization* consists of an attack on the medical profession, past and present:

> On the one hand, madness puts itself at a distance in an objective field where the threats of unreason disappear; but at this same moment, the madman tends to form, with the doctor, in an unbroken unity, a 'couple' . . . As positivism imposes itself upon medicine, this practice becomes more and more obscure, the psychiatrist's power more and more miraculous, and the doctor–patient couple sinks deeper into a strange world. In the patient's eyes, the doctor becomes a thaumaturge . . .[28]

Thus psychiatry is no more than a new form of exploitation:

paradoxically, the liberation initiated by 'Pinel and Tuke' has become 'a gigantic moral imprisonment'.

This argument was pursued in *The Birth of the Clinic* where Foucault writes of 'the contrast between a medicine of pathological spaces and a medicine of the social space'.[29] In French, *clinique* does not mean 'clinic'. It covers all places where clinical medicine is practised, principally hospitals. He challenges the depersonalization of hospital medicine, based on pseudo-science:

> The natural locus of disease is the natural locus of life – the family: gentle, spontaneous care, expressive of love and a common desire for a cure, assists nature in its struggle against the illness, and allows the illness itself to attain its own truth. The hospital doctor sees only distorted, altered diseases, a whole teratology of the pathological.[30]

The hospital 'creates disease by means of the enclosed, pestilential domain that it constitutes, creates further disease in the social space in which it is placed':

> Inversely, if it is left in the free field of its birth and development, [disease] will never be more than itself – as it appeared, so will it be extinguished – and the assistance that is given in the home will make up for the poverty that the disease has caused. The care spontaneously given by family and friends will cost nobody anything; and the financial assistance given to the sick man will be to the advantage of the family. 'Someone will have to eat the meat from which his broth is made, and in heating his tisane, it costs no more to warm his children as well.'[31]

A modern rationale for community care? No. The quotation is from Lanthenas, a Girondiste writing about the health system in Paris in 1792.

In *Discipline and Punish*, the argument is developed: all institutions exist to oppress the people. Factories, schools, mental hospitals, prisons share common characteristics of social control, and exploit the workers. Institutions are 'carceral cities', encapsulating their prisoners – and built to be visible to the outside world, thus providing a warning in architectural form. Prisons exist, not to reform prisoners, but to deter those outside from crime. Mental hospitals exist, not to cure patients, but to show the grim consequences of abnormal behaviour. Professional staff are the agents of social control; and this is the case whether they use the old forms of repression, locks and chains, or the new forms of repression in making people responsible for their own actions. This is why Foucault disapproves so strongly of moral management at the York Retreat. To force people back on themselves, to insist that they control themselves instead of being controlled from outside, is the most insidious and harmful form of control, because there is nothing to fight against except their own disintegrating personalities. There is another haunting image in what he calls 'the play of mirrors': the madman is forced to look at himself:

Freed from the chains that made it purely an observed object, madness lost, paradoxically, the essence of its liberty ... it imprisoned itself in an infinitely self-referring observation. It was finally chained to the humiliation of being its own object.[32]

Psychoanalysts might see this as the way to self-knowledge and ultimate healing; it drives Foucault to fury. He recounts at some length in *Madness and Civilization* the case of one of the patients freed by Pinel in Bicêtre: a former priest, he had the delusion that he was Christ, and gloried in his sufferings. Pinel took the chains off, and made him 'a prisoner of nothing' by removing the cause of his Passion. One can only try to puncture the rhetoric by asking if Pinel would have been more humane to leave the priest in chains; but the question is meaningless to a Foucauldian, since there is no such thing as humane action.

Deeply agnostic and deeply sceptical, lost in Nietzschean nihilism and despair, Foucault sees oppression and repression on all sides. His message was heady stuff for the disillusioned. He occupies a place of his own in the European philosophical thought of the 1960s, somewhere between Sartre, Althusser and Lévi-Strauss. Most of the left-wing 'revisionists' of the 1980s and 1990s are basically Foucauldian in their thinking. In this view, nothing has really changed in two or three centuries: madness is still madness, social control is still social control, psychiatrists are agents of the exploitative state, and self-control is the ultimate weapon of the ruling classes. Foucault said in the concluding sentence of *Discipline and Punish* that he could 'already hear the distant roar of battle';[33] but in view of his total disregard for dates and historical process, it is never quite clear whether he is awaiting a new revolution, or the fall of the Bastille.

Szasz and the non-existence of mental illness

The Myth of Mental Illness had a very different background, and a different message. Thomas Szasz left Hungary at the age of eighteen for medical training in New York. He spent his formative years in a small central European country with a history of repeated invasion and oppression: by Turks, by the Austro-Hungarian Empire, by Nazi Germany, by the Soviet Union. He speaks for the American Way of Life with all the fervour of a successful immigrant from the bad old world to the new: people should be taught to stand on their own feet; state-run health and social services derive from a debilitating Christian ethic which encourages weakness and helplessness.

'Blessed are the poor in spirit' is interpreted 'Man should be poor in spirit', i.e. stupid, submissive: Do not be smart, well-informed or assertive.[34]

The beliefs and practices of Christianity are best suited for slaves. This is hardly surprising when one recalls the oppressed milieu in which this creed emerged.[35]

But if Christianity started as a creed for slaves, it became a creed for oppressors. The Church dominated mediaeval Europe, hunting down the unorthodox, torturing and burning. The ritual persecution of witches was a form of scapegoating – the old Jewish rite of atonement in which a goat was sent into the wilderness by the priests bearing the sins of the people, described in the Old Testament.[36]

Witches and sorcerers, recruited from the ranks of the poor and oppressed, played the role of scapegoats. They thus fulfilled the socially useful role of acting as social tranquillizers . . . by participating in an important public drama, they contributed to the stability of the existing social order.[37]

The 'inverted theological game' of hunting the heretic has been replaced by the 'medical game' of labelling and confining the mentally ill (Szasz is well-versed in Games Theory). It is evident that in his swoops through the centuries from remote Biblical times to the early Christians, to the Inquisition, to Freud's Vienna and Charcot's Paris, to New York in the 1960s, he rivals Foucault in the game of 'Similarities': to Szasz, all these phenomena are simply the age-old process of persecution in different forms. Time and place and motivation are all irrelevant.

The medical case-conference has replaced the auto-da-fé; but mental illness, like witchcraft, is a social construct, not an objective reality. The answer is for free citizens to rid themselves of the apparatus of oppression, and to assume the responsibility for running their own lives:

> Much of what passes for 'medical ethics' is a set of paternalistic rules the net effect of which is the persistent infantilization and domination of the patient by the physician. A shift towards greater dignity, freedom and self-responsibility for the disenfranchised – whether slave, sinner or patient – can be secured only at the cost of honest and serious commitment to an ethic of autonomy and egality.[38]

This bracing prescription involves people in being 'maximally self-reliant and responsible even when ill or disabled'. Much of the book is taken up with an attack on Freud and Charcot, and their definitions of hysteria, and hysteria is considered to be paradigmatic of all mental illness. The argument runs: 'Mental illness is hysteria; hysteria is malingering; malingering is not an illness.'

To Szasz, 'mental illness' is merely a socially acceptable name for 'problems in living'. Everybody has problems in living, and the idea that psychiatric intervention can make for harmonious living is false. Szasz makes use of a very old logical device called the Porphyrian Tree (much used by Jeremy Bentham), which consists of binary classifications: phenomena can be described as either 'A' or 'non-A'. Physical illness is 'A', therefore mental illness is 'non-A' or 'counterfeit A'.[39] The Porphyrian Tree has uses in Logic, but can only be applied to discrete and contradictory terms – black is non-white, white is non-black; it does not offer any help with shades of grey, or with the status of green or purple. To set up physical illness as 'A' and then to argue that mental illness is 'counterfeit' has no basis in logic; one might as well describe dogs as 'counterfeit cats' or a broken leg as 'counterfeit arthritis'.

'Before Charcot's time' the reader is told, 'a person was said to be ill only if his body is physically disordered.'[40] Any history of psychiatry will quickly disprove this. Hippocrates and Aristotle knew about mind–body interaction. A dozen modern textbooks on psychosomatic medicine report solid research on the psychological factors in asthma, diabetes, skin diseases, stomach ulcers, cardiovascular conditions and other illnesses.

The Myth of Mental Illness so outraged the New York State Department of Mental Hygiene that the Commissioner demanded that Szasz should be dismissed from his post in the State University's Department of Psychiatry. The demand was refused by the university authorities in the name of academic freedom, and Dr Szasz continued to hold a public sector appointment, while attacking the public sector, and to profess a subject in which he had proclaimed his disbelief.

In *Law, Liberty and Psychiatry* (1963), Szasz developed his attack on 'the dangers of tyranny by therapy'. He invoked American traditions: the Declaration of Rights, the Constitution, the ideals of the Founding Fathers, to argue that liberty was 'an inalienable human right', and that the mental health movement, by providing excuses for abnormal behaviour, was eroding moral standards and extending the power of the state. This sinister movement was 'hidden under a façade of medical and psychiatric jargon, and ... buttressed by a self-proclaimed desire to help or treat so-called mentally ill persons'.[41] He described involuntary commitment (compulsory detention) as a crime on the grounds that the Declaration of Rights guaranteed 'life, liberty and the pursuit of happiness' to all American citizens.

'Messianic Christianity' is equated with 'messianic psychiatry'. Jews as well as witches were persecuted by the Inquisition, and later by the Nazis. The sweep of horror stories of the persecution of the Jews, through to the Holocaust, is sufficiently powerful to obscure the reality: the Nazis were not Christians, and many American psychiatrists are themselves of Jewish origin. Like Foucault, Szasz is an expert in arousing the senses with horror, gaining the reader's sympathy, and then pursuing a thoroughly illogical argument.

The books continued to pour from this most prolific of writers –

Psychiatric Justice (1965), *The Ethics of Psychoanalysis* (1965), *Ideology and Insanity* (1970), *The Manufacture of Madness* (1970) and others to follow. Perhaps *The Manufacture of Madness* holds the key. Szasz makes it clear in this book that he is opposed to 'institutional psychiatry'. Many readers have assumed that this meant opposition to psychiatry practised in hospitals, but Szasz is using 'institutional' in a different sense – as a service instituted by the state. He makes it clear that 'The most important economic characteristic of Institutional Psychiatry is that the institutional psychiatrist is a bureaucratic employee.'[42] Szasz is not only opposed to mental hospitals; he is equally opposed to the community mental health services which developed in the 1960s:

the mental health . . . of Americans cannot be improved by slogans, drugs, community mental health centers, or even with billions of dollars expended on a 'war on mental illness' . . . the best, indeed the only hope for remedying the problem of 'mental illness' lies in weakening, not strengthening, the power of Institutional Psychiatry. Only when this peculiar institution is abolished will the potentialities of Contractual Psychiatry be able to unfold.[43]

'Contractual Psychiatry' means private practice. Szasz explains elsewhere that he himself operates such a practice, in which people with 'problems in living' can consult him for the payment of a fee. The cash nexus preserves the patient's autonomy, because he is paying for a service. Fees have to be paid promptly: Szasz renders his account monthly, and refuses patients who might find it difficult to pay, because 'strained financial circumstances do not provide a suitable psychological atmosphere for this kind of therapeutic work.'[44] What about people who cannot afford private medicine? Szasz is simply not interested. The 'therapeutic state' is enslaving, and free citizens must learn to accept the consequences of their own behaviour.

Szasz was writing from the point of view of a psychiatrist (or psychotherapist) in private practice. His main target was the development of publicly-funded services which at that time posed a considerable threat to private practice; but his views on 'the therapeutic state' and 'institutional psychiatry' were to provide a rationale for the libertarian movement promoted by the American Civil Liberties Union in the 1960s.

THE IMPACT OF CHANGE

The movement for the abolition of the mental hospital system came suddenly, but it had its antecedents in the 1950s. Enoch Powell was well-known as an early monetarist, a right-wing critic of the post-war growth in the health and welfare services. Deviance theory developed out of the work of the Chicago School of Sociology in the early 1950s, in the seminal work of Edwin Lemert and G.H. Mead, together with phenomenology, ethnomethodology, labelling theory and interaction theory. These academic movements were to dominate sociology in the 1960s. Goffman had applied his ideas on stigma to mental illness as early as 1954.[45] The papers on 'The Characteristics of Total Institutions' and 'The Moral Career of the Mental Patient', which formed the main sections of *Asylums*, were first published in 1957 and 1959 respectively.[46] Ideas about deviance had been filtering across the Atlantic for some years, and had been given expression by a British psychiatrist, Russell Barton, in *Institutional Neurosis* (1959). Barton put forward the theory that most long-term mental hospital patients had two illnesses: the illness which caused their admission, and the illness which resulted from institutional practices.[47] At the Tavistock Clinic, R.D. Laing had published *The Divided Self*,[48], and was already questioning the nature of mental illness and the diagnostic categories used by his fellow-psychiatrists.

All these disparate movements were given a new force and a common direction by the development of the psychotropic drugs. Once the more bizarre symptoms of mental illness could be controlled, mental illness itself seemed to disappear. It could be argued by ultra-conservatives that the heavy expenditure on outdated buildings was no longer necessary – and that there was no need to replace them. It could be argued by Marxists that sending people to mental hospitals was 'labelling', and an act of political oppression. And a new generation of observers, who had never seen untreated mental illness, could visit quiet wards and busy workshops, and come to the conclusion that hospitalized patients were really quite 'normal': it was the system that was wrong.

The pharmacological revolution, the social revolution and the legislative revolution of the 1950s started at the same time; but by 1961, it was evident that the pharmacological revolution had much greater long-term implications than the social and legislative changes of that period. 'Wonder drugs' provided a plausible rationale for the introduction of a hard-line policy based on market economics: the run-down of the hospitals without adequate community care services to replace them.

The logic of the theoretical critics was sometimes flawed and sometimes distorted. Many of the followers of Goffman and Foucault had Marxist sympathies (and some seem to have been under the misapprehension that Szasz shared those sympathies). Most were strongly opposed to powerful drug treatments; but in embarking on a sustained campaign of 'hospital-bashing', (largely based on the description of conditions before 1900) they did not appear to realize that they were supporting a policy which would leave mentally ill people with little else in the way of support.

CHAPTER 11

The Disappearing Services

A year after Enoch Powell's first announcement of the changes in mental health policy, the Ministry of Health issued the *Hospital Plan for England and Wales*. Another year passed before proposals were made for community care.

The *Hospital Plan*[1] proposed the restriction of hospital services largely to the acute sector of medicine. Mentally ill, mentally handicapped, physically disabled and infirm elderly people would no longer occupy hospital beds for long periods. Hospital care would be concentrated in the District General Hospital – a new large hospital which would provide acute treatment in all medical specialisms. Chronic patients would enter hospital only for short periods, for diagnosis and assessment. Their on-going care would be a matter for the community services.

The processes of policy-making were now becoming clearer: the aim was to reverse the decision made when the National Health Service was being planned during the Second World War. Then it had been proposed to leave out the mental health services and other chronic services, and to concentrate the new NHS provision on acute illness. That proposal had been rejected after strong representations from the Royal Medico-Psychological Association and the Royal College of Physicians; but parity of esteem had proved expensive. Nearly 40 per cent of all hospital beds were psychiatric beds, and a good deal of money and effort had gone into upgrading this neglected sector. As a result, there had been pressure from the more prestigious acute sector, which also needed to develop, to return non-acute services to local authorities, leaving funds for the development of new general hospitals.

In the medical enthusiasm for the District General Hospital which followed, arguments that psychiatric patients needed a different kind of architecture and use of space from general hospital patients, because they were ambulant and needed occupation and social activities, were ignored; so was the suggestion that good psychiatric treatment took time, and was more than a matter of prescribing tablets. Some organic psychiatrists were prepared to argue that the only acceptable methods of treating mental illness were those which would be practised in District General Hospitals. Dr William Sargent made a strong plea on these lines to the National Association for Mental Health Conference in 1961:

> most types of patients now being admitted to mental hospitals can be investigated and treated perfectly well in general hospitals ... We even do quite a number of leucotomies every year ... and the advent of the new tranquillizing drugs has enabled us to treat a much larger number of really acute patients ... general hospitals should help to foster a demand for entirely new standards of treatment for the mentally ill, more similar to those provided for and thought essential for the physically ill ...[2]

McKeown, Garrett and Lowe went even further in reporting a survey of psychiatric patients in Birmingham. They concluded that 75 per cent of psychiatric in-patients required 'only limited hospital services consisting of supervision because of their mental state' and no more than 13 per cent required 'the full facilities of a modern hospital'.[3]

This was the period in which it became apparent that the Macmillan Commission's hope of a powerful psychiatric service influencing the general medical service was not going to happen. The power and prestige of general medicine were simply too great. Psychiatrists wanted to be included in the National Health Service, because this meant public acceptance for their work, the reduction of stigma for their patients, and parity with other specialists for themselves; but the inclusion of psychiatry within a framework dominated by general medicine and surgery meant that psychiatry lost much of its distinctive contribution to the understanding of illness. It became one medical specialism among many.

The introduction of the psychotropic drugs strengthened this process. At last psychiatrists had a recognizably medical form of treatment, which gave them standing with other members of the medical profession. Pharmacotherapy did not demand their involvement in extensive social programmes, or in close collaboration with social workers and other non-medical personnel: only the medical practitioner could prescribe, and the psychiatric nurse could monitor medication. It did not demand an understanding of the patient's cultural background – a fact of increasing importance as British society became more diverse, with the formation of West Indian and Asian communities and the prospect of closer ties with Europe.

Pharmacotherapy was generally popular with patients and their relatives, who greatly preferred tablets or injections to lengthy personal enquiries about their life-histories and motivation; with general practitioners, who acquired a new and speedy armoury of treatment for some of their most time-consuming patients; and above all with the drug companies, which made very large profits. While the optimism initially generated by the phenothiazines was later modified, the introduction of this apparently cheap, easy and trouble-free method of treatment radically altered the nature of psychiatry, and virtually ended a promising relationship with the social sciences. The major drug companies promoted their products with lavish medical conferences, scholarships and research grants, and opportunities for travel abroad. Psychiatrists and general practitioners were bombarded with literature promising miraculous results from the prescription of this compound or that. There were no comparable inducements for the social approaches to mental illness.

The companion document to the *Hospital Plan*, entitled *Health and Welfare: The Development of Community Care*,[4] was eagerly awaited. It consisted of 48 pages of general text on the desirability of community care, some glossy photographs, and 321 pages of detailed local authority returns on their future plans. Those who looked for a rationale of community care and a positive lead from central Government were disappointed.

PROFESSIONAL REORGANIZATION

In the next few years, much of the initiative lay with the professional associations. The major associations representing medical practitioners, nurses and social workers were reorganizing their training and qualifications in a way which strengthened their respective power-bases, but made interdisciplinary work more difficult. Power is exercised from the centre of a profession, which tends to be highly orthodox, while growth is often generated by unorthodox activity at the margins.

Sir Keith Joseph, appointed in 1971 as the Conservative Secretary of State for the Social Services (this was the rather confusing title then adopted by the Minister of Health) was strongly in favour of a medically dominated mental health service. He announced with some enthusiasm:

> Psychiatry is to join the rest of medicine . . . the treatment of psychosis, neurosis and schizophrenia have been entirely changed by the drug revolution. People go into hospital with mental disorders and they are cured, and that is why we want to bring that branch of medicine into the scope of the 230 district general hospitals that are planned for England and Wales.[5]

The Royal College of Psychiatrists, replacing the Royal Medico-Psychological Association, was established on 16 June 1971 after some years of negotiation.[6] One of its first tasks was to consider the drafting of a syllabus for the new membership examination of the College. This replaced the Diploma in Psychological Medicine as a post graduate medical qualification, and brought the training of psychiatrists closer to that in other postgraduate medical specialisms. The first Maudsley Lecture to be given under the auspices of the new College was entitled, significantly, 'Morale in Clinical Medicine'.

In 1957, the RMPA had finally handed over responsibility for the training of Registered Mental Nurses to the General Nursing Council, and there too, a new syllabus was developed, bring the training of mental nurses closer to that of general nurses, and making double training easier.

If psychiatry was being absorbed by general medicine, and psychiatric nursing by general nursing, the main hope for community care seemed to lie with social work. Until 1971, there were four separate branches of social work, separately trained: child care, probation, medical social work and psychiatric social work. Most psychiatric social workers opted for work in clinics, where they could join a medically directed team, and there was a strong preference for child guidance; but if community care was not to mean the transfer of psychiatric patients from the care of the trained to the care of the untrained, there was a new need for well-trained social workers. Few PSWs had ever gone into mental hospital work or into local authority work.

Hopes of improved training were raised by the Younghusband Report of 1959, which proposed the training of a second grade of social workers specifically for local authority Health and Welfare Departments;[7] but though the report met with wide public approval, and its recommendations were carried into effect by the Health Visitors' and Social Workers' Training Act of 1962, the majority of the new grade of workers trained in Colleges of Further Education found work in other fields.

In the 1960s, when the Conservative Macmillan and Douglas-Home Governments were succeeded by six years of Labour Government under Harold Wilson, a political divide on health and welfare became apparent. The Conservatives thought in terms of prestigious medical services and services 'supplementary to medicine'. Labour ministers talked in terms of 'health service professionals' rather than of a dominant medical profession, and saw an increasing responsibility for the social services. However, both parties supported the reduction of mental hospital beds. The Seebohm Committee on Local and Allied Personal Social Services (1965–8) was set up and reported under the Wilson Government. Their report was largely concerned with the task of setting up a new managerial framework for local authority social services, and replacing a number of fragmented specialisms with a powerful authority for work in the community. As far as mental health work was concerned, the Committee made some fairly strong strictures about the lack of provision:

despite the national commitment to 'community care' and official plans to run down the number of mental hospital beds, [local authority expenditure] still represents a small fraction of total health service expenditure for the mentally disordered. Although some local authorities have been remarkably successful in developing mental health services, there is a serious lack of staff, premises, money or public concern in other areas. The widespread belief that we have 'community care' of the mentally disordered is, for many parts of the country, still a sad illusion, and judging by published plans will remain so for years ahead.[8]

The Seebohm Committee commented on the 'iceberg problem' – 'needs that are not even expressed in demand for services'. They stressed the fact that many mental health needs were unarticulated and unmet, and that they tended to be unevenly distributed. Decaying city centres could 'carry a fearful burden of social pathology'.

The main question was whether mental health work should be included in the new Social Services Departments, or remain separate because of the need for close collaboration with the health authority. The Committee concluded that mental health services should be included with other social services because mental disorder tended to trigger off a variety of social problems and social disabilities in families, and social workers should be able to take responsibility for the whole family; also, that not to include mental health services would 'mean further segregation of the mentally disordered when in fact the community is becoming ready for their further integration'.[9]

The Local Authority Social Services Act of 1970, which embodied most of the Seebohm Commitee's proposals, received the Royal Assent only a few days before the Wilson Government fell. It established a new structure of Social Services Departments in local authorities with unified and enhanced responsibilities, and set up the Central Council for Education and Training in Social Work. The professional associations which had been responsible for the training of child care officers, medical social workers and psychiatric social workers combined to form the British Association of Social Workers in 1971.

So, while Conservative and Labour placed different emphases on the importance of hospitals and social services, the net result was the disappearance of specialist training in favour of genericism, and the creation of separate health and social services empires. Health authorities, reorganized in 1974 into a structure of Regional Health Authorities, Area Health Authorities and District Management Teams, treated psychiatry simply as one medical specialism among many, and few major decisions were made by bodies on which psychiatrists carried any weight. For psychiatrists and psychiatric nurses, the impact of the managerial revolution was experienced through new staffing structures for all medical and nursing

Year	Resident population (000s)	In-patients per thousand population	Admissions (000s)
1959	(133.2)	(2.9)	(95.3)
1960	–	–	–
1961	135.4	3.0	138.7
1962	133.8	2.9	146.5
1963	127.6	2.7	160.4
1964	126.5	2.7	155.0
1965	123.6	2.6	155.6
1966	121.6	2.5	160.5
1967	118.9	2.5	165.1
1968	116.4	2.4	170.5
1969	105.6	2.2	162.3
1970	103.3	2.1	162.9

Table 11.1 *Mental hospitals, England and Wales: resident populations and admissions, 1959–70*
Source: Annual Reports, Ministry of Health
Note: 1959 figures not strictly comparable; no figures issued for 1960.

staff introduced by the Cogwheel[10] and Salmon[11] Reports. The structures were primarily dictated by the needs and traditions of general medicine and general nursing.

Local authority Social Services Departments inherited severe social problems, many of them involving statutory responsibilities, and were usually headed by Directors who came from Children's Departments or Welfare Departments (the latter dealt with physical disability and infirm elderly). None of the first round of Directors appointed came from the mental health field.[12]

Community care proved difficult to organize as the professional empires drew apart. Health and social services had different responsibilities, different patterns of organization, different styles of management, different planning cycles, different budgeting cycles, different professional personnel and different organizational imperatives.[13] A single specialism which drew on the knowledge and practice of both medical and social service had been chopped in two. Though the reorganizations had many advantages in other areas of work, mental health was the biggest casualty; but the process of reducing mental hospital beds continued (Table 11.1).

By 1970, the number of resident in-patients had fallen from the 1961 peak by 24 per cent, while admissions had risen by 17 per cent. Most mental hospitals developed two quite distinct kinds of work: short-stay care for a rapidly rising number of patients who stayed only a few days to have their medication monitored and prescriptions adjusted, many of them 'revolving door' patients who returned repeatedly; and long-stay care for the chronic population, mainly elderly, who were difficult to discharge. It was this chronic population, together with the population of mental handicap hospitals and geriatric hospitals, which became the target of public concern.

THE HOSPITAL INQUIRIES

The ideas of Goffman, Foucault and Szasz continued to percolate the system, particularly among students and young professionals. R.D. Laing and David Cooper at the Tavistock Clinic developed 'anti-psychiatry'.[14] As the view that all institutional care was oppression, and that all psychiatry was 'social control' spread, there was a general public unease about patients in institutions; and despite the patchy nature of the theoretical work, there was a good practical justification for it. In a period of high employment, mental hospitals and other institutions found it difficult to keep trained staff, and often to recruit any staff at all. Meanwhile the health service unions, like the professional associations, were increasingly concerned with pay and conditions of work, and developed a new militancy. Patient care suffered, and public unease was given a sharp edge by the publication of *Sans Everything: A Case to Answer*,[15] which contained detailed and specific allegations about the treatment of patients in certain hospital geriatric and psychogeriatric wards. The allegations were the subject of a Government inquiry[16] which found many of them not proven: but this inquiry took place long after the alleged events. *Sans Everything* was the work of a pressure-group which had good cause for concern, but possibly did not choose the most convincing cases on which to base a public attack.[17]

Nevertheless, press and television were alerted to the possibility of sensational revelations, and this proved to be the beginning of another 'wave of suspicion and excitement' – or in Stanley Cohen's terms, 'moral panic'.[18] Soon after, the *News of the World* newspaper published a startling and gruesome story of neglect and ill-treatment at a mental handicap hospital, the Ely Hospital, Cardiff, and a flood of allegations, many of them relating to mental illness hospitals, followed. In the next five years, hardly a week went by without press reports of suspected abuse in one hospital or another, and few psychiatric hospitals escaped the process entirely.[19]

A pattern was set: nursing staff, usually male nurses on the 'back wards', would be accused of cruelty and brutality by patients' relatives or former members of staff. It was notable that the latter (like Dr Montague Lomax) were usually outsiders – temporary staff who were not part of the hospital culture. This meant that they felt free to speak, and were not subject to professional or trade union pressure; but it also meant that their status could be challenged, and their evidence more easily discounted. An inquiry would be set up – in minor cases at hospital level, in more serious cases, at regional or national level. The inquiries took place under legal chairmanship, usually months after the alleged events, and were run on lines similar to those of the criminal courts: the aim was to establish the guilt or innocence of accused individuals, not the corporate culpability of health authorities. In some cases, the allegations were proved, and criminal charges followed. In too many, as in the *Sans Everything* inquiry, the investigation took place so long after the alleged events that the trail was cold. Staff often refused to testify against colleagues in the belief that the responsibility for inadequate staffing and inadequate training should have been laid on senior administrators rather than on individual ward staff.

Concern led to some fairly irresponsible popular journalism: though the allegations usually applied only to particular wards, and sometimes to particular shifts, whole hospitals were attacked, with inevitable consequences in the further lowering of staff morale. The impression was created that the hospitals should be closed down, and that any other form of care was preferable – though the attackers rarely specified what that should be, or how the new system was to be set up.

One result of the hospital inquiries was a government commitment to setting up complaints machinery. As early as 1969, the Hospital Advisory Service (now the Health Advisory Service) was established. Interdisciplinary teams of senior staff regularly visit hospitals for periods of two to three weeks' intensive investigation, and advise health authorities, pin-pointing deficiencies and suggesting improvements.

In 1972, the Office of the Health Service Commissioner was

instituted. One of the recommendations in *Sans Everything* had been the appointment of a 'Hospital Ombudsman' who would be able to receive individual complaints and take action on them. Though the work of the Health Service Commissioner and his staff is fairly circumscribed (complaints have to be made within a year of the alleged events, and all other channels of complaint must be exhausted first), it does provide at least a token structure for the investigation of cases of real abuse, and a reminder to health authorities at regional or district level that complaints made to them are to be taken seriously.

In the early 1970s, the 'moral panic' subsided as quickly as it had arisen. Were the new complaints bodies so effective that it was no longer viable? Or did press and television simply lose interest because that sort of story was no longer news? At all events, the wave of accusations was spent, and the energy it had generated was channelled in new directions.

Better services for the mentally ill

In 1975, the year by which Enoch Powell predicted that mental hospitals would have virtually disappeared, a review of progress was due. Community care had been expected to develop along the twin lines of medical and social services. The Department of Health and Social Security duly produced its report,[20] but had to admit that there were failures as well as successes. Mental hospital populations had not been halved. Though overcrowding had been reduced, and resident populations had decreased, no single hospital had closed, and the volume of work was greater than ever: admission rates were still rising.

In a foreword, Barbara Castle, the new Labour Secretary of State, was clearly disturbed by this situation. She forecast that 'some hospitals will continue in use for many years'. Staffing levels were often 'less than adequate', and amenities lacking. Community facilities would need to be built up 'from their present minimal level', and there was a note of warning, echoing Tooth and Brooke's paper, about the limits of public tolerance: the demands made on the community 'must not be greater than the community can accept'. There was little hope of 'the kind of service we would ideally like even within a twenty-five year planning horizon'.

The body of the report, described by one observer as 'a product of the Civil Service',[21] expressed a different philosophy: the belief that the DHSS was planning on the right lines:

> We believe that the failures and problems are at the margins, and that the basic concept remains valid. We believe that the philosophy of integration rather than isolation which has been the underlying theme of development still holds good, and that, for the future, the main aims must continue to be the development of more locally-based services and a shift in the balance between hospital and social services care.[22]

An outline was presented of 'what an ideal service would look like', though it was admitted that it might not be achieved before the year 2000: every District General Hospital would have a department for the mentally ill. This would be very much smaller than existing provision. In 1961, Enoch Powell's proposal was to reduce beds for mental illness from 3.4 per thousand population to 1.8 per thousand. The new proposal was for a hospital service which 'should be responsible for a defined geographical area of about 60,000 population within the district served by the hospital and . . . based on a 30-bed ward'. This proposed a ratio of no more than 0.5 beds per thousand population. The 'specialist therapeutic team' would be hospital-based, and would be responsible for out-patient clinics, hostel provision and day care as well as in-patient work. There would be a crisis service, a mobile team on call twenty-four hours a day for emergencies. In the community, the basis would be the 'primary care team', consisting of the general practitioner, the health visitor, the district nurse and the social worker.

This outline begged several fundamental questions. It was assumed:

1. That 0.5 beds per thousand population – one-seventh of the provision in 1961 – would be enough to meet the needs for hospital treatment.
2. That local authorities would have sufficient resources to provide for those who needed residential care, but whose needs were categorized as 'social' rather than 'medical'.
3. That a primary care team based on general practice, in which no member had a basic training in mental health work, would have the time, the interest and the expertise to diagnose and treat psychiatric conditions.

4. That social workers would be available in sufficient numbers to be attached to medical teams, and that they would wish to work in such teams, rather than in Social Services Departments organized around their own professional skills and providing career opportunities.
5. That the administrative split between health and social services was a minor issue which could be easily overcome.

Mental health services were to be streamlined into an existing pattern of health and welfare services largely designed for other purposes. Had this plan been accompanied by an ambitious training scheme designed to teach new skills for community care on an inter-professional basis, it might have reduced stigma without losing specialization; but no initiative for such a scheme came from either Government or the professional organizations, and medicine and social services were rapidly moving apart.

In the dominant medical model, influenced by the success of the psychotropic drugs, psychiatry was seen primarily as a clinical specialism, to be fitted into the traditions and routines of general medicine and general nursing rather than preserving its own knowledge base. District General Hospitals would provide highly efficient acute services in modern buildings, well placed for transport routes and access to city centres. Mentally ill patients would be admitted for short periods, stabilized on medication, and returned to the care of their general practitioners.

In the dominant social work model, mental illness was seen primarily in terms of social problems demanding skills in social diagnosis and human relations. This might involve family-centred therapy (if clients – not referred to as patients – had families), or be conducted on behaviourist lines, involving a 'contract' with the client aimed at preventing the anti-social behaviour. Since all clients have problems, no special designation would be required for those suffering from mental illness, and separate provision or terminology would be avoided because it involved labelling. Radical social workers went further, following radical sociologists in the view that mental illness had no objective reality. Psychiatrists were seen as agents of social control, and to say that somebody was mentally ill was regarded as an act of political outrage.

As the gap between the two groups widened, politicians interested in cutting public expenditure were able to invoke both views to cut mental health spending. If psychiatry is merely a medical specialism, it can be treated on the same basis as other specialisms. If mental illness is a myth, and definition is not only unnecessary but positively harmful, then no specialized community mental health services are necessary.

The scheme was further spelled out in a Consultative Document in 1976 which commended 'the continued development of community care, with particular emphasis on low cost solutions'. It was stated that 'The closure of mental hospitals is *not* in itself an object of Government policy . . . the possibility of closing a hospital depends . . . on the existence of the necessary range of health and local authority facilities',[23] and there was a commitment 'to continue to raise standards in existing mental illness hospitals'. Though these assurances were to be repeated many times, the Thatcher Government, which took office in 1979, was determined to reduce public sector expenditure. The closures were accelerated, and the necessary range of services failed to develop.

THE AMERICAN SOLUTION

In the 1960s and 1970s, the United States followed a very different path. The mental health reform movement of the 1960s was part of the 'War on Poverty' promoted by the Kennedy–Johnson administration. This started with the major NIMH report, *Action for Mental Health* (1961). In the foreword to this report, Dr Jack R. Ewart posed the question of why advance in the mental health services was so slow, and why 'while each reform appears to have gained sufficient ground to give its supporters some sense of progress, each has been rather quickly followed by backsliding, loss of momentum and public indifference'.[24]

The Commission came to the conclusion that Americans were 'alarm-minded and action-oriented'. When confronted with a deplorable condition, they wanted to 'do something about it':

Our first inclination in practice appears to be to expose, in muckraking fashion, the alarming condition, enumerate the victims, name the 'villain'. But such an attack begs the question of what can be done. Consequently, our second inclination is to appoint a commission to study the problem.[25]

In this case, action did follow, in the form of a new specialist service. The Community Mental Health Centers Acts of 1963 and 1965 offered generous funding for the creation of free-standing Community Mental Health Centers. Each state in the Union prepared a state-wide plan, and some 900 CMHCs were set up. The best of them offered a range of services including pharmacotherapy, individual and group psychotherapy, support groups for relatives, clubs, films, workshops and a variety of 'outreach' activities. These included specialist housing, mental health education and some remarkable experiments in 'storefront psychiatry' (in which an empty shop in a busy shopping area would be used as a base) and 'street psychiatry' (in which psychiatrists worked with local groups in cafés or drug stores or wherever they happened to congregate). The programme was backed by the federal Staff Training College in Washington, and generated great enthusiasm among professionals, who were able to learn new skills in a multi-professional setting. Medical practitioners, psychologists, nurses and social workers became dedicated to 'role-blurring' and 'skill-mix', in which their close collaboration led to the creation of new patterns of service.

The United States started late; but this was the most ambitious and sophisticated social programme for mental health services that any country has so far produced for mentally ill people.[26]

During the Nixon and Ford administrations, the two Republican Presidents, who were opposed to the extension of Community Mental Health services, were repeatedly challenged by Congress. Both the House of Representatives and the Senate, which were controlled by the Democrats, were in favour of extending the Community Mental Health Centers Acts. In 1974, companion Bills were passed by the two Houses near the end of the session, but lapsed because President Ford used a presidential 'pocket veto', refusing to sign them before the end of the session. In 1975, Bills were passed again, and Ford was obliged to sign. This legislation added considerably to the scope and financing of the Community Programs. In 1976, the Democrats won the Presidential election, and President Jimmy Carter set up a major Mental Health Commission within a few months of taking office.

The *Report to the President* was produced within a year, supported by intensive work by thirty-two separate 'task panels'. The conclusion was clearly stated:

a substantial number of Americans do not have access to mental health care of high quality and at reasonable cost. For many, this is because of where they live; for others, it is because of who they are – their race, age, or sex; for still others, it is because of their particular disability or economic circumstances.[27]

The disadvantaged groups included those who lived in decaying inner city areas, and scattered rural populations; ethnic and racial minorities; migrant and seasonal workers; children and old people. The United States devoted only 12 per cent of general health expenditure to mental health, and these limited funds were misallocated. In 1955, 75 per cent of all people receiving mental health care were in institutions; by 1978, this proportion had dropped to 25 per cent, but over half the funds were still being spent on residential care – outdated mental hospitals and inadequate nursing homes, which often lacked the necessary equipment and facilities. Insurance schemes, including the two major US schemes, Medicare and Medicaid, had an inherent bias towards in-patient care, and many offered lower and more restricted benefits for mental illness than for physical illness. The number of people in state mental hospitals had declined from 550,000 to less than 200,000; but many chronic patients had been discharged 'without the basic necessities of life. They lack adequate food, clothing or shelter.'[28]

The recommendations were detailed and forceful: a new Community Support Program (CSP) supported by massive federal funding, to be focused on the 'unserved and underserved'. Grants were to be directed, not to particular organizations, as the earlier CMHC schemes were, but to programmes for particular groups in need. Care would be given on the case management system, which involved utilizing other support agencies to meet a client's varied needs: 'Strategies focussed solely on organizations are not enough: a human link is required.'[29] Insurance mechanisms were to be overhauled. There would be generous new training schemes for the core mental health professions, with particular attention to students from ethnic minority groups, and students wishing to specialize in work with underserved groups.

Congress passed the CSP proposals as part of the Mental Health Systems Act 1980; but President Carter went out of office at the end of that same year. His Republican successors have been concerned to cut welfare funding, and the CSP schemes soon disintegrated. Apart from a few demonstration projects, not much remains of the dynamism and stimulus of the CMHCs and CSPs.

NEW POLICIES IN THE 1980s

Governments in both Britain and the United States had decided to reduce mental hospital populations, but by very different means. Britain utilized existing networks of health and social services to carry new and heavy burdens, without new initiatives. The Federal Government in the USA, lacking a similar infrastructure, developed a new specialized service, with considerable investment in research and training programmes. But by 1980, the political and economic situation had changed. Both had right-wing monetarist and anti-welfarist governments; both continued to reduce mental hospital populations; neither developed an adequate range of community services. Unfortunately, Dr Ewart was right about backsliding, loss of momentum and public indifference.

CHAPTER 12

The New Legalism

When the US Community Programs were at their most stimulating and extensive, they met with a very cold reception in Britain. Conferences were told that the United States had 'only' developed some nine hundred Community Mental Health Centers, and that talk of 'mental health professionals' and 'skill-mix' was dangerous. One distinguished psychiatrist was loudly applauded when he told his audience: 'We don't want to be mental health professionals: we want to be doctors.' Nurses and social workers were similarly uninterested. The Royal College of Nursing and the British Association of Social Workers had become powerful negotiating bodies, and mental health skills were marginal to their interests.

After the introduction of the block grant to local authorities, there was no financial incentive for the development of specialist community services. The Audit Commission was to point out later a continuing 'mis-match of resources' in which local authorities were often penalized for building the very community services which government policy favoured, while expenditure on the declining mental hospital services actually increased.[1]

If mental hospitals were to be closed, the most urgent task was to ensure that there was adequate planning of community services to replace them; that research, training and development were commensurate with the scale of the change, and that there was adequate feedback to identify and deal with new problems as they arose; but these issues were left to local initiatives and – yet again – to local apathy.

Though there was a continuing national public interest in mental health issues, it focused on the important but comparatively narrow issue of the civil liberties of detained patients rather than on the broader problems of expanding the community services. Formally detained patients constituted about 5 per cent of patients in mental hospitals at any one time, and perhaps only a fraction of 1 per cent of all people with mental illness.

In the 1960s, concern grew about the power which new treatment techniques had placed in the hands of psychiatrists. Psychosurgery and the psychotropic drugs could be used for political ends, and there was mounting evidence that both were being employed to suppress dissidence in the Soviet bloc. A text which reflects this anxiety is Malcolm Lader's *Psychiatry on Trial,*[2] which deals with the abuse of psychosurgery and drugs in the Soviet Union, particularly in the Serbsky Institute, and the Kravchenko, the Moscow psychiatric hospital known to be used as a political prison. Dr Lader, himself a psychiatrist, argued that a branch of medicine as inexact and ill-defined as psychiatry was open to political manipulation, and should be subjected to closer controls.

A more immediate public concern was that expressed by a Member of Parliament. Christopher Price, during the parliamentary debate on the new legislation, alleged that the phenothiazines were being used as a substitute for social care.

[Patients] want treatment in the sense of being looked after . . . They do not want treatment which immediately heavily interferes with the whole chemical system of their bodies. That is what the new family of phenothiazines does'.[3]

CHANGE AT NAMH

The view that strong legal safeguards were needed to control the use of these powerful treatments received considerable publicity in late 1969, when the National Association for Mental Health faced an unprecedented and bizarre challenge.

Until that time, NAMH had worked closely in partnership with Government, undertaking public enlightenment campaigns and running training courses for doctors, social workers, mental welfare officers and other groups of mental health workers. In 1969, it faced a take-over bid from the Scientology movement, an American sect led by L. Ron Hubbard, which mixed science fiction and libertarian protest with some fairly unorthodox views on religion and healing. The scientologists started a highly charged campaign against the psychiatric services: one poster which was widely circulated at this time showed Hitler beating a drum labelled 'The Great Psychiatric Front: brain-child of Russia and Eastern Europe' while rats labelled 'Lobomoty', 'Electric Shock', 'Unlawful Seizure' and 'Human Experiments' attacked a terrified golden-haired girl representing 'the Western World'. Mao Tse-tung, Pavlov and Stalin looked on impassively in company with a death's head, while the Universal Declaration of Human Rights went up in flames.[4]

The scientologists were well organized: it was reported that a total of 302 Scientology supporters applied for membership of NAMH, sending in their subscriptions, and making nominations for senior posts in the organization, including the chairmanship. When the subscriptions were refused, eight representatives sought a High Court injunction to prevent NAMH holding its Annual General Meeting without the would-be members. At the High Court hearing in March 1970, their application was rejected. The Annual General Meeting was postponed until July,when the existing members of NAMH turned out in force to defeat the challenge. Elderly psychiatrists and psychiatric social workers came surging up from the shires, and after a noisy meeting the scientologists' take-over bid was beaten off.[5]

But NAMH felt the need to respond to the new demand for the protection of the civil rights of patients and the restriction of psychiatric power. In September 1971, the journal *New Society* reported that 'That determinedly twin-setted organization the National Association for Mental Health' was undergoing radical change, and that 'balancing royal patronage with an aggressive concern for the consumer' was likely to be difficult.[6] The NAMH journal *Mental Health* was re-christened *MIND*, despite the fact that this was already the name of a well-known philosophical academic journal. The editor, a psychiatrist, was moved to the post of 'consultant', and a professional journalist was appointed in his place. The first issue of the newly constituted journal had a cover picture of 'a seaside fat lady', and *New Society* commented that 'the well-meaning but slightly stuffy image was almost gone'.

The next step was a national campaign. David Ennals (now Lord Ennals), a former Labour Minister of Health, was recruited as Campaign Director, and a successful national MIND Campaign was held in 1971; but change was to go much further. In 1973, Tony Smythe, formerly Director of the National Council of Civil Liberties, became the Director of NAMH, now known as MIND. The journal was re-titled *MINDOUT*. This was a period in which a number of voluntary organizations adopted titles thought to have media impact: for instance, the National Association for the Care of Old People became Age Concern, and the National Association for Mentally Handicapped Children became Mencap.

Tony Smythe had spent some time in the United States in 1973, acting as Field Director for the American Council of Civil Liberties. In 1975, he was joined at MIND by an American lawyer, Larry Gostin, as Legal Director. MIND became primarily a civil rights organization, abandoning most of its training programmes and embarking on an American-style campaign for reform through legal advocacy. In doing so, it rejected the duchesses-and-twin-set image, alienated some of its professional supporters, and introduced new techniques of lobbying and media publicity.

THE AMERICAN PATTERN

The American Civil Liberties Union (ACLU), predominantly a lawyers' organization, represented a very different strand in the US mental health movement of the 1960s and 1970s from the Community Mental Health Centers. Its tactics are described in a handbook, *The Rights of Mental Patients*[7] one of a series of paperbacks which also includes publications on the rights of the poor, the rights of gay people, women, students, racial minorities, suspects, ex-offenders and other groups deemed to be in special need of legal support.

The American Constitution specifically provides that no citizen shall be deprived of life, liberty or property without 'due process'.[8] 'Due process' means a procedure of the kind which in Britain is followed in the criminal courts: legal representation, judgement by peers (a jury rather than 'experts') and an adversarial procedure, including the making of allegations by the prosecution and their attempted rebuttal by the defence. Since most American citizens in mental hospitals were subject to 'involuntary commitment' (compulsory detention), it was possible to plead 'due process' and to demand a full legal procedure to 'defend' them against the 'charge' of insanity. Other legal cases cited in the ACLU handbook deal with such issues as the right to treatment, the right to refuse treatment, the right to privacy, the right to communication, and the right to refuse to work. Many of these cases were heard by state courts, and state laws differed, so there was ample scope for litigation. Lawyers are advised in the handbook how to deal with psychiatrists as hostile witnesses, and are warned:

> Psychiatrists are not stupid. It is unlikely that any of the techniques suggested here will ever 'trip up' an opposing psychiatrist, or force him to admit that he was mistaken. But if you are willing to spend the time, you should be able to lessen the impact of his testimony very substantially.[9]

Much emphasis is placed on the doctrine of the 'least restrictive alternative', a doctrine which seems to derive from Ockham's Razor. In the American context, this means that commitment to hospital, transfer to a closed ward or particular forms of treatment may be declared unconstitutional by a court on the grounds that the action would unnecessarily restrict the patient's liberties. For instance, if 'a period of residence in a half-way house would be sufficient, forced residence in a hospital would be unconstitutional'.[10] The alternative may be a purely theoretical one: it is not necessary for a place actually to be available in a half-way house, or even for a half-way house to exist, for a 'least restrictive alternative' ruling to be made. Courts 'can be reminded of the basic rule that lack of financial resources is no defense when state action or lack of action abridges a constitutional right.'[11]

The ideas of 'due process', 'the least restrictive alternative' and opposition to the psychiatric profession, evolved in a different culture and in the context of a very different legal system, found considerable support in Britain in the 1970s. A strong attack came from a lawyer, Professor Ian Kennedy, who used the occasion of the Reith Lectures in 1980 to develop a general critique of the medical services in *The Unmasking of Medicine*.[12] Kennedy's main theme – that doctors hold too much power – is developed on familiar grounds in relation to general medicine: the over-emphasis on curative medicine and the need for preventive medicine; the split into smaller and smaller specialisms, and the need for a holistic approach; the concentration on hospital-based technology instead of community care; the undue influence of the pharmaceutical industry. These considerations, backed by statistics, are used to support the general assertion that 'medicine has taken the wrong path'.

By contrast, Kennedy's chapter on mental illness is simplistic and biased. He writes that 'Large numbers of people seek the refuge of the status "ill" . . . Lacking the faith that fortified their predecessors, they turn to the new religion of mental illness.'[13] He is prepared to concede that there should be some sort of service for people who are dangerous to others, for those who request assistance, and for those who 'appear helpless'. In this last case, 'paternalistic action' would be warranted, but should be subject to a formal hearing in which lay people are involved. He appears to be unaware that the Mental Health Act 1959, which was in force at the time, covered all these issues in some detail.[14] His only positive recommendations are that 'due process' should be followed, and that people who wish to commit suicide should be allowed to do so, 'otherwise you undermine their sense of responsibility'.[15]

AMENDING THE MENTAL HEALTH ACT

In 1975, Larry Gostin produced the first volume of *A Human Condition*.[16] This deals with the general case for extended human rights for all mental patients, and consists largely of a thorough and detailed critique of the Mental Health Act 1959 as it related to compulsorily detained patients: the procedures for formal admission to hospital, the working of Mental Health Review Tribunals, the rights of detained patients, and the question of consent to treatment. It ends with a proposal for an extensive advocacy system to enforce patients' rights, with regional and national Committees on the Rights and Responsibilities of Staff and Patients in Mental Hospitals (CORR) to act as review bodies. It was suggested that this organization might be placed under the supervision of the Lord Chancellor's Department to keep it clear of 'indirect pressures' from the DHSS. Advocates need not necessarily be lawyers, but would need 'special and rare abilities': verbal proficiency, skill in writing, understanding of the needs of the resident (patient), and the ability to identify the violation of rights, to lobby successfully, and to present a cogent argument. There should be at least one advocate for every hospital, and one for every five hundred patients in the larger hospitals.

The proposal to re-involve the Lord Chancellor's Department, the language of 'violation' and 'enforcement', and the scheme for a body of advocates with lawyer-like skills was a major step in what Dr Clive Unsworth terms 'the New Legalism'.[17] Though this differed from the 'Old Legalism' of the 1890 Act in many ways (particularly in the strength of American influence), it embodied the same demands that the treatment of mentally ill people should be viewed primarily as a problem of the deprivation of liberty, and hedged with legal safeguards and precautions.

On the political front, Gostin pursued his campaign with great energy. In Britain, there was no written constitution, and no specific constitutional guarantee of life and liberty to be enforced by 'due process'. Class action suits, common practice in the United States, where one court decision might be held to apply automatically to similar cases, did not exist. Larry Gostin vaulted over these difficulties by taking two individual cases of patients at Broadmoor to the European Commission of Human Rights, claiming that conditions at the hospital breached the Human Rights Conventions to which Britain was a signatory, and in one case amounted to 'inhuman and degrading treatment';[18] but this procedure was slow and costly. A quicker path to change existed through amendments to the Mental Health Act 1959.

The working of the 1959 Act was already under consideration at the DHSS. In 1976, an interdepartmental committee of civil servants from the DHSS, the Lord Chancellor's Department and the Welsh Office produced a consultative document, *A Review of the Mental Health Act 1959* which raised many of the issues with which MIND was concerned, but left them open for debate. Larry Gostin commented that the DHSS thinking was 'static and resistant to change', and that the limited suggestions from DHSS represented 'first aid rather than surgery'.[19] The Royal College of Psychiatrists had had its own committee on the working of the Act since 1972,[20] but in Gostin's view 'tended to equate the rights of patients with, at best, inconvenience to themselves, or at worst, with an assault on their professional integrity'.

The Chairman of MIND was to claim later that two-thirds of the new provisions in the 1983 Mental Health Act were based on proposals first made in Larry Gostin's *A Human Condition*.[21] The main issues which emerged were those of the detained patient's right to treatment, and to refuse treatment; special provision for irreversible and hazardous treatments such as psychosurgery and hormone implants; the tightening of formal admission procedures; the powers and procedures of Mental Health Review Tribunals; and some method of advocacy or inspection – though it soon became clear that this was unlikely to be as extensive as Gostin's proposals for CORR.

MIND played a leading part in the lengthy and protracted negotiations. The negotiators for the Royal College of Psychiatrists took up a defensive position in order to protect professional standards and medical autonomy. Other professional associations – the British Association of Social Workers, the Royal College of Nursing and the British Psychological Association – were also involved, and BASW put up a strong case, backed by MIND, for special training for social workers and for 24-hour crisis services in local authorities. Early in 1978, Larry Gostin wrote:

> Aside from the Royal College of Psychiatrists, other organisations were slow to comment, but over recent months, the floodgates have opened, and advice has been showered on the Secretary of State from various quarters. Gradually the debate and it seems the position of the DHSS has become more susceptible to the special pleading of the professionals and the groups that represent them.[22]

MIND's position was ostensibly anti-professional and libertarian; but it was based on a very strong belief in law as the safeguard of liberties, and the legal profession as the guardians of the law. Dr Unsworth, commenting after the events, suggests a basic conflict between those who wish to subject 'the purveyors of the mental health services, and especially psychiatrists, to a tight legal régime of rules, so defining the relationship in terms of rights and duties' and those who 'insist that such an ambition mistakes the essentially individualized and discretionary nature of the therapeutic enterprise, and threatens to impose a legal strait-jacket'.[23] MIND, like Dr Unsworth, took the first view, which involved an adversarial relationship between psychiatrist and patient rather than a co-operative one. British and American lawyers are trained and practise in an adversarial framework. The professional mental health organizations, trained in a framework of co-operation in the patients' interests, were resistant to the legal strait jacket.

In 1918 and 1959, the Board of Control had given a strong lead in reform, but the DHSS now adopted the role of arbiter rather than initiator. An inter-departmental committee of civil servants representing the DHSS, the Home Office, the Lord Chancellor's Department and the Welsh Office held consultations, and in 1978 a White Paper was issued[24] which dealt with the technical details of possible revision without mentioning issues of principle or the existence of conflict.

MIND advocated human rights and lay (or legal) representation. Larry Gostin was reported to be 'disturbed by the lack of control and knowledge available' on psychosurgery.[25] BASW wanted human rights and stronger involvement by social workers.[26] The Royal College of Psychiatrists was concerned about proposals for multidisciplinary panels[27] in what psychiatrists regarded as matters for medical judgement, and about the delays to treatment which could result from lengthy consultation processes. Professor Robert Bluglass estimated that a system of second opinions recommended by MIND in cases where a patient refused consent to treatment would have meant about 15,000 second opinions in England and Wales in 1972 alone.[28] He was quoted as saying 'What was worrying us was having to get a second opinion every time we did anything'.[29] In the final proposals, the procedure for second medical opinions in cases where patients refused consent for treatment was limited. The Mental Health Bill which went to Parliament was a 'compromise package'[30] in which there was something for all the interested parties, but about which all had reservations.

THE MENTAL HEALTH BILL IN PARLIAMENT

Norman Fowler, then Secretary of State for Social Services, introduced the second reading of the Mental Health Amendment Bill in Parliament on 22 March 1982 with the statement that the 1959 Mental Health Act was 'a landmark in the care of the mentally disordered' and that the Bill did not 'seek in any way to overturn the principles of the 1959 Act'.[31] It concerned 'only a small number of people' who presented 'problems which have no parallel among the physically ill' because their behaviour could constitute a danger to other people or themselves.

The main issues relating to mental illness were the introduction of a test of treatability (a formulation of the 'right to treatment'); restriction of the section 29 emergency order to genuine emergencies; the replacement of mental welfare officers by Approved Social Workers 'who will have to be specially designated and trained in the care of mental disorder'; improvements in Mental Health Review Tribunal procedures; new safeguards on the consent to treatment – 'a carefully thought out scheme'; and 'the single most important innovation in the Bill', a multidisciplinary Mental Health Act Commission whose members would visit hospitals, interview individual patients, and draw up a Code of Practice. The debate was far from over. The organizations which had taken part in framing the Bill had many Members of Parliament to represent their interests, and many amendments were introduced at the Committee stage – notably the clause relating to controls over irreversible and hazardous treatment, and the right of patients in mental hospitals to establish residence for a postal vote. Opposition criticism focused on the need for additional financial resources for local authorities. The Secretary of State's reply was 'We shall keep the matter under review.' Good local authorities, he argued, already allocated adequate funds to the development of mental health services. Those local authorities which were not already making such allocations would have to find their own extra resources.

In its final form, the Mental Health Amendment Bill was passed in 1982, and then consolidated with the Mental Health Act 1959 to form the Mental Health Act 1983.

THE MENTAL HEALTH ACT 1983

The new Act was long and complicated, and left much room for legal argument over its interpretation. The conflicts involved in its framing are reflected in the fact that different and lengthy accounts of its provisions were subsequently published for MIND, for the legal profession, for psychiatrists and for social workers.[32] The main terms are as follows:

1. *Definition of mental disorder.* This was narrowed in three respects. First, a new category of 'severe mental impairment' applies only to those mentally handicapped people who exhibit 'abnormally aggressive or seriously irresponsible conduct'. The effect is to remove nearly all mentally handicapped people from the provisions of the Act, and to restrict its operation substantially to mental illness. Second, psychopathy and severe mental impairment are subject to the 'treatability' criterion: formal detention in hospital is

only applicable if treatment for the condition exists, and is available. Third, the clause of the 1959 Act providing that no-one could be dealt with under the Act 'by reason only of promiscuity or other immoral conduct' is strengthened by the specific exclusion of sexual deviance, alcoholism or drug abuse unless there is also evidence of demonstrable mental disorder.

2. *Compulsory admission to hospital.* The three principal forms of admission in the 1959 Act are retained, but with modifications. An Assessment Order (section 2, duration 28 days) specifically includes provision for 'treatment' as well as 'observation'. The duration of a Treatment Order (section 3) is halved from one year, one year and then two years at a time to six months, six months and then one year at a time. An Emergency Order (section 4, duration 72 hours) is restricted so that it can only be used in genuine emergencies: the petition may be made by an Approved Social Worker or the nearest relative (no longer by any relative); the petitioner is required to have seen the patient personally within the previous 24 hours, and the patient must be admitted to hospital within 24 hours of the doctor's examination and certificate: the previous provision allowed three days for either process.

3. *Discharge from hospital.* Provisions for discharge are extended: patients admitted on Assessment Orders or Treatment Orders may be discharged by the Responsible Medical Officer (RMO), that is, the consultant psychiatrist in charge of the patient's case; by the nearest relative; by the hospital managers; or by a Mental Health Review Tribunal. Patients have an automatic right to regular review by a Mental Health Review Tribunal (previously, the patient had to apply). The nearest relative's power is still subject to a 72-hour barring certificate if the RMO takes the view that the patient is 'likely to act in a manner dangerous to other persons or to himself'. Nurses have a new 'holding power' for six hours if the RMO is not immediately available.

4. *Consent to treatment.* These clauses are new. Patients detained under Assessment or Treatment Orders may be treated without their consent for the first three months after admission (a notable concession to the Royal College of Psychiatrists, since most patients are discharged within three months. This greatly reduced the number of second opinions). 'Treatment' in this case refers primarily to ECT or medication. If the patient remains in hospital for more than three months, and is incapable of consent or refuses

consent, section 58 provides that treatment may only be given with
the written approval of a 'second opinion doctor', an independent
psychiatrist who must consult two other persons concerned in the
patient's treatment, one a nurse, and one neither a medical practitioner nor a nurse (in practice, usually a social worker, but the Act
does not specify this).

Psychosurgery and other 'irreversible or hazardous' treatments
as defined by the Secretary of State require the patient's consent,
and the confirmation of this consent by three people appointed by
the Mental Health Act Commission: one a medical practitioner,
and two who are not medical practitioners. The medical practitioner
must consult two other persons concerned in the patient's treatment, one a nurse, and the other neither a nurse nor a medical
practitioner, before confirming that treatment 'has the likelihood
... of alleviating or preventing a deterioration of the patient's
condition'. 'Irreversible or hazardous' treatments are relatively
rare, and carried out in only a few specialist hospital units.

Section 58, the usual 'second opinion' procedure, applies only to
formally detained patients. Section 57, the procedure for 'irreversible and hazardous' treatments, applies to all patients, formal or
informal. The procedures for non-medical consultation were described by one Member of Parliament during the second reading of
the Mental Health Amendment Bill as resembling the complexities
of the Hampton Court Maze.

5. *Guardianship.* The concept of guardianship, seen as 'a way of
protecting persons who are vulnerable because of their mental
disorder from exploitation, ill-treatment or neglect, and ensuring
that a responsible person is empowered to make important decisions
on their behalf', had been introduced in relation to mentally ill
people in the 1959 Act, but had been little used.[33] Guardianship
may be exercised by a relative or other suitable person, or by a local
authority. The local authority Social Services Department has a duty
to act as guardian when no other suitable guardian is available. The
powers of guardians are limited to control of where the patient
resides, requiring him or her to attend centres for treatment,
education, occupation or training, and requiring access to the
patient to be given to medical practitioners or Approved Social
Workers. The guardianship order confers no other powers on the
guardian, and the only sanction is that the patient may be 'taken into
custody' and brought back if the residence requirement is broken.

6. *The Mental Health Act Commission.* The MHAC is a special health authority, an independent inspectorate which inherits some of the responsibilities of the Lunacy Commissioners and the Board of Control. The Board of Control had been abolished in 1959, with the establishment of Mental Health Review Tribunals; but though Mental Health Review Tribunals dealt with applications for discharge from hospital, and there were other inspecting bodies, they did not replace the Board's function in relation to the rights of the individual patient while in hospital.

The MHAC consists of some eighty to ninety people drawn primarily from the medical, legal, nursing, psychology and social work professions. Its remit is confined to detained patients in hospital, though the Secretary of State has the power to extend the remit to informal patients. Members have a duty to visit and interview detained patients in private, and to investigate complaints from patients or other interested parties. The MHAC is also responsible for appointing 'second opinion' doctors and other persons concerned in consent to treatment; for reviewing the 'second opinion' procedure, and for publishing an annual report on its activities, to be laid before Parliament. Its initial duties included the preparation of a Code of Practice on the operation of compulsory admission and treatment.

7. *Social work responsibilities.* Social Services Departments of local authorities are required to appoint 'a sufficient number' of Approved Social Workers 'having appropriate competence in dealing with persons who are suffering from mental disorder'. The qualifications of ASWs must be approved by the Central Council for Education and Training in Social Work. The ASW has a duty to make application for a patient to be detained in hospital under the procedure for an Assessment Order or a Treatment Order where this is not done by the nearest relative. Before making such an application, the ASW must interview the patient 'in a suitable manner', and be satisfied that there is no other practicable way of providing the necessary care and treatment (the least restrictive alternative). The ASW, like the Duly Authorized Officer under the 1890 Act and the Mental Welfare Officer under the 1959 Act, has a duty to convey the patient to hospital. ASWs may enter and inspect premises where a patient is thought to be housed (with a magistrate's warrant, and accompanied by a constable and a doctor) and the patient may be removed to a 'place of safety'.

The Act also requires hospital authorities to inform Social Services authorities of patients admitted on petition by the nearest relative, and requires social workers (not necessarily ASWs) to provide the managers 'as soon as practicable' with a report on the patient's social circumstances. Health and Social Services authorities have a duty to provide after-care for patients who have been detained on a Treatment Order and certain categories of offender patient. Arrangements are to be made in co-operation with voluntary agencies.

THE WORKING OF THE NEW ACT

The revised admission and discharge procedures have on the whole worked well; but apart from the consent procedure for 'irreversible and hazardous' treatment, the new civil rights provisions, which were the main innovations, apply only to formally detained patients, and give no protection to the majority of patients in mental hospitals, who are technically of informal status. The distinction, though clear in law, is not clear in practice. Patients with informal status may be too deluded or too confused or too heavily medicated or simply not intelligent enough to be able to question their right to refuse treatment or to leave hospital; they may have nowhere else to go; they may know, or think, that if they try to leave hospital, they will be 'sectioned' – that is, subjected to a formal order of detention. Such '*de facto* detained' patients are not protected by the treatability criterion or the section 58 consent to treatment provisions. As Larry Gostin points out, mental patients, like other citizens, have common law rights: to treat any patient without consent except in cases of 'urgent necessity' (which may be defined by the courts if the decision is challenged) constitutes a prima facie case of assault.[34]

But if common law is held to protect informal patients, it offers the same protection to formally detained patients; and if common law is not sufficient to protect formally detained patients, then it will not protect informal patients either. The new factor introduced by the phenothiazines is that if prescribed long-term, for instance to patients with chronic schizophrenia, they can cause tardive dyskinesia as a side-effect: patients who would normally be capable of making a decision about treatment may become too apathetic or muddled to do so.

It is not suggested that patients' rights in respect of treatment are commonly abused in mental hospitals. Psychiatrists, like other medical practitioners, do not wish to treat unwilling patients, and the pressure to discharge is now so great that they have no possible incentive to keep in hospital patients who are fit to be discharged; but if the threat to patients' rights is real enough to require special procedures in addition to common law protection, the provisions in the 1983 Act are inadequate to prevent it: 'second opinion' procedures should be available for all patients in mental hospitals from the moment they are admitted. If the threat is not a real one, the whole expensive and complex 'second opinion' procedure under section 58 is unnecessary. The final form of the provisions is a compromise between the interests of the civil rights lobby and the anxieties of the psychiatric profession, but it misses the mark on both counts.

The Mental Health Act Commission was set up within a few months of the passing of the 1983 Act. Some ninety members – psychiatrists and other medical practitioners, lawyers, psychiatric nurses, psychologists, and 'lay' members, including people with considerable mental health experience, such as NHS managers – met at Sunningdale in September 1983. Though the lawyers were initially most concerned with the interpretation of the Act, and the psychiatrists with the 'second opinion' procedures, interdisciplinary co-operation has worked well, and without conflict.

The work of the MHAC involves regular visits by multidisciplinary teams to all NHS hospitals with detained patients at least once a year, and to the special hospitals, Broadmoor, Rampton and Moss Side (now Ashworth), once a month. Commissioners have the right to interview patients in private; to inspect documents and records; and to hold such inquiries as they see fit. Hospitals have generally welcomed MHAC visits as part of a policy of increased openness, and Commissioners have, in the tradition of their predecessors, the Lunacy Commissioners and the Board of Control, tried to be helpful rather than acting as fault-finding 'inspectors.'

A Central Policy Committee composed of Commissioners receives reports, discusses issues of policy, monitors the 'second opinion' procedures and compiles the annual report to Parliament.

However, it would be misleading to assume that the MHAC has inherited the mantle of Lord Shaftesbury. Commissioners are part-time, and the work is expected to occupy only one day a week. Most are appointed only for four years, so that there is little opportunity to build up experience. By contrast, the Scottish Mental Welfare Commission has a core of full-time professional members. The terms of reference for the MHAC are so constructed that Commissioners may spend more time on checking the niceties of legal procedure and possible rule infringement than on the major concerns of patient care.

The reduction of mental hospital populations has meant that Commissioners have fewer patients to visit, but they are more scattered, since detained patients may be found in general hospitals and small units as well as in the remaining mental hospitals.

The remit has never been extended, and is still confined to formally detained patients in hospital. The MHAC has identified some cases of abuse, and some hospitals in which conditions are less than desirable, but it has no sanctions, and no power of redress apart from reporting the matter to the Secretary of State.

The MHAC has 'aimed to be a catalyst of good practice' and to 'contribute to the climate of learning and discussion'.[35] A good deal of work went into the initial task of preparing a Code of Practice; but the result, in which all ninety Commissioners had a hand, was very long and complex, and ran into difficulties with the professional organizations. Eventually the DHSS prepared its own much shorter and less contentious version for the use of mental hospital staff.

The parts of the 1983 Act relating to the work of Social Services Departments have had very limited success. Hopes that the provisions for Approved Social Workers might result in a social work specialism comparable to that of the former psychiatric social worker were not fulfilled. The training pattern which evolved bore much more relation to the work of the old Mental Welfare Officer, with a heavy emphasis on the exact interpretation of the Act, 'knowing your sections', and the statutory duties in connection with formal detention.[36] A proposal for a national qualifying examination was resisted by the British Association of Social Workers, and discreetly dropped.

Guardianship under the 1983 Act met the same fate as under the 1959 Act. Local authorities have not been anxious to take on extra work, and the provisions, which are limited in scope, have been little used.

Larry Gostin's *Practical Guide to Mental Health Law* is concerned for seventy one of its seventy six pages with the legal rights of detained patients in hospital. In the last few pages, he considers 'Mental Health Rights in the Community'. Every citizen has a right to health care, care from social services and housing provision. The new clauses relating to the after-care of detained patients do not add any more rights for patients or duties for local authorities. Gostin's conclusion is that what is needed is 'a massive shift of resources from hospital care to care in the community' and that there has been a 'failure to provide *real* alternatives to hospital care'.[37] The civil rights movement has discovered that prescriptive law is a useful weapon in establishing 'rights against' various kinds of abuse, but that it is much less effective in establishing 'rights to' services and support.[38]

How much did the New Legalism actually achieve? The possibility of extending the provisions of the Act, notably the section 58 second opinion procedure and the work of the Mental Health Act Commission, to all patients in mental hospitals is remote on the grounds of expense and the unwieldy size of the operation required; yet without such an extension, the procedures are little more than tokenism. Was the whole debate, which occupied the energies of the mental health movement for the best part of a decade, little more than a diversion from the major task of providing effective community care for all patients, irrespective of questions of hospital admission and legal status?

CHAPTER 13

Distractions and Placebos

In the 1980s, while much interest and effort went into securing the rights of detained patients under the 1983 Mental Health Act, the great majority of people with psychiatric problems, whether in hospital or out, received relatively little attention from would-be reformers. There was an enthusiasm for 'normalization', or treating mentally ill people like everyone else, and a popular interest in the 'Italian Experience' after Italy attempted to abolish mental hospitals altogether. Meanwhile, government publications continued to exhibit a remarkable blandness as both hospital and local authority conditions deteriorated.

NORMALIZATION

This concept, sometimes described as 'mainstreaming', was originally developed in Copenhagen in relation to mental retardation. The basic aim was to restore human dignity and full social participation to people who had previously been stigmatized and segregated.[1] The idea spread to other parts of Scandinavia, and was carried into law with excellent results for mentally retarded people in Denmark in 1959 and in Sweden in 1968.[2]

Wolf Wolfensberger's *Normalization*, published by the Canadian Institute of Mental Retardation, applied the principle in the English-speaking world, and proposed its extension to many other social groups, including mentally ill people. Drawing on deviance theory and labelling theory, Wolfensberger and his colleagues argue that 'a deviant person' has in the past been treated as 'a Subhuman

Organism', 'a Menace', 'an Unspeakable Object of Dread' or one of a number of similarly pejorative categories. The contention is that 'deviance' is 'in the eye of the beholder', and has no objective reality.[3] The approach is strongly anti-professional. Wolfensberger admits that even in Scandinavia, the principles of normalization have not been applied in the field of mental illness, but brushes aside all existing agencies as 'futile', and proposes a 'systemic' approach in which clients would be cared for by 'persons with modest and often no degree of 'certification' (academic degrees, boards etc.)'.[4]

> Because of the nature of their training and the rigidity of their functioning, I doubt seriously whether most *current* mental health workers could play highly effective roles ... Mental health is dominated by a large, highly-trained and highly 'certified' élite .[5]

Robust common sense and humanity would take the place of professional training:

> After all, the non-professional is apt to be a 'four-square retired farmer or his wife, a student working his way through college in the old-fashioned way, or a person of low income toiling to make an honest living'.[6]

Wolfensberger's text, which is not easy to obtain in Britain, is much more often cited than read. Normalization theory and practice has done much to free services for people with learning difficulties from the medical framework imposed on them by the National Health Service Act 1946. The transfer to a framework of care based on principles drawn from education and psychology has been beneficial, though there are now signs of second thoughts about the limits of integration:

> Normalization, because it persists in denying difference, or viewing it negatively, may entrap the individual in a constant cycle of dealing with stigma: encouraging individuals to 'pass', to disaffiliate from their peer group and suffer the loneliness involved, and to put up with discriminating job opportunities because a poorly paid job is at least more highly valued than nothing at all . . . .[7]

'Mainstreaming' has benefited many people with mild learning difficulties, particularly those with Down's Syndrome, whose distinctive appearance may lead to preconceptions about the limits of their abilities. It is much more questionable in relation to people with severe learning difficulties: there is a point at which refusal to admit that they have special problems, insistence that they behave like 'normal' people, creates more pressures than it relieves.

The uncritical application of normalization to people with severe and chronic mental illness, the demand that they behave in a 'normal' manner, coupled with heavy doses of medication, is even more questionable. It can amount to a very strong form of social control, denying them the right to 'act out', or give vent to their often very explosive feelings. The result may not be an increase in public tolerance, but the reverse: a new form of suppression.

'Normalization' rejects the idea that abnormality or deviance has an objective reality, but paradoxically relies heavily on a concept of normality, the way most people behave and are regarded by others. Whatever the policy implications of Wolfensberger's ideological dream (which included the elimination of poverty) might have been for mental illness, the practical outcome has been that governments committed to the reduction of public sector expenditure have seen it as a means of cutting commitments on mental health. If advanced professional training is unnecessary, and special services are unnecessary, it can be claimed that services are actually improved by abolishing or down-grading special facilities. The theory is very easily distorted by economic pressures. It was reasonable enough in the 1960s and 1970s to argue that underprivileged people should share in the general prosperity; but in the 1980s, when it became 'normal' for large numbers of people to live in poverty, to be unemployed or homeless, mentally ill people were often the first to lose their jobs, or to drift into sub-standard accommodation. The fact that they were not separately designated was hardly a consolation.

THE 'ITALIAN EXPERIENCE'

In the late 1970s, considerable interest was aroused in Britain by mental health developments in Italy. In 1978, Law No. 180 (now part of general health law No. 833) was designed to abolish mental hospitals and replace them with 'alternative structures' in the community. No new patients were to be admitted to mental hospitals. All patients already in hospital were to be reviewed with a view to discharge. The mental hospital system was to be replaced by Diagnosis and Cure (D and C) units in general hospitals, where compulsory admission was expected to last only forty eight hours, renewable for a further seven days on the signature of a judge. There would be one D and C unit of fifteen beds for every 150,000 inhabitants, designed as emergency short-stay accommodation. 'Alternative structures' were left undefined.

Early British observers reported in glowing terms. Patients had been released from depressing mental hospital settings, and enabled to live normal lives in the community. There was an atmosphere of carnival and gaiety: mental hospital walls were symbolically breached, and in Trieste, a papier-mâché Trojan Horse was pushed out through the hospital gates to general rejoicing.[8] In the new day centres (*centri psicho-sociali*) there was a 'buoyant Left Bank atmosphere', with warm human relationships between staff and former patients.[9] Staff had responded enthusiastically to the informality and dynamism of the new setting.[10] Ron Lacey, deputy Director of MIND, praised the scheme as 'Europe's most radical approach to psychiatry' and concluded that 'It is possible to provide a credible service for mentally disordered people without mental hospitals. In this, Italy is at least ten years ahead of Britain'.[11]

A team from the Italian organization Psichiatria Democratica toured western Europe and North America with an exhibition, contrasting pictures of apathetic patients in bleak and dingy wards with others of bronzed and smiling former patients, now called 'users', at the seaside, enjoying a glass of wine at an open air café, or sailing along the Adriatic. If Italy could achieve this miracle, reducing psychiatric beds to 0.1 per thousand population and actually benefiting the patients, why could it not be done in Britain and elsewhere?

Empirical observation, undertaken in two study tours with an Italian-speaking colleague,[12] presented a very different picture. As so often happens, a model scheme which succeeded brilliantly in one small area involved special features which made it impossible to replicate in most others. The centre where the model scheme was based was Trieste, where Professor Franco Basaglia, Medical Director of the San Giovanni Hospital, reduced the patient population from 1,200 to 500 between 1971 and 1976. Basaglia, a charismatic

218   *Asylums and After*

and creative psychiatrist, blended the ideas of Foucault and other European and North American left-wing thinkers with the revolutionary spirit which was sweeping Italy at the time. Powerful trade unions and student organizations were convinced that mental hospital patients were 'emarginated' or cut off from normal society, and that they must be liberated. Basaglia set up five 'alternative structures' or psycho-social centres, which were more like social clubs than clinics. Patients were re-housed, sometimes in groups of three or four sharing a flat, and supported by visiting nurses and psychiatrists.

In 1974, Basaglia founded the national Italian organization Psichiatria Democratica, which embarked on a sophisticated media campaign to change the Italian mental health laws. Press and television were bombarded with information about the *abbandonnati* – the patients locked away in mental hospitals. As one Republican politician commented, 'They made great use of the horrible and pathetic.' Politicians of all parties were lobbied, and all except the Movimento Socialista Italiano, generally regarded as the successor to Mussolini's Fascist Party, were prepared to support the reform. In 1978, a Bill was brought forward, together with the threat of a referendum on the existing law if the Bill failed. If a referendum decision had been against the existing law, Italy would have been left with no mental health law at all. In a country where political support is fragmented, and coalitions unstable, this was a recipe for chaos. Law 180 was passed in both Houses of the Italian Parliament in the record time of twenty three days.

But Trieste is not Italy, and for most of its history has not even been Italian. It is situated on a peninsula on the borders of Slovenia, and was part of the Austro-Hungarian Empire until the Second World War. It was under United Nations control for some years after the war, and only ceded to Italy in 1956. To call the Trieste experience 'the Italian Experience' was rather like claiming as 'the British Experience' an experiment developed in Gibraltar or the Isle of Man. Trieste was in a particularly favourable position: the local administration, which was Euro-Communist, gave Basaglia strong financial backing for what became an exercise in political ideology; and in the 1970s, when housing shortages were acute, Trieste was one of the few cities in Europe (perhaps in the world) which had surplus housing. Large numbers of workers were going back to what was then Yugoslavia, so prices were low, and there were empty houses and flats which could be utilized for discharged patients.

Under Law No. 833, budgetary control for the health services has been pushed down to the local level, and the health districts are very small. There are twenty separate districts in Milan, and more in Rome. Each makes its own decisions on how to allocate resources, and while a few have followed the Trieste example (notably Parma, Arezzo, Perugia and one district in Milan), many have other priorities. There is no overall mental health planning, and statistics are of very poor quality.

In study tours which took us from Como on the Swiss border to Reggio di Calabria in the 'toe' of Italy, my colleague and I visited Trieste, Como, Milan, Ferrara, Florence, Lucca, Pisa, Rome, and Naples. We found that the rhetorical claims of Psichiatria Democraticà bore very little relation to reality.

The mental health service in Trieste had genuinely innovative features. The informal atmosphere of the psycho-social clubs was both warm and supportive, a sharp contrast to the chilly atmosphere of the average out-patient clinic, Italian or British. Former patients re-housed in group flats, and known as 'users', were able to live something approaching a normal life with the help of young and informal community nurses who would help with the shopping and cleaning, share in the cooking, and use these simple household tasks as a means of promoting group interaction and providing support. 'Users' were able to help each other through quite acute schizophrenic or depressive episodes. Psychiatrists provided informal back-up, making unscheduled (and unpaid) domiciliary visits, and discussing cases at length with the community nurses.

Basaglia himself recognized that it would be difficult to replicate his scheme elsewhere, and that it 'could hardly serve as a model in other social circumstances'.[13] In 1978, he moved from his successful Trieste service to be *primario*, or psychiatrist in charge, of the Lazio Region, which includes Rome. He hoped to disseminate his ideas in the heart of Italy; but he told a colleague that the situation there was 'catastrophic', and seemed disheartened. After his death two years later, Psichiatria Democratica, led by his widow Franca Ongaro Basaglia, a deputy in the Italian Parliament, became a mixture of a political pressure-group and a cult based on the memory of a dead leader.

Outside Trieste, though there were a few good experiments and some very committed workers, the odds against them were over-whelming. Mental hospitals had been left to decay, but could not be emptied. There were technically no patients, because the law forbade the existence of patients, but there were many *ospiti* or 'guests' who had nowhere else to go, and new *ospiti* were still being added. By British standards – and even by the standards of St Elizabeth's, Washington, DC in Goffman's time – conditions in many hospitals, particularly in the south, were very bad, and had become worse since the passing of Law no. 180. *Ospiti* drifted about aimlessly, or sat vacantly, drumming their heels, banging their heads or in a near-comatose state, with no occupation of any kind. They were not allowed to work, because work for the capitalist system was said to be exploitative. There were no ward orderlies. Nurses, usually untrained, and few in numbers, spent their time mopping the floors, changing the incontinent, serving meals and medication. The sounds, the sights and the smells were indescribable. One would have to go back to Bethlem in 1815 to find parallels. Some hospitals were literally falling down because there had been no repairs and no administration since 1978. Some 'guests' were in restraint, tied to chairs or in straitjackets. One *ospito* was seen strapped to a bed by his wrists and ankles. The psychiatrist in charge confirmed that he was technically free to leave. There was no compulsion. All he had to do was to apply in writing – which, in the circumstances, presented difficulties.

Psychiatrists, psychiatric nurses and social workers described how Law no. 180 had created an avalanche of apparently insuperable problems. Most of the 'new' Diagnosis and Cure Units turned out to be in sub-standard hospital accommodation – disused geriatric wards or isolation wards. These were locked because, as staff pointed out, they took the 'heavy psychiatry' – the violent cases, the would-be suicides and homicides, all the results of acute social breakdown. Patients often stayed for months – mayors and judges signed committal orders on request, without investigation. Psycho-social centres, even in districts which had been commended to us as 'enlightened' frequently turned out to be orthodox out-patient clinics, where dispirited rows of patients sat waiting for interviews with psychiatrists in white coats. In some areas, particularly in southern Italy, there were no psycho-social centres, and no out-patient clinics. Many patients had been discharged, but without any kind of community support. The Italian press, which had once headlined the problems of the *abbandonnati* in mental hospitals, had turned to headlining the problems of the *abbandonnati* in the community: the family breakdowns, the alleged murders (often not by patients, but of patients whose relatives could no longer cope with the situation), the homeless who haunted airports and railway stations. Italy has some very sensational newspapers: they had changed sides, from attacking the hospitals to attacking the lack of 'alternative structures' or community services.

There is unlikely to be a new mental health law in Italy for a long time. The campaign which led to the passing of Law no. 180 was a confrontational manoeuvre which scored because it was unexpected, and could not be repeated. Though many attempts have been made to introduce revisions into the Italian parliament, the unstable nature of Italian government has frustrated them; and while budgetary control remains with the small health districts, there is no possibility of reform on a national scale. Psichiatria Democratica has blamed the failure to implement the vague provisions in the law about 'alternative structures' on capitalist obstruction, administrative inefficiency and lack of resources. The gap between the reformers' intentions and the reality has left many Italian mental health workers (and at least two British observers) angry and despairing.

As far as Britain is concerned, the main question is why politically biased accounts of the success of 'the Italian Experience', based on very selective information, carried such weight at the time. To many people in Britain, 'Italy' means sunshine, holidays, art treasures, the glories of Rome. The thought that these desirable features could co-exist with less than adequate social conditions was unwelcome. Perhaps it was merely wishful thinking. If it had been possible to abolish stigma and deprivation by law, to empty all the hospitals and accept all the patients into the community, there would indeed have been 'lessons for Britain'. In the event, the only 'lessons for Britain' are that extreme Left-wing reform movements can very easily be turned to Right-wing ends, and that it is much easier to destroy the existing services than to create better ones.

COMMUNITY POLICIES AND PROBLEMS

Until 1985, the policy of reducing mental hospital beds and placing reliance on community care continued almost unchallenged in

England, but despite decades of discussion about the necessity for collaboration, health authorities and local social services authorities in many areas were still failing to co-operate in the joint tasks involved. Attitudes on both sides were hardening. The Hospital Service was rapidly becoming an acute service with little interest in the continuing needs of chronic patients, while local authority Social Services had many other responsibilities – not least in the field of child abuse, which had a high public profile, and in the care of the elderly infirm.

The National Health Service Reorganization Act of 1973 had attempted to bring the two sides closer together by law. Section 10 states: 'In exercising their respective functions, health authorities and local authorities shall co-operate with one another. There shall be committees, called Joint Consultative Committees . . .'

The Joint Consultative Committees were duly formed, but the health and social services representatives still did not speak the same language, or share the same priorities. The only common vocabulary they had was the vocabulary of finance, and on financial issues, their interests were in conflict. Government exhortations to collaboration continued. The 1975 White Paper *Better Services for the Mentally Ill* included The statement that 'the hallmark of a good service for the mentally ill is a high degree of local co-operation'.[14] In 1977, *Joint Care Planning* proposed that health and local authorities should 'secure the best balance of services and make effective use of the resources available'.[15] In 1978, a discussion document, *Collaboration in Community Care,* acknowledged that this process might present difficulties: '. . . there is often a lack of contact between health and social services . . . the obvious and important implication is that services need to collaborate'.[16]

Labour and Conservative governments alike had consented to the streamlining of the mental health services into the general pattern of health and welfare services; but the Thatcher Government, which took power in 1979, broke new ground by its open commitment to an anti-welfarist policy, and its attack on the power of the local authorities.

The reorganization of local government which took place in 1974 had led to the creation of powerful, Labour-dominated metropolitan authorities in the major cities, and these, like the trade unions, became prime targets for Government attack.[17] In the 1980s, grants to local government no longer kept pace with galloping inflation. Local authorities' power to borrow was severely restricted by 'rate-capping'. The Greater London Council and the other large metropolitan authorities were abolished in 1986. Property values soared, and the Government decided to replace the domestic rating system, which provided a large part of the income of local authorities, with a flat rate tax on individuals. The Community Charge Act of 1989 introduced the 'poll tax', which applied to almost the whole of the adult population, including sick and disabled people, unemployed, pensioners and full-time housewives with small children. The principle was that every citizen must pay something – though the obvious unfairness of the scheme, and its unpopularity with the public, soon forced concessions for needy categories. Not surprisingly, the community charge proved difficult to collect. Local authorities had to spend much time and money in identifying and prosecuting defaulters, and well over a million people officially disappeared, because they could not be traced for tax purposes.

Eventually it was realized that a tax on property had certain advantages over a tax on individuals: people move, houses do not. The 'poll tax' was gradually phased out after 1989, to be replaced by a new 'council tax'. Meanwhile, local authorities were going through a period of acute financial difficulty. Asset-stripping became common: land and property were sold off to balance the books. Some local authorities sold their own town halls, and leased them back again. Others played the stock market, with varying degrees of success and failure. Some invested in apparently safe financial enterprises like BCCI and Barlow Clowes, which crashed, and lost millions of pounds.

The full story of what happened to local government in the 1980s has still to be told, and circumstances have improved since, with the reduction of inflation and a less drastic central government policy. The main point for the present narrative is that, during this period of financial turmoil, when all local authority services were cut and cut again, central government continued to countenance the reduction of mental hospital beds, and to leave the hard-pressed local authorities with the responsibility for community care, offering little more than general advice and exhortation. Central government, in the shape of the Department of Health and Social Security, kept a low profile. This 'hands-off' policy, it was argued, would improve the quality of local decision-making, and ensure that the services provided 'value for money'.

In 1980 came *Care in Action*, a brief and generalized Government document which contained only four pages on mental illness services, in which it was admitted that 'the NHS, local authorities and voluntary bodies will need to develop co-ordinated and complementary services' and acknowledged that both NHS and local authority services were 'patchy'.[18] The Secretary of State who promoted this document, Patrick Jenkin, subsequently advocated a high priority for mental illness services, but declined to say how it was to be achieved:

> You will see that I have referred to health and social services together. Although run by different authorities, they are part of a broad spectrum of health care ... I want to see as close a collaboration between health authorities and local government as possible. How this should be done must be for you and your colleagues [to decide].[19]

The situation was summed up in less mellifluous terms in *Social Work Today*. In a leader comment headed 'PRIORITIES IN THE WILDERNESS', *Care in Action* was described as 'a blueprint for a welfare system run on hot air and platitudes, and most of all political humbug'. The Government message was translated:

> Well, we know you people are into priorities and things like that. So we have issued this little handbook that tells you that community care, the elderly and the handicapped are all terribly important. Obviously you may have other priorities, and that is for you to decide. The last thing we want to do is to interfere in local decision-making ... as long as you understand there is not going to be any money.[20]

THE SOCIAL SERVICES COMMITTEE REPORT

A highly critical report from the House of Commons Social Services Committee, under the chairmanship of the Labour MP Renée Short, spelled out the problems in 1985. This standing committee, which had an all-party membership, was appointed in 1983 'to examine the expenditure, administration and policy of the Department of Health and Social Security'.[21] Although its terms of reference were very different from those of the old nineteenth-century Select Committees on Lunacy, it was to display something of the same temper.

Community care was described as 'virtually meaningless . . . a slogan, with all the weakness that that implies'. The term should not be used as 'a catch-all phrase' to describe 'saving money on the present costs of hospital care by getting people out of hospital', or 'care by families and volunteers rather than statutory care'.[22] The Social Services Committee pointed out that, though public opinion had turned against the 'custodial' asylums, they had represented a necessary form of care in their day.

The great asylums signified Victorian social concern . . . they protected inmates from the community as much as the community from the inmates. They also represented what was in retrospect an astonishing commitment of money, on staff and building. If the focus of the service is to undergo a further radical switch, we are under a moral obligation at least to match the degree of commitment shown by earlier generations.[23]

Members of the Committee had studied both the results of the US Community Mental Health Programs and those of the 'Italian Experience', and drew the lesson that they offered a powerful warning 'against closing down one set of facilities, however imperfect, until there is a firmly established alternative set of facilities'.[24] Funding must be adequate and secure, since much harm had been done in the USA and Italy by 'hasty, erratically-funded' schemes.

Community care had been seen as a cheap alternative; but the effects of turning people out of hospital without making adequate provision for them were clear to see:

There are hundreds if not thousands of mentally ill people living unsupported in the community, many of them former hospital patients. Large numbers are sleeping rough in archways and under railway bridges, some within hailing distance of the Palace of Westminster.[25]

This was literally true; for this was the time when central London became 'Cardboard City'. When the mobile soup kitchens went round in the small hours of the night, figures would emerge from dark corners in the most prosperous districts – along the Embankment, from the back of hospitals and hotels, where warm air came from gratings over basement kitchens and offered some protection against the cold, from under Charing Cross bridge, in Lincoln's

Inn Fields, in Hanover Square: crowds of hungry and homeless men, and a few women, of a kind who had not been seen since the Great Depression of the 1930s. Voluntary organizations which provided emergency services reported 'a high, and rising, proportion of their clients who were mentally ill'. Of the thousand or so people in Church Army hostels, over a quarter had recently been discharged from mental hospitals. The Salvation Army estimated that its workers came into contact with some five thousand people a year with some form of mental disability. The Cyrenians thought that between a quarter and a third of their residents suffered from mental illness, and that the proportion was as much as half in their short-stay hostels.[26]

Pressure had been put on health services to close hospitals without any serious attempt to ensure that alternative facilities existed for the patients. This was 'putting the cart before the horse'.[27] It was necessary to face the fact that 'some people need asylum'.[28]

> The stage has now been reached where the rhetoric of community care has to be matched by action, and where the public are understandably anxious about the consequences.[29]

Community care was not a cheap alternative. It involved 'a lot more than reducing hospital beds'. It involved developing new supportive services, redeploying thousands of workers, switching capital resources, and educating the general public. No real effort had been put into these major tasks: 'the frontiers are still relatively unexplored'.[30]

The Committee believed that central Government's 'hands-off' policy was an abdication of responsibility:

> Our analysis and the evidence we have heard lead us to believe that the Department [DHSS] is not in every respect living up to its duties of central management.[31]

The report was understandably not popular in Government circles – nor with the health authorities, which tended to see the run-down of mental hospitals, and the sale of hospital sites, as a means of balancing their own precarious budgets as the squeeze on public sector spending continued.

Some attempts were made to modify the rush to wholesale demolition. A British architect, John Burrell, developed a scheme for 'New Communities', pointing out that in physical planning terms, mental hospital sites were often attractive to developers. The Lunacy Commissioners' insistence on good sites had meant that the hospitals were often built on rising ground, surrounded by extensive and well-wooded estates, and, under modern transport conditions, within easy reach of urban centres. 'New Communities' involved urban planning to create 'an environment with a sense of place and a human scale' where new mental health facilities, ranging from sheltered flats and hostels to clinics and residential units, might be provided in the context of an urban quarter. Selective demolition and high-density development would allow for the sale of some land for a supermarket, a library, a leisure centre, car parks and some upmarket housing (to counteract stigma). Piazzas, parks and walkways would make it a pleasant environment, and access roads would open up the site to the local community.[32] The principle was that the community would be brought in, rather than that the patients should be dispersed; and the money raised from the sale of land would be devoted directly to the improvement of facilities for the former patients.

Though 'New Communities' aroused a degree of interest, and some feasibility studies were undertaken, the sites were also very attractive to speculative builders, and the outright sale of the land had considerable attractions to hard-pressed health service administrators as property values continued to soar. Figures of £40 million or £60 million for hospital sites were commonly quoted as the boom reached its peak. Discussions of the subject tended to be finance-led: the awkward problem of what to do with the patients received much less attention.

The Department of Health and Social Security made no attempt to intervene. The criticisms of the House of Commons Social Services Committee on the lack of central management were answered, but not with action. The report seems to have been considered as the work of a few parliamentary malcontents, and the DHSS took the unusual step of issuing an official reply. This defended the 'hands-off' policy:

The Government . . . has initiated a major drive to secure acceptance of management responsibilities at all management levels, to give managers the tools ... that they need, and to hold them accountable for their results.[33]

Community care was 'a matter of marshalling resources'. 'Fear of change and pessimism about the possibility of change' were being challenged by 'what has been achieved, and is being achieved and by the achievable plans for substantial progress now being produced'. No details about these achievements were given. There was 'no pre-packaged kit for community care'. Authorities must work out their own network of services at local level.

What we cannot afford is to waste resources on buildings, land and services which have increasingly little relationship to needs and priorities, and which make an increasingly small return in quality of service.[34]

The parliamentary committee's comments about the build-up of alternatives to precede hospital closure and the need to take account of patients already in the community were dismissed briefly:

All this has been recognized and implemented as good practice. Closures of mental hospitals will often be simply rationalizing hospital services in the light of falls in the in-patient population which have already taken place. Authorities are aware of their obligations to the substantial majority of mentally ill and mentally handicapped patients already 'in the community'.[35]

THE AUDIT COMMISSION REPORT

The next contribution to the debate came from a body which could not be suspected of over-sympathetic attitudes to people in need of care: the Audit Commission for Local Authorities in England and Wales. This body, which existed to ensure that local authority finance was properly accounted for, produced a solid and workmanlike document which pointed to a considerable mis-match of resources, and 'poor value for money'.

Community care policies, it was pointed out, related to a very large number of people: about a million elderly and infirm people; half a million younger people either physically or mentally handicapped; and a large number suffering from mental illness.[36] (The

Audit Commission quoted the figures from *Better Services for the Mentally Ill*: five million a year consulting their general practitioners, and 600,000 referred to the specialist psychiatric services: it is notable that in 1985, no better estimate was available than these very vague 1975 figures). Many more people could be cared for at home if the services were available. Most of the funds available for caring for these people were locked up in payments for care in hospitals and residential homes. Local authorities had an impossible task, because they were told to expand their services, but financially penalised by rate-capping if they did so. 'Local authorities cannot be expected to play their full part given the loss of grant incurred for expanding services'. There was 'considerable organizational fragmentation and confusion' between services, and arrangements for training community-based staff were inadequate.

In the services for mentally ill people, mental hospital beds had been reduced by some twenty five thousand, while the community facilities, in terms of day hospital and day centre places, had increased by only nine thousand.

> These global figures mask the reality for patients and their families. It must be a matter for grave concern that . . . no-one knows what has happened to many of those who have been discharged. Some, of course, have died. Others are likely to be in some form of residential care; the rest should be receiving support in the community. But no-one has the necessary information to confirm whether or not this is in fact the case.[37]

Local authority expenditure on these services varied considerably, from slightly over £7 per head of population per annum in Newcastle to less than 20 pence per head in Cornwall, Gloucestershire, Northumberland and Oxfordshire.[38] The disparity was to some extent due to the greater incidence of need in inner city areas, but the figures for the London boroughs did not reflect the concentration in the metropolis; and the areas with the lowest expenditure on community care did not have the highest expenditure on hospital beds. There was simply 'no correlation between the two'.

'The Commission has concluded that the slow and uneven progress towards community care is due to some fundamental underlying problems which need to be tackled directly.' These included the failure to direct resources where they were needed; the inadequacy of short-term bridging finance to fund the transition from hospital to community care; and the increasing use of social security funds to pay for residential care in the private sector, often the only option available. As local authority and hospital services were financially squeezed, there were 'perverse incentives' for local authorities to delay building up their community services. Patients who could not afford to pay the cost of private care (and few could, for long periods) could be off-loaded on to the Social Security budget by being transferred into private sector homes. Government policy had had the 'perverse effect' of greatly inflating Supplementary Benefit board and lodging payments, which had risen in consequence from £6 million in 1978/9 to £200 million in 1984/5, and were forecast to reach £489 million in 1986/7.[39] Much of this expenditure would not be necessary if people could be adequately cared for in their own homes – and most would prefer to stay at home, given the option.

Clearly some action had to be taken. The Government appointed a businessman as trouble-shooter: Sir Roy Griffiths, Deputy Chairman of Sainsbury's food chain, and of the NHS Management Committee, was asked 'to review the way in which public funds are used to support community care policy', and to advise the Secretary of State on the options for action.

THE GRIFFITHS REPORT

The remit was accepted in December 1986, and the report was published in March 1988. The conclusions reached by Sir Roy Griffiths were blunt and forthright. He accepted the evidence of the Social Services Committee Report and the Audit Commission Report, and endorsed the view that there was a wide gap between political rhetoric and the realities of the situation. Community care was 'a poor relation: everybody's distant relative, but nobody's baby'.[40] Resources were inadequate, bridging finance was inadequate, and responsibility was fragmented. The local authorities, in particular, 'certainly felt that the Israelites faced with the requirement to make bricks without straw had a comparatively routine and possible task'.[41]

Central government could not opt out of responsibility. 'The role of the public sector is essentially to ensure that care is provided'.[42] A new focus would be the appointment of a minister 'clearly and publicly identified as responsible for community care'. A specific grant should be provided 'amounting to say 50 per cent of the costs of an approved programme'. Central government approval for programmes would only be given if the plans were cost-effective; if they met the needs of the locality; if adequate provision was made for the support of voluntary groups, and for their participation in planning; if informal carers were properly supported; and if the housing and health authorities were making suitable contributions to the plan. The need was for 'a clear framework properly costed, and with timescales for action'.[43]

At the local level, 'packages of care' from whatever sources were appropriate – statutory, voluntary or private – should be devised for individuals in need, and care managers should be appointed to manage them. The local authority would be responsible for costing the care provided. The 'perverse incentive' to residential care in the private sector would be removed: Social Security payments for board and lodging would be fixed, and where residential care was judged to be the right solution, additional costs would be met by the local authority.

I believe that the above will provide an acceptable framework. It substitutes for the discredited refuge of imploring collaboration and exhorting action a new requirement that collaboration and action are present normally as a condition for a grant. It places responsibility for care clearly within the local community which – subject to minimum provisions for all disadvantaged groups – can best determine where money should be spent.[44]

Sir Roy criticized 'the present lack of refined information systems and management accounting' which 'would plunge most organizations in the private sector into a quick and merciful liquidation'.[45] If this was a businessman's prescription, readers could reflect that a food store chain like Sainsbury's had plenty of experience in meeting consumer demand and controlling quality.

The reception of Sir Roy Griffiths' findings by Government was distinctly unenthusiastic. Though he had acknowledged the importance of efficiency, 'value for money' and the involvement of the private sector, his comments on the failures of central Government and the need for adequate resourcing were trenchant. The report was published in March 1988. There was no press conference, and it was prefaced by a statement from the Secretary of State to the effect that the DHSS would put forward its own proposals 'in due course'.

CARING FOR PEOPLE

The DHSS proposals finally emerged in November 1989. The full title of the document was *Caring for People: Community Care in the Next Decade and Beyond*, and it began with a metaphorical flourish of trumpets: a letter printed over the personal signatures of four Secretaries of State. While paying tribute to Sir Roy Griffiths' 'valuable work', the letter starts defensively, with references to pride in 'the progress that has been achieved', the work of 'dedicated staff' and 'the many innovative and successful schemes in existence'. It is claimed that gross expenditure on core community care services has increased by 68 per cent over the ten years since 1978/9;[46]; but this is calculated from a very low base, and it is not possible to tell how much of the additional money has been available for mental health needs. It is estimated that 'more than six million adults of all ages' have some physical, mental or sensory disability – but more than four million of them are over sixty five years of age, so the emphasis is fairly heavily on the elderly infirm.

The section on mental illness runs to four pages out of 106,[47] and stresses the successes of the new drug treatments which have 'transformed the prognosis of the most serious mental illnesses' and made 'the traditional large and often remote mental hospital' redundant. It is admitted that 'there are legitimate concerns that in some places hospital beds have been closed before better, alternative facilities were fully in place' and that it has been suggested that 'at times, patients have been discharged without adequate planning to meet their needs in the community'. This is followed by a clear statement:

> the Government emphasizes that the number of hospital beds should be reduced only as a consequence of the development of new services. Ministers will not approve the closure of any mental hospital unless it can be demonstrated that adequate alternatives have been developed.[48]

Ministers had, of course, made a number of earlier pledges on the
same lines. Though there is the predictable statement about the
importance of co-ordination between services, this appears to have
been recognized as a losing battle, for mental health needs are
neatly divided into 'health care' and 'social care'. In the area of
'health care', the Royal College of Psychiatrists is to issue a code of
good practice which 'should materially improve standards of practice in the discharge of patients'. 'Finance from the sale of mental
illness and mental handicap hospitals can provide valuable capital
for replacement facilities', though it is officially recognized that the
money may be diverted for other purposes: mental health facilities
have to 'compete with other priorities in regional authorities'
building programmes'.[49] Asset-stripping is described as a 'problem',[50] but health authorities will still be able to close a mental
hospital and apply the money to other services – or to the relief of
their growing deficits. Local authorities will be responsible for
'social care', and a specific grant for community care services will
be provided. However, this only involves the transfer of Social
Security funds for private sector residential care to the local authorities. This money was previously used for the care of elderly infirm
people with limited resources. Since their numbers are increasing,
there is unlikely to be much to spare for people suffering from
mental illness.

Despite Sir Roy Griffiths' plans for a clear structure, there is no
clearly-identifiable Minister for Community Care. The responsibility has simply been added to the others carried by one of the junior
Health Ministers. What has come through the process of consultation is not the recognition of the responsibilities of central
Government, but an additional burden for local authorities
without adequate finance to match it.

Sir Roy's recommendation that local authorities should be responsible for 'a proper assessment of the individual's needs, and in
particular whether they could be met while enabling the individual
to continue to live independently' has been adopted, together with
the view that the authorities' role should be 'as arrangers and
purchasers of care services rather than as monopolistic providers'.[51]
Social workers are to make an assessment of need with the understanding that residential care is to be regarded as a last resort.
After that, they will be 'arrangers and purchasers', and will not
undertake direct social work with clients. 'Social care' is defined[52]

as 'help with personal and domestic tasks such as cleaning, washing and preparing meals . . . transport, budgeting and other aspects of daily living'. Richard Titmuss was not far wrong when he predicted the move 'from the care of the trained to the care of the untrained' in 'the cottage garden of community care' back in 1961.

THE HEALTH OF THE NATION

The National Health Service and Community Care Act, 1990, provided for the transfer of community care responsibilities to local authorities. The date of implementation was twice postponed as a result of protests from health authorities and local authorities that provision would not be adequate. Before the transfer finally took effect in April 1993, a new White Paper came from the Department of Health on *The Health of the Nation*. This specified five 'key areas': coronary heart disease and stroke, cancer, accidents, HIV/AIDS and mental illness. The Key Area Handbook for mental illness, sent to 'purchasers' in January 1993, does not share the blandness of previous Government documents; but its recommendations and specifications might be puzzling to anyone who knew nothing of the contradictions and confusions which preceded it, or the forces which went into its drafting.

The handbook is a document in a series on health, designed to assist the development of 'local strategies for reducing mortality and morbidity';[53] but it was published at a time when the major part of the care of mentally ill people was shifting from the health services to the social services. Though the organizational framework has changed, the conceptual framework of the book is that of the public health doctor and the medical statistician. The concepts of mortality and morbidity, so familiar and measurable in physical medicine, do not easily fit the work of the Social Services. In order to make them relevant, a heavy emphasis has been placed on the prevention of suicide. The three primary targets are as follows:

1. To improve significantly the health and social functioning of mentally ill people.
2. To reduce the overall suicide rate by at least 15 per cent by the year 2000.
3. To reduce the suicide rate of severely mentally ill people by at least 33 per cent by the year 2000.[54]

The first of these targets is unexceptionable, if vague. The second is laudable, but tangential to the first and the third. Not at all mentally ill people are suicidal. Not all people who wish to commit suicide are mentally ill (the coroner's court formula 'while the balance of his/her mind was disturbed' is often a kindness to relatives of the deceased rather than a retrospective diagnosis). It seems likely that the considerable space devoted to considerations of suicide is a reflection of the need to find something measurable in a field unamenable to medical statistics rather than an attempt to address the real issues of social care.

Health agencies and local authorities are referred to jointly as 'NHS and SSD management' or 'purchasers'. They are to 'detect at risk groups', which include unemployed or retired, the bereaved, single parents, social isolates, homeless or badly housed people, the physically disabled and the victims of child abuse.[55] They are to concentrate on early diagnosis and treatment in order to 'reduce rates of hospitalization and the need for costly on-going care', and to 'develop coping strategies' with carers and people with long-term mental illness.[56] They are to 'use brief standardized assessment procedures' to establish local social-demographic profiles for the assessment of needs.[57] They are to develop computerized information systems – but not the use of case registers, which cause 'great concern among service users and is seen as a means of labelling people'.[58]

They are also to 'provide practical support for user involvement' and 'support the work of independent advocacy services', though it is recognised that 'involving users with the most severe mental illness and the most long-standing health and social problems' may be difficult. User involvement and advocacy may also raise expectations of a response, so 'a clear explanation of the constraints on action should . . . be given when people's views are sought'.[59]

'Purchasers' are to develop better co-operative working among themselves, and to 'develop alliances' with a variety of other bodies–in housing, education, employment and the voluntary social service sector.[60] Two points stand out: first, privatization and plurality have created far more bodies which need to co-operate and develop alliances than in the past – hospital trusts, fund-holding general practices, educational trusts and housing associations, among others, complicate the situation; second, mental hospitals are virtually ignored. There is some mention of '24-hour NHS accommodation', but the term 'mental hospital' is used only in the context of 'old-style mental hospitals', fourteen of which were 'replaced' between 1985 and 1992, or 'outdated mental hospitals' which are to become redundant as the new comprehensive services develop. There is much more in the way of specification and advice. The hanbdbook sets very ambitious aims for local authorities. How far they will be able to live up to them remains to be seen.

VOLUNTARY ORGANIZATIONS

MIND took a leading part in the libertarian movement which led up to the 1983 Mental Health Act, and publicized a very optimistic view of the 'Italian Experience'. More recently, MIND has adopted a less confrontational mode, typified by the change of the journal title from *MINDOUT* to *OPENMIND*. It has consistently supported Good Practices in Mental Health,[61] an organization which publicizes constructive local experiments in mental health care, and has supported the Consumers' Movement, arguing for 'user involvement' and 'empowerment' in the planning of services.[62] The model is one adopted in the Netherlands, where many hospitals have Patient Advocates who may work with or against the hospital authorities. Confrontations can occur in situations where the doctor prescribes treatment, the patient resists, and the advocate takes the patient's side. The scheme has many similarities with that recommended by Larry Gostin in *A Human Condition* in 1975.[63] The endorsement of this model in the Key Area Handbook illustrates the continuing influence of MIND on Department of Health policy.

MIND has carried out a number of demonstration projects in community care, with the object of influencing health and local authorities in their decision-making. In recent years, MIND publications have become increasingly critical of the limitations of Government provision, sponsoring such publications as *Mental Health Care in Crisis* and *Waiting for Community Care*.[64]

While MIND's work is largely with mentally ill people who are capable of benefiting from community care, the National Schizophrenia Fellowship has concentrated on the needs of people with chronic and severe conditions, and of their carers. The NSF has consistently made representations about the closure of mental hospital accommodation, and the plight of those whom community care fails – mentally ill people who are homeless, living in squalid circumstances, sent to prison for minor crimes, or an unwarranted burden on relatives.[65] Much of the support for the NSF comes from relatives of 'sufferers', who have stories to tell at conferences of almost unbelievably tangled lives and official indifference.

In 1985, *The Times* newspaper ran a campaign on schizophrenia through the initiative of Marjorie Wallace, a journalist who had no previous experience of mental illness problems, and was appalled by what she found:

> I had already, through my time in television and journalism, seen the desperate situation of the thalidomide victims, the old and the handicapped, and the families who struggle to support them. But schizophrenia moved me even more deeply . . . the scale of the problems is so daunting and unexpected.[66]

Marjorie Wallace investigated people who 'lived miserable lives in sordid boarding houses'; the 'loneliness and horror' of relatives unable to cope with 'a life sentence for the entire family'; the 'bedsit despair of the mental hospital outcasts'; and publicized schizophrenia – which affects one person in a hundred – as 'the Forgotten Illness'. In a *Sunday Times* supplement, Lord Snowdon provided illustrative photographs.[67] There were documentary programmes on television. Then the issue again ceased to be news.

This time, there was a positive outcome: the setting up of a new organization entitled SANE (Schizophrenia – a National Emergency), which works in partnership with MIND and the NSF. With Marjorie Wallace as Director, SANE has been highly successful in raising funds for medical research from the business community, and has established a telephone helpline in the London area.

And on the last day of 1992, all the confusions and all the contradictions came into focus, when a young man with schizophrenia, Ben Silcock, climbed into the lions' cage in the London Zoo.

CHAPTER 14

Consequences

New Year's Day is a public holiday, and in 1993 it fell on a Friday. There was a long weekend of activity on the Silcock case before the newspapers provided full reportage on the following Tuesday. Ben Silcock, the son of a well-known journalist, Bryan Silcock, suffered from chronic schizophrenia. He had asked to return to hospital on a number of occasions, but had been refused admission. His father said that the family had had to cope with him – nobody had helped, and the professionals had been uninterested in the family's experience. Though he was capable of violent action, Ben was basically a gentle person who loved animals, and he apparently thought that he could communicate with the lions – which led him to scale a 20 foot wire fence and attempt to feed them with chicken carcases. He was badly mauled by a lion, and surgery to repair his injuries was reported to take eight hours. One newspaper correspondent noted the irony of a situation in which a lion which could survive in the wild was caged, while a young man who could not survive in the community was denied shelter.[1]

The case had all the features of a *cause celèbre* – the involvement of a journalist, a dramatic stage (the London Zoo was under threat of closure, and the subject of much debate by environmentalists and Animal Rights groups) and the right timing – there was little other domestic news over the holiday period. The Secretary of State for Health, Virginia Bottomley, tackled the issues over the long holiday weekend. In press and television interviews on Sunday 3 January, she commented that 'Once again a case has hit the public eye which can be used responsibly to take forward the debate.' She added that the aim of Government policy was to get patients out of 'bleak old Victorian institutions' and to provide a more sensitive service; that a small number of mentally ill people were 'not taking advantage of the services'; and that the law might have to be changed so that such people could be recalled to hospital for treatment.

The policy of making patients subject to compulsory medication outside hospital by a Community Treatment Order (CTO) had been much debated. A CTO would apply to people like Ben Silcock, who had refused to take his medication, and was not responsible enough to take decisions for himself. Parents and other carers (few people with severe mental illness marry, and even fewer have intact marriages) have no authority to take decisions on their behalf. If the patients will not come to the services, the services can take no action until there is demonstrable evidence that they are 'sectionable' – physical violence, a suicide attempt or a public act which involves the police. (Causing a public disturbance on a railway station, or pouring tomato sauce over the customers in a supermarket, usually produces results. Reasoned argument by a carer may only produce a case-note: 'The mother/father/ brother/ sister is a very anxious person', or a high rating for Expressed Emotion in the family.) Even when admitted in emergency, patients may be discharged from hospital again within a few days. But, though a CTO is a means of securing continuity of treatment, it is a very obvious form of social control, forcing medication which has marked side-effects on people who do not want it, and who are not in hospital. Patients often say that it makes them feel 'like zombies'.

On Monday 4 January, Mrs Bottomley summoned a series of representatives of mental health organizations for consultation, and most of them subsequently gave television interviews. The reactions, as reported in the press,[2] were extremely varied.

The chief executive of the National Schizophrenia Fellowship, Martin Eede, said that the first need was to stop the reduction of mental hospital beds, and the second was to cope with a chronic lack of resources. He noted that in Mrs Bottomley's own constituency (Surrey South-west), £476 a year was spent on average on individuals with learning difficulties, and only 67p on those with mental illness.

The chief executive of the Mental Health Act Commission,

William Bingley, took the view that a legal power to recall patients to hospital 'might distract attention from a number of fundamental difficulties' in relation to professional attitudes and adequacy of service organization.

The legal director of MIND, Ian Bynoe, wanted patients to have more extensive rights to after-care, but thought that a CTO would be an unacceptable breach of civil liberties.

A spokesman for the Association of Metropolitan Authorities pointed out that the AMC had estimated a £200 million shortfall in the funds necessary to implement community care.

The Royal College of Psychiatrists stated that it had set up a working party on CTOs in 1987, that opinion among College members was divided, but that another working party would shortly propose a modified scheme for Community Supervision Orders.

The British Medical Association reported the findings of a recent survey: more than 90 per cent of general practitioners were not aware of a formal hospital discharge policy; 81 per cent were not aware of any mechanism for formal collaboration between agencies over community care cases; over 90 per cent thought there would not be enough funding; and 64 per cent thought that community care plans would not be ready by April 1993, the final date for the handover to local authorities.[3]

The *Guardian* in a leader headed, 'The Grim Lesson of the Lion's Cage' commented that it was time for a pause. 'There is nothing more dangerous than policy-making on the hoof. All ministers are prone to it, particularly during a parliamentary recess.'

The *Times* devoted a whole page to recalling its campaign of 1985, and Marjorie Wallace's articles on 'Schizophrenia – the Forgotten Illness'. The leading article commented:

> Plans were laid to empty the hospitals, but no plans were made to provide alternative care . . . the accelerated run-down of the hospitals sent into the community people with severe conditions whose needs were never met, and are still not being met . . . To most patients it matters little where they are cared for, how or by whom. It is the quality of care that counts.

A week later, an article by Bryan Silcock on his son's treatment by the mental health services[4] told a story only too familiar to mental health organizations, particularly the National Schizophrenia Fellowship and SANE: of intolerable tensions at home; of short periods when Ben was in hospital, and sudden unplanned discharges without notice; of periods when he was sleeping rough; of placements in bedsits and hostels and bed and breakfast accommodation which never lasted; of his attempts to live alone in a flat, and how 'the community' turned hostile – his furniture was smashed and his possessions were stolen; of a hospital actually discharging him because he threatened a member of staff – though violence was a symptom of his illness, and an indicator of his need for treatment; and of the 'smug bureaucratic evasion of responsibility' by one hospital authority which deemed that he lived outside their catchment area because his family had been forced to change the locks on the front door, 'making him technically homeless'.

Bryan Silcock's analysis of the situation led him to a number of general conclusions about the care of people with severe mental illness: return to hospital must be made easier, and hospitals must accept the responsibility; the family must have a right to know what is happening, and to co-operate in care, rather than being ignored or made to feel guilty; some means of helping people who stop taking their drugs must be devised (but not forcible medication). The major long-term needs are identified as the regular follow-up of chronic patients by a named case manager; and 'long-term accommodation, similar to sheltered accommodation for the elderly'.

None of these very reasonable points was taken up in public discussion. Within a few days, press and television had moved on to other preoccupations. After all, a man does not climb into a lion's cage every day of the week, and the inadequacy of local authority funding is difficult to keep in the headlines.

The Silcock case raises many issues: if there was any consensus on what the problems were, they would be more easily resolved; but even the Royal College of Psychiatrists' modified proposal for a Community Supervision Order (CSO) presents difficulties. A CSO would make patients liable to be recalled to hospital if they refused medication. Some patients, like Ben Silcock, have asked to be taken back into hospital, and have been refused admission. It is not unknown for patients to commit a minor theft (stealing a newspaper or a bottle of milk) in order to get the care and treatment they know they need; and where the patient is genuinely resistant to going into hospital, a CSO involves using compulsory admission as a threat. This runs counter to every development in mental health policy since 1926.

William Bingley's reference to 'fundamental difficulties' in professional attitudes and service organization, the BMA survey, and the repeated references to inadequate after-care provision suggest that the CSO issue indicates only the tip of a sizeable iceberg, and the dimensions of the iceberg are unknown.

MENTAL HEALTH STATISTICS

What have been the results of the run-down of psychiatric hospital beds? To the exasperation of journalists and scholars, information is simply not available. Government statistical services were severely cut following the Rayner Report's recommendation in 1981 that 'information should not be collected primarily for publication. It should be collected because Government needs it for its own business.'[5] Calls for an independent body to monitor the use and accuracy of Government statistics have so far been unsuccessful in reversing this policy.[6]

At the same time, the collection of mental health statistics has become much more difficult. When mental hospitals were separately designated, and most patients stayed in hospital for comparatively long periods, admissions, discharges and average length of stay could be calculated with some confidence. Now that many acute patients stay for very short periods of time, accurate compilation even of hospital data has become much more difficult.

The detailed Mental Health In-Patient Enquiry was last published in 1977, with 1976 figures. The annual patient census of mental hospitals, which showed the number, age, sex, diagnosis and length of stay of actual patients under the hospital roof at midnight on 31 December of each year, no longer operates. Table 14.1 gives generalized figures for the numbers of patients in mental hospitals, which are now the only figures issued.

The figures in Table 14.1 are not directly comparable with tables in earlier chapters, for several reasons. Welsh health statistics are separately collected in Cardiff, not necessarily on the same basis as in England, and are no longer aggregated with the English figures. Table 14.1 figures do not include psychiatric patients in district

1976	83,320	1984	66,040
1977	80,686	1985	63,970
1978	78,205	1986	60,279
1979	76,364	1987/8	n/a
1980	74,831	1988/9	56,200
1981	73,174	1989/90	56,900
1982	70,881	1990/1	48,700
1983	69,030	1991/2	45,100

Table 14.1 *Residents in mental illness hospitals, England, 1976–92*
Source: SD2A Department of Health

general hospital units; and from 1986, figures have been collected for the financial year, not for the calendar year. These changes have only relatively minor implications, but they do mean that there is not an accurate run of figures available for the period since the introduction of the Powell policy in 1961. Calculations can only be approximate; but in round terms, it is reasonable to estimate that the number of beds in mental hospitals has been reduced by more than two-thirds since 1960.

Statistics for all psychiatric patients in hospital, including those in general hospital units, are now only collected in terms of generalized estimates of 'beds available', not actual patient occupation. (It should be noted that official classifications are made in terms of 'beds', as for other hospital specialisms, though most psychiatric patients are ambulant, and occupy the beds only at night.) The bed occupancy rate, which used to be estimated at approximately 86 per cent of available beds, is now not estimated at all. Table 14.2 shows available beds for given years, together with admission figures and an estimate of 'bed turnover' – that is, the number of patients occupying a particular hospital place over the year.

If there were 55,000 'beds available' in 1990/1, and the 86 per cent occupancy rate were maintained, this would imply that there were some 47,300 patients undergoing psychiatric in-patient treatment in all types of hospital at any one time; but according to the Department of Health's own figures, there were 48,700 patients in mental hospitals alone (see Table 14.1). This suggests (a) that the number of psychiatric patients in general hospital psychiatric units was not large; (b) that such mental hospital accommodation as was still in use was considerably overcrowded by previous standards; and/or (c) that the figures may not be very reliable.

	I Beds available (000s)	II Admissions (000s)	III Annual turnover
1976	97	179	1.8
1977	93	175	1.9
1978	91	171	1.9
1979	89	165	1.9
1980	87	174	2.0
1981	85	176	2.1
1982	84	186	2.2
1983	82	192	2.3
1984	79	197	2.5
1985	76	204	2.7
1986	72	204	2.8
1987/8	67	304	4.5
1988/9	63	212	3.4
1989/90	59	215	3.6
1990/1	55	219	4.0

Table 14.2 *Beds available for mental illness, admissions and bed turnover, England, 1976–91*
Source: (cols I and II): SD2A Department of Health, KH03 returns.

Since 1991, the number of mental hospital beds available has decreased sharply with further hospital closures, and the decrease is continuing; but it is notable from Table 14.2 that the fall in 'bed numbers' has been counterpointed by an equally marked and continued rise in admissions: as patient numbers decreased between 1976 and 1991, the work became more than twice as intensive. Hospital statistics still record events, not people, so it is not clear how many of these are 'revolving door' admissions.

Professor Steven Hirsch comments: 'The rate and extent of bed closures in the United Kingdom is only equalled by that in Italy, while psychiatric bed provision in most continental countries has decreased only slightly.'[7]

Mentally ill people in the community go to many different kinds of accommodation – to their own homes, relatives' homes, hostels, lodgings, bed and breakfast accommodation, group flats, sheltered accommodation or nursing homes. They may move from one kind of accommodation to another – and some move frequently. They may be homeless, or go to prison. They may be cared for in the public sector, the private sector, the voluntary sector or the 'informal sector', which means such care as relatives and friends can provide; or any of these at different times; or none at all. They may attend day hospitals, out-patient clinics, sheltered workshops, training centres, day centres or drop-in centres, or not attend any of these. They may visit, or be visited by, psychiatrists, community psychiatric nurses, social workers, housing officials, social security officials, police (as victims or offenders) or voluntary workers, or not be visited by anybody. We have little idea of the patterns of help which are being formed, or of when and how the system fails. The only evidence on the gaps in the services and the ways in which people 'fall through the net' relates to particular cases, like that of Ben Silcock, or the cases highlighted by Marjorie Wallace. There is no reliable statistical evidence. The only evidence is anecdotal.

The blurring of the distinction between mental illness and other categories of need in the health and social services, intended to reduce stigma, has made the routine collection of statistics impossible. Once former patients go out into the community, they are no longer 'patients', but 'clients' or 'residents', largely indistinguishable from others. Normalization, streamlining or mainstreaming: whatever the policy is called, it has the effect of destroying the evidence of its own processes.

Many people have argued that this is as it should be – that once a psychiatric patient leaves hospital, he or she becomes an ordinary citizen, who should not be specially marked or traced; but the results are that a major measure of social policy affecting over a hundred thousand very vulnerable citizens was introduced, and there is no national information on its effects.

MENTAL HEALTH RESEARCH

Until 1993, research funding on the run-down of mental hospitals was largely concentrated on projects recording the placement of long-stay patients in non-hospital settings. These patients, some very institutionalized and most elderly, were transferred directly from hospital to hostels and similar settings (from which, given their age and disabilities, they are unlikely to move). The TAPS Project directed from the Institute of Psychiatry has demonstrated the effects of running down the long-stay population of two large London mental hospitals, Friern and St Bernard's Southall (formerly Colney Hatch and the Hanwell Asylum);[8] but the research did not extend to other mental hospitals, which might be more summary in their discharge policies, or to the younger chronic

patients who now have only brief periods in hospital, and whose
experiences in the community are more fragmented and often more
traumatic.

In April 1993, following on from the 'Health of the Nation'
initiative, an official research project on the prevalence of mental
illness was at last announced. The work will be undertaken by the
Office of Population Censuses and Surveys (OPCS):

> The survey will estimate the prevalence of different types of
> mental illness among adults, and will investigate their associated
> social disabilities; the variation in the use of health, social and
> voluntary care services, and the risk factors associated with
> mental illness – for example, the death of a spouse or other close
> relative. It will also try to measure the smoking, drinking and
> drug-taking habits of people with mental illness.[9]

The method to be used is that of quota sampling: separate
samples will be established for adults living in private households,
adults in institutions 'catering for people with mental illness', and
institutions 'which do not specifically cater for people with mental
illness – concentrating on various types of hostels for homeless
people'.

The final samples will comprise about 2,000 people living in
private households who are suffering from neuroses such as
anxiety or depression, and about 600 'who *may* be suffering from
a psychosis, such as schizophrenia or manic-depression'; 1,500
people in institutions for mentally ill people; and about 1,000 in
hostels for the homeless, or sleeping rough. People in the samples
will be interviewed if they give 'their written and informed
consent'. The survey, which covers Scotland and Wales as well
as England, is scheduled to be completed by mid-1995. It is intended that it should 'enable those responsible for providing services for mentally ill people to set local needs into a national
context'.

The emphasis is primarily on medical statistics, and while the
survey should provide much useful information, it necessarily has
certain limitations. Quota-sampling hardly justifies the claim that it
is 'a national survey of mental illness'. The results will not necessarily be capable of extrapolation to the whole population of Britain.
Subjects will be interviewed at one point in time, so the results will

provide a snapshot rather than a moving picture of their experiences. The proportion of responses may not be high, since some will not be able to respond, and some may refuse to do so. Questions are likely to be pre-set and standardized: there will be little opportunity for the kind of sensitive and time-consuming depth interview which yields the best results with mentally ill people.

Nevertheless, the survey represents a distinct advance in research – not least in the official recognition that the run-down of mental hospitals has left a very large gap in our knowledge of where mentally ill people are, and how they live. It is to be hoped that this basic study will be complemented by other research which can explore the social factors in greater detail.

The greatest need is for social data on seriously mentally ill people who have never been allowed to become institutionalized. At a conference on Community Care in Schizophrenia hosted by SANE at Nuffield College, Oxford, in July 1990, a list of projects on the following lines was suggested[10]

Proposals for research on community care

1. *Follow-up studies of patient cohorts* to determine the outcome after hospitalization. What is the length of stay for different groups? How many return, how often, and for how long? To what type of setting do they go on discharge? How long do they stay there? What does 'a package of care' involve in practice? What patterns of care are emerging?
2. *Longitudinal studies of patient careers.* Most care is now episodic. How do people with chronic mental illness fare in the community over time – say, five or ten years? What are their major problems as they and their relatives (if any) experience them?
3. *Typologies of care.* Who gets what care, and why? Differences by age, sex and social class – what other indicators are employed in practice, and what works best for what kinds of patient? Do the most serious cases get the best care – or the worst?
4. *Planning studies.* How have local authorities planned to take over community care responsibilities? On what basis of factual knowledge? What consultation has taken place, with what agencies? What training has been instituted for staff?
5. *Comparison of residential settings*, such as private homes, NHS

hostels, local authority homes, voluntary homes; both between institutions of the same kind, and between institutions of different kinds accommodating comparable patients: siting, accommodation, management, staffing, community contacts, patterns of living, selection procedures, turnover, etc.

6. *Cost–benefit studies* of different kinds of provision (how do authorities know if they are getting value for money?).

7. *Housing studies*. Are people with mental illness significantly worse housed than other members of the community? Compared to the rest of the population, what proportion are home owners / have had their houses repossessed / live in rented accommodation / are subject to eviction orders? What policies do housing authorities follow in dealing with them?

8. *Employment and income studies*. Are people with mental illness more likely to be unemployed or under-employed than other people of their age / sex / qualifications? Does Employment Training help some categories of former patients, and if so, who? What are employers' attitudes? How do mentally ill people find their way through the maze of Income Support and other benefits? What is their experience of applying for benefits? Do they get advice, and if so, from whom?

9. *Comparative studies of district services*. If Health Districts are to experiment with different patterns of provision, what works best, in what circumstances? These studies need to be linked to tracer studies of patients' experience.

10. *Quality of Life studies*, systematically comparing patient care and treatment in different community settings with care and treatment in hospital.

Research workers were interested and concerned, but without official encouragement and official funding, the probability is that many will be diverted to less expensive and less taxing subjects of investigation. The kinds of social care studies envisaged would be methodologically exacting, but a start has been made on some of the problems.[11] Meanwhile, there are other major policy issues which need to be tackled now: multidisciplinary training and education; the state of the remaining mental hospitals; and the problems of local authority services.

PROFESSIONAL TRAINING AND EDUCATION IN COMMUNITY CARE

Like planning, training and education for professional personnel must depend on the identification of problems and the systematic sharing of information. It must also depend on opportunities for workers from different professional backgrounds to learn and develop new approaches together: not at occasional day conferences where they achieve little more than stating their respective positions, but in sustained and creative contact.

Professional education is a socialization process. Each profession develops its own frame of reference, concepts and technical vocabulary. Members of a profession come to see their own contribution as central to the task in hand, and that of other professions as peripheral. The result may be a genuine inability to understand another professional point of view; and the more highly trained the workers, the greater their inability to cross professional boundaries. Psychiatrists, psychologists, lawyers, general practitioners, social workers, psychiatric nurses and administrators all encounter these problems in communication, and official exhortations to 'collaborate' do not break down the barriers.

In the 1970s and 1980s, the professional organizations in medicine, in nursing and in social work became powerful. Because they were powerful, they were challenged. The answer of Government, supported by MIND, has been to 'de-professionalize' the mental health services, on the grounds that what is needed is more common sense and less professional pretension. This policy has made the professions more defensive of their individual positions, and less inclined to encourage inter-professional dialogue and the pooling of skills. Existing expertise in mental health care, focused largely on hospital-based practice, has been lost. So far, there has been little new expertise to replace it.

When the National Health Service was reorganized in 1975, the DHSS spent very large amounts of money on inter-professional courses, held in four universities and the King's Fund College, designed to re-orient senior staff to the structure and aims of the new administrative framework. Medical consultants, general practitioners, nursing administrators, lay administrators, and other professionals came together for three weeks to hammer out their common problems. Some developed research ideas, and met again to compare their findings. No similar national exercise has so far been mounted in relation to community care. Currently the Department of Health supports a university postgraduate course, at MA level, for professionals in the field of learning disability (mental handicap). So far, there has been no similar opportunity for advanced multi disciplinary work in the much larger and much more difficult field of mental illness.

THE REMAINING MENTAL HOSPITALS

Most psychiatrists, increasingly committed to clinics and consultancies outside the hospital, no longer take much interest in the administration of intra-hospital services. Administration has devolved on generalist health service administrators, for whom this is a diminishing sector of the NHS or Trust provision. 'Management' has become a branch of accountancy rather than a specialized human relations skill.

One conference for administrators on the future of mental hospitals in 1986 was entitled 'Odd Bins: rundown and disposal'. The participants, when challenged on the implications of this pejorative title, and told that the real problem was the build-up and provision of modern services for mentally ill people, were very nice about it. When some possible schemes for the administration of modern community-based mental health services had been explained, they became enthusiastic, and wanted to know, 'Where is it all written down?' There is nothing available on the shelves of Her Majesty's Stationery Office which gives them any practical guidance.

Some old mental hospitals have been allowed to decay while the patients are still on the site. A television programme on the Hackney Hospital in March 1993 described 120 per cent overcrowding on decrepit and dismal wards, allegations of inadequate security and sexual abuse, and the finding of a patient's body in a maze of tunnels under the hospital three weeks after he disappeared. No maintenance work or upgrading was in progress, because the hospital is scheduled for closure in two years' time. There are over 40,000 patients still in mental hospitals. Many of them represent the 'hard core' of patients difficult to discharge because they are potentially violent or self-destructive. The task of the medical and nursing staff must be all but impossible in such circumstances.

The National Health Service has been shedding any responsibility for mental illness which cannot be dealt with by a few days in hospital to adjust medication. The problems have been handed to the local authorities, who have to make decisions – often at short notice, and under pressure – without the expertise which can only be provided at national level.

LOCAL AUTHORITY SERVICES

The transfer of community care responsibilities to the local authorities finally took place on 1 April 1993. The local authorities were hardly in good heart for the changes. The American sociologist Alvin Schorr, in a survey undertaken for the Joseph Rowntree Foundation in 1992, pointed out that 60 per cent of Directors of Social Services had left their jobs in the previous four years, and that the turnover of social workers was rising. The social services had been asked to carry too many burdens, and remained substantially under-resourced. They had become disorganized and demoralized.

> The danger is not that the personal social services may fail to perform, but that in failing, they may become so badly disorganized that there is no road back ... the time will come when no one knows how to restore these departments to sound functioning.[12]

The local authority associations have repeatedly protested that the amount of money being transferred from Social Security funds will be inadequate to meet the many and varied needs they are expected to assume. The House of Commons Select Committee on Health (an all-party committee with a Conservative majority) pointed out that at least one local authority in five would receive less money in the first year than had been budgeted for. For the first few years at least, the needs of permanent residential care for elderly infirm people will have to take priority, as existing commitments are maintained. Extra resources for mentally ill and mentally handicapped people are unlikely to be available. The Select Committee was unable to reach firm decisions on the adequacy or otherwise of funding, because of 'a lack of transparency' in the assumptions made by the Department of Health.[13]

In March 1993, these assumptions were made a little clearer in a letter from an Assistant Chief Inspector at the Department of Health to certain local authorities.[14] This amended previous official guidance about the assessment of unmet need: in order to avoid being sued for failure to provide services listed in section 2 of the Chronically Sick and Disabled Persons Act 1970, it is suggested that authorities might list in their records 'unmet *choice*' rather than 'unmet need', and the recording of that 'choice' would 'not carry any validation by the LA of any unmet need'. The local authority might meet its obligations with regard to needs assessment 'by having a service deficiency form for internal purposes only'; and if the authority is concerned that this might reach the public domain through access to information legislation, the list of deficiencies might 'be done in an aggregate way' rather than recording information about individual cases.

The implications of this play with words are troubling. If access to information legislation leads to the concealment of need from the general public, what is its value? And if 'choice' means the worker's assessment of needs, what has happened to 'patient choice'?

Some local authorities are already being very cautious. A report on two local authorities studied shortly before the implementation of the community care provisions describes the assessment process in action: social workers had very limited time, and usually devoted no more than half an hour to an assessment. Approaches were sometimes insensitive, and responses stereotyped. Assessors tended to be highly defensive: 'People who were knowledgeable about their entitlements were frequently characterized as "demanding" or even "grabbing", those expressing preferences as "fussy". Clients were "expected to be grateful, and ready to accept the response advanced by the assessor".'[15]

THE CASE FOR A ROYAL COMMISSION ON MENTAL ILLNESS

Sir Roy Griffiths pin-pointed the gap between official rhetoric and action, and made a 'key statement' that 'the role of the public sector is essentially to see that care is provided'. It is becoming increasingly clear that the care of mentally ill people cannot be provided by a 'hands-off' policy on the part of central Government, and that a much greater input is needed in research, in training and in the development of new principles of care.

Mentally ill people who can lead their own lives with regular medication, or who suffer brief acute episodes, have benefited from advances in pharmacology and extra-hospital services, and are now spared the necessity of mental hospital admission; but governments have too easily assumed that the policy which is advantageous for some is sufficient for all. In the rush to condemn the mental hospital, the enthusiasm for new drugs and normalization and Italian-type 'solutions', politicians and civil servants have been led to believe what they wanted to believe: that the problems of severely mentally ill people do not exist.

The urgent need is for a Royal Commission: a body of experts who can survey the whole field, and recommend a new and positive set of principles for policy. It is ironic that, while the mental health services rated Royal Commissions in 1924–6 and 1954–9, the subject has since been downgraded to the level of departmental committees, and often left to civil servants with many other responsibilities – to the point where Parliament intervened in the shape of a Select Committee of the House of Commons in 1985. The Select Committee has again become an instrument of democratic protest, as it was in the nineteenth century.

The answer has often been that Royal Commissions 'take too long'; but when the policy of running down a hospital-based service has been in operation for over thirty years with little attempt to provide a viable alternative means of care, three or four years of deliberation to secure a clear and publicly-backed policy does not seem excessive. The *Guardian* warning about policy made 'on the hoof' was timely.

Nobody seriously argues for the return of the old mental hospital system; but its abolition has left a chasm between intentions and performance. From the 1930s to the 1950s, British mental health policy set a standard for the rest of the world. Only positive action at the highest level can repair the damage of the past three decades.

CONCLUSION

By any reckoning, this is a remarkable story. In the eighteenth century, mentally ill people were scattered in workhouses and poorhouses, in prisons, in private madhouses, in a few subscription hospitals, in their own homes, or wandered as vagrants. The problems were largely hidden until the parliamentary reformers

254 *Asylums and After*

dragged them into the light of public debate. Abuses were publicized, vested interests were fought, and the lunatics were brought into purpose-built asylums where they could be cared for without stigma. Thirty years of campaigning went into the creation of the national Lunacy Commission, which monitored the system and set national standards.

Somehow, in the second half of the nineteenth century, the whole enterprise went badly wrong. The asylums became huge, overcrowded monoliths, stigmatized in their turn. The Lunacy Commission became bureaucratic and remote. The revisionist tendency to blame 'the capitalist system', or the supposed machinations of the medical profession, does not provide adequate explanations for such a wholesale defeat of good intentions.

Sheer numbers swamped the system; but even without the population pressures, Shaftesbury's system would inevitably have become outmoded. Many attempts were made to humanize it, and some held a promise of success. In 1954, the moment of reality came, when the Government recognized that the replacement of the old, outdated asylums was likely to cost 'many, many millions'; and those millions were never found (though the Government appears to have had no great difficulty in finding millions to build new prisons).

Three new factors provided a rationale for destroying the system and dispersing the patients: the new pharmacology of the 1950s, the libertarianism of the 1960s (in both its Left-wing and Right-wing manifestations), and the flimsy philosophy of 'normalization' which took root in the 1970s. Most people in a populist democracy were happy to be told that mental illness did not really exist, or that it could be dealt with by low-paid and largely untrained staff. If symptoms could be suppressed by drugs, and inappropriate behaviour could be stopped by the threat of compulsion, that might be seen as good enough. The nagging sense that such a policy was *not* good enough for a civilized society could always be appeased by turning moral outrage on the old asylums or their staff.

The policy of drift and don't care served a number of very powerful vested interests. Government did not have to spend money on an unpopular cause unlikely to provide returns in the form of votes. Shares in pharmaceuticals stood high on the Stock Exchange. NHS and Hospital Trust administrators were able to concentrate on the needs of the acute sector, and dispose of some embarrassing building stock to balance their budgets.

So the problems of the patients, clients, 'users' or 'customers' were hidden again in a new conspiracy of silence; and after many protests, and many demonstrations of failure, we seem to have come again to the point we reached in 1842, when Lord Shaftesbury and his colleagues on the Metropolitan Commission in Lunacy undertook the first national survey of lunatics, and laid the facts before Parliament. The OPCS survey of 1993–5 could just possibly be the start of a new chapter in the history of the mental health services. It is long overdue.

References

INTRODUCTION

1. *Lunacy, Law and Conscience, 1744–1845* (1955); *Mental Health and Social Policy, 1845–1959* (1960); *A History of the Mental Health Services* (1972).
2. E.g. A.T. Scull, *Museums of Madness*, p. 14; 'The social history of psychiatry in the Victorian Era' in A.T. Scull (ed.) *Madhouses, Mad-doctors and Madmen*, p. 5; 'Psychiatry and its historians', in *History of Psychiatry*, vol. 2, part 3, no. 7, pp. 239–40; *Social Order/Mental Disorder*, pp. 34 and 143, n. 78. See also comment by W.F. Bynum, Roy Porter and Michael Shepherd (eds), *The Anatomy of Madness*, vol. I, editors' introduction, p. 2.
3. The term 'Whig historians' has a precise meaning in British historiography. It has nothing to do with mental illness or psychiatry, and very little to do with scientific progress. The 'Whig historians' wrote in the second half of the nineteenth century. Their aim was to correct the bias of 'Tory historians' who stressed the power of Crown and Church and City, and virtually ignored Radical movements. See G.P. Gooch, *History and Historians in the Nineteenth Century*, p. 332.
4. Of the writers cited by Scull as 'Whig historians', all those except the present writer are or were Americans, wrote from an American viewpoint, and published in the United States. Albert Deutsch, author of *The Mentally Ill in America* and *The Shame of the States*, was a writer and journalist. Zilboorg and Henrey's *History of Medical Psychology* is concerned with the medical treatment of mental illness. Norman Dain's *Concepts of Insanity in the United States* deals with American alienists in the late eighteenth and early nineteenth centuries, and their changing definitions and diagnoses.

5. Roy Porter. 'History of psychiatry in Britain', *History of Psychiatry*, vol. 2, part 3, no. 7, September 1991, pp. 271–80.

CHAPTER 1   FIRST MOVES

1. M.W. Flinn, *British Population Growth, 1700–1859*, pp. 17 *et seq.*
2. Eva Hubback, *The Population of Britain*, p. 20.
3. Keith Thomas, *Religion and the Decline of Magic: Studies in popular Beliefs in Sixteenth and Seventeenth Century England*, p. 681.
4. Irvine Loudon, *Medical Care and the General Practitioner, 1750–1859*, pp. 14–17.
5. ibid.
6. Michael MacDonald, *Mystical Bedlam: Madness, Anxiety and Healing in Seventeenth Century England*, p. 7.
7. Benjamin Rand (ed.) *The Life, Letters and Philosophical Regimen of the Third Earl of Shaftesbury*, p. 96.
8. Patricia Allderidge, 'Management and mismanagement at Bedlam, 1547–1633', in Charles Webster (ed.), *Health, Medicine and Mortality in the Sixteenth Century*, p. 142.
9. John Aubrey, *A Natural History of Wiltshire* (written 1656–91), 1847 edition, p. 93.
10. Patricia Allderidge concludes from her study of the Bethlem records that genuine Bedlamites were few in number.
11. 'Loving Mad Tom', Giles Earle's Song Book 1615, and broadsheets.
12. In the early 1950s, I was officially informed that all the Bethlem records had been destroyed in an air raid during the Second World War.
13. Patricia Allderidge, 'Bedlam: fact or fantasy?' in Bynum, Porter and Shepherd, op. cit., vol. II, pp. 17–33.
14. E.G. O'Donoghue, *The Story of Bethlehem Hospital from its Foundation in 1247*, p. 251.
15. Jonathan Andrews, 'Bedlam Revisited: a history of Bethlem Hospital c.1634 – c.1770', Ph.D. thesis, University of London, 1991, p. 115.
16. *John Wesley's Journal*, ed. Nehemiah Curnock, vol. III, p. 455.
17. Sidney and Beatrice Webb, *English Poor Law History*, vol. I, *The Old Poor Law*, p. 155.
18. Anon., *An Account of Several Workhouses in Great Britain in the year 1732, shewing their original number and the particular management of them at the above period. With many useful remarks on the state of the poor.*
19. E.E. Butcher (ed.), *Bristol Corporation of the Poor: Selected Records 1696–1834.*
20. S. and B. Webb, op. cit., p. 86.
21. John Howard, *The State of the Prisons* (1777), Everyman edition, 1929, p. 1.

22. ibid.
23. Howard, op. cit., p. 6.
24. Howard, op. cit., p. 5.
25. For a discussion of this point, see Kathleen Jones and A.J. Fowles, *Ideas on Institutions: Analysing the Literature on Long-term Care and Custody*, pp. 30–1.
26. Michel Foucault, *Madness and Civilization: A History of Insanity in the Age of Reason*, p. 39.
27. Richard Hunter and Ida Macalpine, *Three Hundred Years of Psychiatry, 1535–1860*.
28. W.F. Bynum, 'Tuke's Dictionary and psychiatry at the turn of the century', in G.E. Berrios and H. Freeman (eds), *150 Years of British Psychiatry, 1841–1991*, pp. 163, 170.
29. W.Ll. Parry-Jones, *The Trade in Lunacy*, p. 7.
30. Parry-Jones, op. cit., p. 2.
31. ibid.
32. Jonathan Andrews, 'In her Vapours . . . [or] in her Madness? Mrs Clerke's case: an early eighteenth century psychiatric controversy', *History of Psychiatry*, vol. 1, part 1, no. 1, March 1990, pp. 125–44.
33. *English Reports* (Law Reports), vol. 97, p. 741.
34. op. cit. vol. 97, pp. 875–6.
35. *Gentleman's Magazine*, January 1763, vol. XXXIII, pp. 25–6.
36. *Report on Private Madhouses in this Kingdom, 1763*, House of Commons reprints, vol. 25, pp. 3–11.
37. ibid.
38. I. Macalpine and R. Hunter, *George III and the Mad-Business*.
40. John Brooke, *King George III*.
41. Macalpine and Hunter, op. cit. p. 235.
42. J. Heneage Jesse, *Memoirs of the Life and Reign of George III*, vol. 3, p. 45.
43. Jesse, op. cit., p. 91.
44. Jesse, op. cit., p. 257.
45. The Duke of Buckingham and Chandos, *Memoirs of the Court of George III*, vol. I, p. 170.
46. *The Times*, 31 January 1820, 31j2b.

CHAPTER 2   MORAL TREATMENT AND COUNTY ASYLUMS

1. *Considerations upon the usefulness and necessity of establishing an hospital as a further provision for poor lunatics in London*, St Luke's Hospital, 1817.
2. William Battie, *A Treatise on Madness*, J. Whiston and B. White, London, 1758.
3. John Monro, *Remarks on Dr Battie's Treatise on Madness*, Bridewell, London, 1758. Richard Hunter and Ida MacAlpine's *A Psychiatric*

Controversy reproduces both Battie's text and Monro's, but the introduction (pp. 10, 20–1) tends to minimize the controversy. In the same authors' *300 Years of Psychiatry*, the contentious passages are omitted.
4. *Raffald's Manchester Directory* and contemporary maps.
5. Manchester Royal Infirmary, *Rules for the Government of the Infirmary, Lunatic Hospital and Public Baths in Manchester*, 1791.
6. J. Ferriar, *Medical Histories and Reflections*, pp. 83–112.
7. Ferriar, op. cit., p. 111.
8. D.H. Tuke, *Chapters in the History of the Insane in the British Isles*, p. 112, gives the date as 1791. H.C. Hunt, *A Retired Habitation: A History of the Retreat, York*, p. 5 and n., gives it as 1790.
9. D.H. Tuke, op. cit p. 115
10. Samuel Tuke, *A Description of the Retreat* (1813), 1964 reprint, ed. Richard Hunter and Ida MacAlpine, p. 111.
11. S. Tuke, op. cit., pp. 146–7.
12. Case-book of the Retreat.
13. Sidney Smith, 'Mad Quakers', *Edinburgh Review*, 1817, pp. 431–71.
14. H.C. Hunt, op. cit., pp. 49–50.
15. G. Berrios and H. Freeman (eds.), *150 Years of British Psychiatry*, editors' introduction, p. xi.
16. Michel Foucault, *Folie et déraison: histoire de la folie à l'âge classique*, tr. Richard Howard as *Madness and Civilization: A History of Insanity in the Age of Reason*, pp. 242–3.
17. Foucault, op. cit., p. 245.
18. S. Tuke, op. cit., pp. 148–9, 157.
19. Foucault, op. cit., p. 247.
20. Foucault, op. cit., p. 249.
21. Foucault, op. cit., p. 247.
22. S.Tuke, op. cit., p. 101.
23. Foucault, op. cit., p. 251.
24. For a discussion of this point, see K. Jones and A.J. Fowles, *Ideas on Institutions*, pp. 31–5.
25. Anne Digby, 'Moral treatment at the Retreat, 1796–1846', in W.F. Bynum, Roy Porter and Michael Shepherd (eds), *Anatomy of Madness*, vol. II, pp. 53, 55.
26. Anne Digby, *Madness, Morality and Medicine*, p. 13.
27. Andrew Scull, *Museums of Madness: The Social Organization of Insanity in Nineteenth Century England*, pp. 132–4.
28. Digby, *Madness, Morality and Medicine*, pp. 57–8.
29. Digby, op. cit., p. 59.
30. Fiona Godlee, 'Aspects of non-conformity: Quakers and the lunatic fringe', in Bynum, Porter and Shepherd, op. cit., vol. II, pp. 73–85.
31. S.E. Finer, *The Life and Times of Sir Edwin Chadwick*, p. 14.
32. Jeremy Bentham, *The Works of Jeremy Bentham*, ed. J.Bowring, vol. 4, p. 40.

33. *Suggestions of Sir George Onesiphorus Paul, Bart, to the Secretary of State*, 1806. Published as an appendix to the *Report of the Select Committee on the State of Criminal and Pauper Lunatics in England and Wales, 1807*, (1807 Report).
34. *1807 Report*, p. 17.
35. A. Aspinall, *Politics and the Press, 1780–1850*, p. 163.
36. H.C. Hunt, op. cit., p. 27. Certificate for a patient admitted to the Retreat.
37. *Reports of the Select Committee on Madhouses, 1815*, first report, evidence of Mr William Finch, p. 51.
38. Scull, *Museums of Madness*, pp. 14–16.
39. Trevor Turner, 'Not worth powder and shot': the public profile of the Medico-Psychological Association, c. 1851–1915. chapter 1 in Berrios and Freeman, op. cit., pp. 3–16.

CHAPTER 3   THE PARLIAMENTARY REFORMERS

1. Godfrey Higgins, *A Letter to the Right Honourable Earl FitzWilliam respecting the Investigation which has lately taken place into the Abuses at the York Lunatic Asylum, together with various Letters, Reports etc.* This volume contains minutes of the Governors' Meetings of the York Asylum, newspaper correspondence and other relevant material.
2. *Report of the Select Committee on Madhouses, 1815*, first report of Minutes of Evidence (hereafter cited as 1815 Report, 1R, ME): p. 12, evidence of Edward Wakefield. A picture of Norris in confinement was submitted to the Select Committee.
3. Patricia Allderidge, 'Bedlam: fact or fantasy?', in Bynum, Shepherd and Porter, op. cit., vol II, pp. 25–7.
4. *1815 Report*, 1R, ME, p. 63, evidence of John Haslam.
5. E. Baines, *History of the County of York*, p. 55.
6. J. Thurnam, *Observations on the Statistics of Insanity*, Appendix I, p. 3.
7. *Dictionary of National Biography*.
8. Godfrey Higgins, op. cit., p. 8 and appendix.
9. Higgins, op. cit., p. 10.
10. *York Herald*, 9 December 1813. Higgins, op. cit., pp. 17–18.
11. Higgins, op. cit., pp. 19–20.
12. E. Baines, op. cit., p. 55
13. Higgins, op. cit., p. 13.
14. *1815 Report*, 1R, ME, p. 1, evidence of Godfrey Higgins.
15. ibid.
16. *York Herald*, 30 March 1814.
17. Letter from S.W. Nicol, a Governor, in Higgins, op. cit.
18. Letters, *York Herald*, 12 and 19 December 1814.
19. ibid.
20. Bryan Crowther, *Practical Remarks on Insanity*, pp. 102–9.

21. *1815 Report*, 1R, ME, p. 104, evidence of John Haslam.
22. *Dictionary of National Biography*. Edward Wakefield was the father of Edward Gibbon Wakefield.
23. *1815 Report*, 1R, ME, p. 11, evidence of Edward Wakefield.
24. op. cit., p. 55, evidence of Henry Alexander.
25. op. cit., pp. 56–7, evidence of Henry Alexander.
26. *1815 Report*, 3R, ME, p. 17, evidence of Sir Jonathan Miles.
27. Parry-Jones, *The Trade in Lunacy*, pp. 222–3.
28. Parry-Jones, op. cit., p. 244.
29. Parry-Jones, op. cit., pp. 15–16.
30. Parry-Jones, op. cit., p. 175.
31. Parry-Jones, op. cit., p. 81.
32. *1815 Report*, 1R, ME, p. 17, evidence of Edward Wakefield.
33. *1815 Report*, 1R, ME, p. 78, evidence of Dr Powell.
34. Andrew Scull, *Museums of Madness*, pp. 63–4.
35. *Hansard*, vol. XL First Series, col. 1345.
36. *Dictionary of National Biography*.
37. T. Monro, *The Observations of Dr Thomas Monro upon the evidence taken before the Committee of the Hon. House of Commons for Regulating Madhouses*.
38. A Constant Observer, *Sketches in Bedlam*. See also Rajendra D. Persaud, 'A Comparison of Symptoms recorded from the same patients by an asylum doctor and "A Constant Observer" in 1823', *History of Psychiatry*, vol. 3, part 1, no. 9, March 1992, pp. 83–8, which gives information on probable authorship and the pamphlet's reception by the Governors of Bethlem.
39. Andrew Halliday, *A General View of the Present State of Lunatics and Lunatic Asylums in Great Britain and Ireland and some other Kingdoms*, p. 17.
40. *Report of Select Committee on Pauper Lunatics in the County of Middlesex, and on Lunatic Asylums, 1827* (1827 Report), p. 30, evidence of Richard Roberts.
41. *1827 Report*, p. 37, evidence of John Nettle.
42. *Hansard* vol. XVII, Second Series, cols 576–8, 19 February 1828.
43. *The Times*, 20 Feb. 1828, 20f2c; *1827 Report*, pp. 114–6, 149–52, evidence of Mr Cordell.
44. *1827 Report*, pp. 134–5, evidence of Sir Alexander Frampton.
45. *1827 Report*, p. 15, evidence of Mr John Hall, Guardian of the Poor for the Parish of St Marylebone.

CHAPTER 4   CREATING THE ASYLUM SYSTEM

1. James Gerard *et al.*, *Address to the Magistrates of the County of Lancaster on the Situation Proposed for the intended County Lunatic Asylum*.

2. First Visitor's Book of Cornwall Asylum, report of the Metropolitan Commissioners in Lunacy, 1842.
3. Andrew Halliday, *A General View of Lunatics and Lunatic Asylums*, p. 23
4. M.Bettelle, *Rapport au Conseil-Général des Hospices de Paris sur les établissements alienés d'Angleterre*, p. 22.
5. E.P. Charlesworth, *Considerations on the Moral Management of Insane Persons*, 1828.
6. First Minute Book of Cornwall Asylum, 1810.
7. Paul Slade Knight, *Observations on the Causes, Symptoms and Treatment of Derangement of the Mind* (Knight on Insanity).
8. *1815 Report*, IR, ME, evidence of the Rev. J.T. Becher, pp. 177–80.
9. R. Gardiner Hill, *The Non-Restraint System of Treatment in Lunacy*. Gardiner Hill's lecture on 'The Total Abolition of Personal Restraint' is reproduced in Hunter and Macalpine's *Three Hundred Years of Psychiatry*, but there is no mention of Dr Charlesworth's claims, though Charlesworth is described in passing as 'kindly and progressive' (p. 887).
10. Gardiner Hill, op. cit., in Hunter and Macalpine, op. cit., p. 889.
11. ibid.
12. G. Thane, *Medical Biographies*. (The lectures of Sir George Thane, Professor of Anatomy at University College Hospital, London: a student's notes in manuscript, in UCH Library.)
13. John Conolly, First Report to the Visiting Committee at Hanwell Asylum, quoted by D.H. Tuke, *Chapters in the History of the Insane*, p. 207.
14. Andrew Scull. 'A Victorian Alienist; John Conolly' in Bynum, Porter and Shepherd, op. cit., vol. I, pp. 103–150.
15. Nancy Tomes, 'The great restraint controversy: a comparative perspective on Anglo-American psychiatry in the nineteenth century', in Bynum, Porter and Shepherd, op. cit., vol. III, p. 197.
16. Tomes, op. cit., p. 190.
17. G.M. Burrows, *Commentaries on the Causes, Forms, Symptoms and Treatment, Moral and Medical, of Insanity*, p. 7.
18. W.A.F. Browne, *What Asylums Were, Are, and ought to Be* (1837). Reprint A.T. Scull (ed.), *The Asylum as Utopia: W.A.F. Browne and the Mid-Nineteenth Century Consolidation of Psychiatry*, p. 69.
19. Browne, op. cit., 1991 reprint, p. 70.
20. Report of the Metropolitan Commissioners in Lunacy, 1844, p. 185.
21. Browne, op. cit., pp. 150–1.
22. Caleb Crowther, *Observations on the Management of Madhouses*, vol.1.
23. Reports of Visiting Justices, Surrey Asylum, 1844–6.
24. ibid.
25. Nicholas Hervey, 'A slavish bowing down: the Lunacy Commission

and the psychiatric profession, 1845–60', in Bynum, Porter and Shepherd, op. cit., vol. II, pp. 101–3.

26. *Hansard*, vol. LXXXII, Third Series, cols. 410–13, 11 July 1845.
27. County returns, quoted by D.H. Tuke, op. cit. p. 173.
28. *Annual Report of the Poor Law Commissioners*, 1845, pp. 186–7; *Report of the Metropolitan Commissioners in Lunacy, 1844*, statistical appendix.
29. *Report of Select Committee on the Poor Law Amendment Act, 1838*, ME, pp. 10–11, evidence of Edward Gulson.
30. *Annual Report of the Poor Law Commissioners*, 1845, pp. 186-9.
31. Printed directive of the Poor Law Commissioners, 5 February 1842, in *Report of the Metropolitan Commissioners in Lunacy*, 1844, pp. 95–6.
32. D.J. Mellett, *The Prerogative of Asylumdom*, pp. 96–7.

CHAPTER 5   THE NATIONAL LUNACY COMMISSION

1. *Hansard*, vol. LXI, col. 804, 17 March 1842.
2. John Walton, 'Pauper lunatics in Victorian England', in A.T. Scull (ed.) *Madhouses, Mad-Doctors and Madmen*, p. 171.
3. E. Hodder, *The Life and Work of the Seventh Earl of Shaftesbury, K.G.*, Cassell, London, 1887, p. 308.
4. *Report of the Metropolitan Commissioners in Lunacy to the Lord Chancellor, 1844* (1844 Report), pp. 11–12.
5. *1844 Report*, pp. 29–30.
6. ibid.
7. *1844 Report*, p. 33.
8. *1844 Report*, p. 53.
9. *1844 Report*, p. 54.
10. *1844 Report*, p. 96.
11. *Hansard*, vol. LXV, col. 223, 16 July 1842.
12. *1844 Report*, p. 141.
13. *An Epistle addressed to Mr Ewart, MP, on his withdrawing his Notice of Motion for an Enquiry into the Total Abolition of all Restraint on the Pauper Lunatics at Hanwell*, by a Rev. Gentleman not under Restraint.
14. *Hansard*, 23 July 1844, vol. LXVII, col. 1279.
15. *Westminster Review*, London, vol. 43, no. LXXXIV, March 1845, pp. 162- 92.
16. *Hansard*, 23 July 1844, vol. LXVII, col. 1271.
17. *The Times*, 24 July 1844 24j2b; editorial, 25 July 1844.
18. op. cit., correspondence columns.
19. *English and Empire [Law] Digest*, vol. 33, pp. 189–230.
20. *Hansard*, 6 June 1845, vol. LXXXI, col. 194.
21. Nicholas Hervey ('A slavish bowing down: the Lunacy Commission and the Psychiatric Profession, 1845–60', in Bynum, Porter and Shep-

herd, op. cit., vol. II, 1985, p. 103) states that 'The Lunacy Commission
established in 1845 consisted of six full-time professionals (three medical
and three legal)'. This omits the five lay Commissioners – Lord Ashley,
Lord Seymour, Vernon Smith, Robert Gordon and Francis Barlow.
22. e.g. Andrew Scull, *Museums of Madness*, pp. 15–17, 148–53; *Social
Order Mental Disorder*, pp. 118–61; Joan Busfield, *Managing Madness*,
pp. 114–17; David Mellett, *The Prerogative of Asylumdom*, pp. 164–5.
23. Mellett, op. cit., pp. 134–58.
24. Mellett, op. cit., p. 163.

CHAPTER 6   THE TRIUMPH OF LEGALISM

1. *J. Ment. Sci.*, October 1858, vol. V, p. 146.
2. Nicholas Hervey, 'Advocacy or folly: the Alleged Lunatics' Friend
Society', *Medical History*, vol. 30, 1986, pp. 245-75.
3. J.C. Bucknill, 'An open letter to Samuel Trehawke Kekewich, Esq.,
MP', *J. Ment. Sci.* March 1859, vol. V, pp. 421–30. (Mr Kekewich was
the Chairman of the Visiting Committee of the Devon County Asylum,
and Dr Bucknill the Physician Superintendent).
4. D.H. Tuke, *Chapters in the History of the Insane*, p. 190.
5. *Report from the Select Committee on Lunatics, 1859* (1859 Report), pp.
1-101, evidence of the Earl of Shaftesbury.
6. *1859 Report*, pp. 218–19, evidence of Gilbert Bolden.
7. Charles Reade, *Hard Cash* (1863), Cassell, 1909 edition, p. 353.,
8. Malcolm Elwin, *Charles Reade: A Biography*, Jonathan Cape, 1931, p.
145.
9. *Report of the Select Committee on the Lunacy Laws, 1877* (1877
Report), p. 532.
10. E. Hodder, *Life and Works of the Seventh Earl of Shaftesbury, KG*,
p. 100.
11. *J. Ment. Sci.*, January 1878, vol. XXIII, pp. 510–11.
12. Hodder, *Shaftesbury*, p. 700.
13. *1877 Report*, Proceedings of the Committee, p. x.
14. ibid.
15. J. Mortimer Granville, *The Care and Cure of the Insane*, Reports of
Lancet Commission on Lunatic Asylums, 1875–6–7, p. 120.
16. Granville, op. cit., pp. 218–19. Present author's italics.
17. *The Times* Law Reports 1884. See especially 18 March–2 April. The
various actions are fully listed in *The Times* Index for that year.
18. Dr Lyttelton Stewart Forbes Winslow was the son of a former President
of the Medico-Psychological Association, Dr Forbes Benignus Winslow. Hunter and Macalpine do not include any documents on the
Weldon case in *Three Hundred Years of Psychiatry*, and mention Dr
Lyttleton Stewart Forbes Winslow only in passing as the gifted son of

a gifted father, two of whose medical papers are included (pp. 964–5 and 1074–9). Parry-Jones deals with the Weldon case in four lines in *The Trade in Lunacy* (p. 232), and does not mention either the father or the son, though the legal actions must have been much discussed among medical proprietors of private asylums at the time.

19. Dr Elaine Showalter (*The Female Malady: Women, Madness and English Culture, 1830–1990*, p. 126) does mention one of Mrs Weldon's many treatises – *How I Escaped the Mad-Doctors* (1878) – but does not mention the law cases.
20. *The Times* 1 December 1884, 1d3e.
21. *J. Ment. Sci.*, October 1884, vol. XXX, p. 131.
22. Hodder, *Shaftesbury*, p. 762.
23. *Hansard*, 5 May 1884, vol. CCLXXXVII, col. 1268–9.
24. Report on Winslow v. Semple, *The Times*, 11 July 1884, 11j2f.
25. *Hansard*, 31 January 1887, vol. CCCX, col. 738.
26. *Hansard*, 2 March 1888, vol. CCCXXXIII, col. 7.

CHAPTER 7   STAGNATION

1. Clive Unsworth, *The Politics of Mental Health Legislation*, pp. 19, 33. 80.
2. See H.L.A. Hart, *The Concept of Law*, pp. 27 *et seq.*
3. W.A.F. Browne, *What Asylums Were, Are and Ought to Be*, 1991 edition, ed. Scull, p. 52.
4. *1859 Report* – evidence of Lord Shaftesbury, p. 7.
5. *29th Annual Report of the Commissioners in Lunacy*, 1875 p. 55 and appendix M. See also Sidney Webb, *Grants in Aid: A Criticism and a Proposal*, p. 43.
6. Browne, op. cit., p. 68.
7. Elaine Showalter, *The Female Malady: Women, Madness and English Culture, 1830–1980*, pp. 52–3.
8. Showalter, op. cit., p. 53.
9. *1807 Report* p. 7.
10. John Walton, 'Pauper lunatics in Victorian England', in A.T. Scull (ed.), *Madhouses, Mad-Doctors and Madmen*, pp. 183, 191.
11. Richard Russell, 'The lunacy profession and its staff in the second half of the nineteenth century, with special reference to the West Riding Lunatic Asylum', in Bynum, Porter and Shepherd, op. cit., vol. III, p. 311.
12. David Cochrane, 'Humane, Economical and Medically Wise': the LCC as administrators of Victorian lunacy policy, in Bynum, Porter and Shepherd, op. cit., vol III pp. 247–272.
13. Cochrane, op. cit., p. 262.
14. J. Mortimer Granville, *The Care and Cure of the Insane*, vol. I, p. 120.

15. For a fuller account of the eugenics movement, the Radnor Commission and the Mental Deficiency Act of 1913, see K. Jones, *A History of the Mental Health Services*, pp. 182–225.
16. Personal communication from Dr Alexander Walk (1901–82), Librarian of the Royal Medico-Psychological Association, who held discussions on the subject with several members of the Radnor Commission.
17. On Galton's death in 1911, he bequeathed £45,000 to University College, London for the foundation of the first Chair in Eugenics. His colleague and friend, Karl Pearson, became the first Galton Professor of Eugenics in the same year.
18. R.L. Dugdale, *The Jukes: A Study in Crime, Disease and Heredity*.
19. Arthur H. Estabrook, *The Jukes: A Study in Crime, Pauperism, Disease and Heredity*.
20. H.H. Goddard, *The Kallikak Family*.
21. Mrs Hume Pinsent (later Dame Ellen Pinsent) was a member of the Radnor Commission. Her daughter, the late Lady Adrian, was kind enough to lend me Dame Ellen's papers. These included notes on the Radnor Commission, with several sketches of Juke and Kallikak-type family trees.
22. J. McKeen Cattell, 'Address before the American Psychological Association', *Psychological Review*, vol. III, 2, 1896.
23. See Peter Townsend's introduction to Pauline Morris, *Put Away: A Sociological Study of Institutions for the Mentally Retarded*.
24. William Booth, *In Darkest England: or, The Way Out*.
25. *Report of the Royal Commission on the Care of the Feeble-Minded*, Cd 4215–21 and 4202 (8 vols), 1908.
26. 5th Annual Report of the Board of Control for year 1918.
27. 8th Annual Report of the Board of Control, for year 1921.
28. Report of Annual Conference of the National Association for Mental Health, NAMH 1955.

CHAPTER 8 INTO THE COMMUNITY

1. Trevor Turner, 'Henry Maudsley: psychiatrist, philosopher and entrepreneur', in Bynum, Porter and Shepherd, op. cit., vol. III, pp. 151–89.
2. Patricia Allderidge, 'The foundation of the Maudsley Hospital', in Berrios and Freeman, *150 Years of Psychiatry*, pp. 79–88.
3. 4th Annual Report of the Board of Control for year 1917.
4. Rev. H. Hawkins, 'A plea for convalescent homes in connection with asylums for the insane poor', *J. Ment. Sci.*, vol. XXIII, 1877, pp. 10–16; 'After-Care', *J. Ment. Sci.*, vol. XXV, 1879, pp. 358–67.
5. Presidential Address to the Mental After-Care Association, quoted in MACA information leaflet.
6. Transfer of Powers Order, 1920.

7. 7th Annual Report of the Board of Control, for year 1920.
8. Montague Lomax, *Experiences of an Asylum Doctor.*
9. Ministry of Health, *Report of Departmental Committee on the Administration of Public Mental Hospitals, 1922* (Cobb Report).
10. T. W. Harding, 'Not Worth Powder and Shot': a reappraisal of Montague Lomax's contribution to mental health reform, *B.J. Psychiat.* (1990), vol. 156, 180–7.
11. *Report of the Royal Commission on Lunacy and Mental Disorder, 1924–6*, (Macmillan Report), para. 13.
12. *Macmillan Report*, para. 38.
13. op. cit., paras 38, 39.
14. op. cit., paras 42, 50.
15. op. cit., para. 46.
16. op. cit., paras 43, 48.
17. op. cit., para. 49.
18. op. cit., para. 53.
19. op. cit., para. 104.
20. M. Ashdown and S.C. Browne, *Social Service and Mental Health.*
21. *Hansard*, vol. 237, cols. 2527–600, 11 April 1930.
22. See K. Jones, *The Making of Social Policy*, pp. 104–14.
23. 24th Annual Report of the Board of Control for year 1937, p. 15.
24. 18th Annual Report of the Board of Control for year 1931, p. 12.
25. 19th Annual Report of the Board of Control for year 1932, p. 7.
26. 24th Annual Report of the Board of Control for 1937, pp. 6–7.
27. Ministry of Health, *Report of Committee on the Voluntary Mental Health Services, 1939* (Feversham Report).

CHAPTER 9   A NEW SERVICE FOR A NEW AGE

1. Personal information from Dr Alexander Walk. The *Lancet* had a number of papers and letters on the subject of the psychological effects of warfare in 1939 (vol. 1, 1939, pp. 189, 297, 496, 1163, 1288, 1395), but made no direct reference to this report, and I cannot trace any published references elsewhere. The report was presumably classified information.
2. *Lancet*, 1939, vol. 1, p. 1163.
3. H.V. Dicks, *Fifty Years of the Tavistock Clinic.*
4. Ministry of Health, Ministry of Labour, Ministry of Pensions etc. *Report of Committee on Social Insurance and Allied Services, 1942* (Beveridge Report).
5. *Hansard*, vol. 388, col. 1401, 15 April 1943: written answer to Parliamentary Question from Mr Sorensen.
6. *A National Health Service*, Cmd. 6502, 1944, p. 9.
7. Royal Medico-Psychological Association, British Medical Association,

Royal College of Physicians, *The Future Organization of the Psychiatric Services*, reviewed in the *Lancet*, 16 June 1945. pp. 763–5.

8. Kathleen Jones, 'Problems of mental after-care in Lancashire', *Sociological Review*, July 1954.
9. This section is drawn from K. Jones, 'The culture of the mental hospital', in Berrios and Freeman, *150 Years of Psychiatry*, pp. 17–28.
10. *Hansard*, vol. 523, col. 2293, 19 February 1954.
11. op. cit., col. 2307.
12. op. cit., col. 2371.
13. G.C. Tooth and E.M. Brooke, 'Needs and beds: trends in the mental hospital population and their effect on future planning', *Lancet*, 1 April 1961, pp. 710–13.
14. G.M. Carstairs, 'Advances in psychological medicine', *The Practitioner*, 1961, vol. 187, pp. 495–504.
15. World Health Organization, *Report of Third Expert Committee on Mental Health, 1953*.
16. T.F. Main, 'The hospital as a therapeutic community', *Bulletin of the Menninger Clinic*, X (1946), pp. 66–70.
17. Maxwell Jones, *Social Psychiatry; Social Psychiatry in the Community, in Hospitals and in Prisons; Social Psychiatry in Practice*.
18. W.R. Bion, 'Experiences in groups', *Human Relations*, vols 1–4, 1947–51, published as a book with other papers under the same title.
19. S.H. Foulkes and E.J. Anthony, *Group Psychotherapy: A Psychoanalytic Approach*.
20. R. Rapoport, *Community as Doctor*.
21. W.A.J. Farndale, *The Day Hospital Movement in Great Britain*.
22. J. Bierer, 'A review of modern trends in psychiatry and their consequences for the psychiatric services', in *Proceedings of the Thirteenth International Hospital Congress* Paris, International Hospital Federation, 1963, pp. 161–3.
23. J. Bierer, *Therapeutic Social Clubs*.
24. Milbank Memorial Fund, Proceedings of the Thirty-Sixth Annual Conference, *Steps in the Development of Integrated Psychiatric Services*, p. 18.
25. op. cit. pp. 83–4.
26. Ministry of Health, *Royal Commission on Mental Illness and Mental Disorder, 1954–57*, Minutes of Evidence, Day 3, 16 June 1954, qu. 466, p. 97, question by Mr Hylton-Foster.
27. *Report of Royal Commission on Mental Illness and Mental Disorder, 1959* (Percy Report).
28. *Hansard*, vol. 598, col. 704, 26 January 1959.
29. *Hansard*, vol. 605, cols. 405–6, 6 May 1959.
30. *Hansard*, vol. 438, col. 519, 4 June 1959.

CHAPTER 10   THE IDEOLOGIES OF DESTRUCTION

1. Conservative MPs' analysis, 'The Social Services – needs and means', *The Times*, 17 January 1952, 3c; leading article, 7b. Iain MacLeod and Enoch Powell, *The Social Services – Needs and Means*.

2. For full text, see the Report of the Annual Conference of the National Association for Mental Health, 1961, pp. 4–10.

3. ibid.

4. Ministry of Health Circular HM(61)25, March 1961.

5. G.C. Tooth and E.M. Brooke, 'Needs and beds: trends in the mental hospital population and their effect on future planning', *Lancet*, 1 April 1961, pp. 710–13.

6. R.M. Titmuss, *Commitment to Welfare*, chapter IX, pp. 104–12.

7. A.A. Baker, 'Pulling down the Old Mental Hospital', *Lancet*, 7179, 25 March 1961, pp. 656–7.

8. G.F. Rehin and F.Martin, *Psychiatric Services in 1975*, PEP. (Political and Economic Planning), vol. XXIX, no. 468, 1963.

9. Alan Norton, correspondence, *Lancet*, 25 March 1961, p. 884.

10. Kathleen Jones and Roy Sidebotham, *Mental Hospitals at Work*, pp. 11–21.

11. Ministry of Health, Annual Reports; Jones and Sidebotham, op. cit. pp.18–19, 126–8.

12. Erving Goffman, *Asylums: Essays on the Social Situation of Mental Patients and Other Inmates*.

13. Michel Foucault, *Madness and Civilization*, tr. Richard Howard.

14. T.S. Szasz, *The Myth of Mental Illness: Foundations of a Theory of Personal Conduct*.

15. Goffman, *Asylums*, p. 11.

16. op. cit., p. 20.

17. op. cit., pp. 69–70.

18. op. cit., p. 9.

19. op. cit., p. 305.

20. op. cit., p. 11.

21. Jason Ditton (ed.), *The View from Goffman*, *passim*.

22. Peter Laslett, review in *New Society*, vol. 42, pp. 474–5, 1 December 1977.

23. For a fuller commentary, see Kathleen Jones and A.J. Fowles, *Ideas on Institutions: Analyzing the Literature on Long-term Care and Custody* chapter 2 *passim*.

24. Foucault, *Madness and Civilization*, pp. 33, 35.

25. Alan Sheridan, *Michel Foucault: The Will to Truth*, p. 6.

26. Michel Foucault, *Surveiller et punir*, published as *Discipline and Punish*, tr. Alan Sheridan.

27. René Semelaigne, *Aliénistes et philanthropes: les Pinel et les Tuke*, p. 1 and elsewhere.

28. Foucault, *Madness and Civilization*, pp. 274, 275. A thaumaturge is a wonder-worker.
29. *Naïssance de la clinique*, Presses Universitaires de France, Paris, 1963; published as *The Birth of the Clinic*, tr. Alan Sheridan, p. 38.
30. Foucault, *Birth of the Clinic*, p. 17.
31. Foucault, *Birth of the Clinic*, p. 19.
32. Foucault, *Madness and Civilization*, p. 265.
33. Foucault, *Discipline and Punish*, p. 308.
34. T.S. Szasz, *The Myth of Mental Illness*, p. 182.
35. ibid.
36. Leviticus XVI.
37. Szasz, *The Myth of Mental Illness*, p. 199.
38. op. cit., p. 174.
39. op. cit., pp. 50–64.
40. op., cit. p. 58.
41. T.S. Szasz, *Law, Liberty and Psychiatry: An Inquiry into the Social Uses of Mental Health Practices*, p. 38.
42. T.S. Szasz, *The Manufacture of Madness: A Comparative Study of the Inquisition and the Mental Health Movement*, p. xiii.
43. T.S. Szasz, *The Ethics of Psychoanalysis: The Theory and Methods of Autonomous Psychotherapy*, p. 165.
44. ibid.
45. M. Greenblatt, D.J. Levinson and R.H. Williams, *The Patient and the Mental Hospital*, report of a symposium held by the American Psychological Association in 1954, p. 507, note 1.
46. Jason Ditton, 'A bibliographic exegesis of Goffman's sociology', in J. Ditton (ed.), *The View from Goffman*, pp. 7–11
47. W. Russell Barton, *Institutional Neurosis*. See K. Jones and A.J. Fowles, *Ideas on Institutions*, pp. 71–7.
48. R.D. Laing, *The Divided Self*.

CHAPTER 11   THE DISAPPEARING SERVICES

1. Ministry of Health, *A Hospital Plan for England and Wales*, Cmnd 1604, 1962.
2. William Sargent, Report of Annual Conference, 1961, National Association for Mental Health.
3. F.N. Garratt, C.R. Lowe and T. McKeown, 'Institutional care of the mentally ill', *Lancet*, 29 March 1958, pp. 682–4.
4. Ministry of Health, *Health and Welfare: The Development of Community Care*, Cmnd 1973, 1963.
5. *Hansard* vol. 879, col. 280–1, 7 December 1971. Written answer to Dr Stuttaford.
6. John G. Howells, 'The establishment of the Royal College of Psychia-

trists', in Berrios and Freeman (eds), *150 Years of Psychiatry*, pp. 117–34.

7. Ministry of Health, *Report of Working Party on Social Workers in the Local Authority Health and Welfare Services*, 1959 (Younghusband Report).

8. Interdepartmental report (Ministry of Health, Home Office etc.), *Report of the Committee on Local Authority and Allied Personal Social Services* (Seebohm Report) Cmnd. 3703, 1968, para. 339.

9. *Seebohm Report*, para. 334.

10. Ministry of Health, *Report of Committee on the Organization of Medical Work in Hospitals*, 1967, (Cogwheel Report).

11. Ministry of Health, *Report of Committee on Senior Nurse Staffing Structure*, 1968 (Salmon Report).

12. Jef Smith, 'Top jobs in the Social Services', in Kathleen Jones (ed.) *The Year Book of Social Policy in Britain 1971*, pp. 16–30.

13. Neil Thomas and Brian Stoten, 'The NHS and local government: cooperation or conflict?', in Kathleen Jones (ed.) *The Year Book of Social Policy in Britain 1973*, pp. 48–70.

14. R.D. Laing and A. Esterson, *Sanity, Madness and the Family*; R.D. Laing, *The Politics of Experience and the Bird of Paradise*; David Cooper, *Psychiatry and Anti-psychiatry*; *The Death of the Family*.

15. B. Robb (ed.), *Sans Everything: A Case to Answer*.

16. Ministry of Health, *Findings and Recommendations following Enquiries into Allegations concerning the Care of Elderly Patients in Certain Hospitals*, 1968.

17. K. Jones and A.J. Fowles, *Ideas on Institutions*, pp. 101–8.

18. Stanley Cohen, introduction to *Folk Devils and Moral Panics*.

19. V. Beardshaw, *Conscientious Objectors at Work*; John Martin, *Hospitals in Trouble*.

20. Department of Health and Social Security, *Better Services for the Mentally Ill*, Cmnd. 6233, 1975, foreword by the Secretary of State for the Social Services.

21. Professor Hugh Freeman, *New Society*, vol. 45, p. 709, 26 September 1978.

22. *Better Services for the Mentally Ill*, op. cit., para. 2.19, p. 17.

23. Department of Health and Social Security, *Priorities for Health and Personal Social Services in England: A Consultative Document*, 1976.

24. US Department of Health, Education and Welfare, Joint Commission on Mental Health, *Action for Mental Health*, 1961, p. xxix.

25. ibid.

26. Murray Levine, *The History and Politics of Community Mental Health*; Bernard Bloom, *Community Mental Health: A General Introduction*. For a short introduction, see Kathleen Jones, *Experience in Mental Health* Sage, 1989, pp. 7–29 and 154–55.

27. The President's Commission for Mental Health, *Report to the President*, 1978, p. vii.

28. op. cit., p. 5.
29. op. cit., p. 24.

CHAPTER 12   THE NEW LEGALISM

1. The Audit Commission for Local Authorities in England and Wales, *Making a Reality of Community Care*, 1986, pp. 2–3.
2. Malcolm Lader, *Psychiatry on Trial*.
3. *Hansard* vol. 688, col. 728, 22 March 1982.
4. This poster bears no mark of its origin.
5. *New Society*, vol. 399, p. 863, 21 May 1970.
6. *New Society*, vol. 469, p. 573, 23 Sept. 1971
7. Bruce Ennis and Richard D. Emery, *The Rights of Mental Patients* (ACLU Handbook).
8. The Fifth Amendment refers to federal procedures, and the Fourteenth to state procedures.
9. ACLU Handbook, p. 185.
10. op. cit., p. 57.
11. op. cit., p. 58.
12. Ian Kennedy, *The Unmasking of Medicine*.
13. Kennedy, op. cit., p. 107.
14. See the Mental Health Act 1959, sections 5, 25, 26, 29, 122.
15. This was a British version of the ACLU's rebuttal of the 'thank you theory': that if one saved a mentally ill person from suicide, he or she would subsequently be grateful. The freedom to commit suicide was a major issue in the ACLU campaign.
16. Larry O. Gostin, *A Human Condition: The Mental Health Act from 1959 to 1975: Observations, Analysis and Proposals for Reform*, vol. 1. Vol. 2, published later, dealt with the rights of mental patients of violent or aggressive tendencies, many of them criminal offenders, in the special hospitals (Broadmoor, Rampton and Moss Side), following the recommendations of the Butler Report (Cmd 6244, 1975).
17. Clive Unsworth, *The Politics of Mental Health Legislation*, p. 4.
18. Larry O. Gostin, *Is It Fair? The Mental Health Act, 1959*, p. 37.
19. Gostin, *Is It Fair?*, p. 3.
20. Robert Bluglass, *A Guide to the Mental Health Act 1983*.
21. Lady Bingley, Chairman of MIND, foreword to Gostin, *A Human Condition*, vol. 1.
22. Gostin, *Is It Fair?*, p. 3.
23. Unsworth, op. cit., p. 4.
24. Ministry of Health, *Review of the Mental Health Act 1959*, Cmnd 7320, 1978.
25. *New Society* vol. 56, p. 18, 2 April 1981.
26. Rolf Olsen, 'The case for giving more rights to the mentally ill', *New Society*, vol. 59, pp. 347–8, 4 March 1982.

27. *New Society*, vol. 47, p. 425, 26 Feb. 1979.
28. M.A. Beedie and R. Bluglass, 'Consent to psychiatric treatment: practical implications of the Mental Health (Amendment) Bill', *British Medical Journal* vol. 284, pp. 1613–16).
29. Jeremy Laurance, *New Society*, vol. 61, p. 25, 8 July 1982
30. Kenneth Rawnsley, foreword to Robert Bluglass, *A Guide to the Mental Health Act 1983*.
31. *Hansard*, vol. 20, col. 688, 22 March 1982.
32. Larry O. Gostin, *A Practical Guide to Mental Health Law: The Mental Health Act 1983 and Related Legislation*; Brenda Hoggett, *Mental Health Law*; Richard Jones, *The Mental Health Act 1983*, (an annotated edition of the Act); Robert Bluglass, *A Guide to the Mental Health Act 1983*; Rolf Olsen (ed.) *Social Work and Mental Health: A Guide for the Approved Social Worker*.
33. Bluglass, *A Guide to the Mental Health Act*, p. 38.
34. Gostin, *A Practical Guide to Mental Health Law*, p. 48.
35. First Biennial Report of the Mental Health Act Commission, 1986.
36. See Rolf Olsen (ed.) *Social Work and Mental Health: A Guide for the Approved Social Worker*.
37. Gostin, *A Practical Guide to Mental Health Law*, p. 75.
38. See Kenneth Minogue, in E. Kamenka and A.E. S. Tay, *Human Rights* pp. 15–31.

CHAPTER 13   DISTRACTIONS AND PLACEBOS

1. Wolf Wolfensberger *et al.*, *The Principle of Normalization in Human Services*, p. 27.
2. ibid
3. op. cit., p. 28.
4. op. cit., pp. 118–19.
5. op. cit., p. 118.
6. op. cit., p. 115.
7. Sue Szivos, 'The limits to integration?' in Hilary Brown and Helen Smith, *Normalization: A Reader for the Nineties*, p. 127.
8. C. Heptinstall, 'Psichiatrica Democratica: Italy's revolution in caring for the mentally ill', *Community Care*, 1 March 1984 pp 17–19.
9. C. Hanvey, 'Italy and the rise of democratic psychiatry', *Community Care*, 25 October 1978 pp 22–4.
10. Shulamit Ramon, 'The Italian job', *Social Work Today*, 14 December 1982, p. 14.
11. Ron Lacey, 'Where have all the patients gone?', *Guardian*, 4 July 1982.
12. Kathleen Jones and Alison Poletti, 'Understanding the Italian experience', *B. J. Psychiat.* vol. 146, 1985, pp. 341–7; 'The Italian experience reconsidered', *B. J. Psychiat.*, vol. 148, 1986, pp. 144–50. The 1986 study was funded by the British Academy.

13. Franco Basaglia, 'Problems of law and psychiatry: the Italian experience', Report of Fourth Congress on Law and Psychiatry, *International Journal of Law and Psychiatry*, 1980, vol. 3, p. 17.
14. *Better Services for the Mentally Ill*, Cmnd 6233, 1975, para. 1.31.
15. DHSS, *Joint Care Planning: Health and Local Authorities*, Circular HC (77) 17, LAC (77) 10, 1977.
16. DHSS, Central Health Services Council/Personal Social Services Council, *Collaboration in Community Care: A Discussion Document*, 1978, pp. 48–9.
17. Hugo Young, *One of Us: A Biography of Margaret Thatcher*, pp. 330, 377, 434, 499, 538–9.
18. DHSS, *Care in Action: A Handbook of Policies and Priorities for the Health and Personal Social Services in England*, DHSS, 1981, Secretary of State's introduction.
19. Patrick Jenkin, Secretary of State for the Social Services, address to chairmen and members of the newly formed District Health Authorities, 1981, reported in *Social Work Today*, 10 March 1981, p. 10.
20. *Social Work Today*, editorial comment, 10 March 1981.
21. House of Commons: second report from the Social Services Committee, session 1984–5: *Community Care with Special Reference to Adult Mentally Ill and Mentally Handicapped People*, vol. 1: *Report together with Proceedings of the Committee*, p. ii.
22. op. cit., paras 8 and 9.
23. op. cit., para. 13.
24. op. cit., para. 18.
25. op. cit., para 162.
26. op. cit., para. 163.
27. op. cit., para. 30.
28. op. cit., para. 26.
29. op. cit., para. 27.
30. op. cit., para. 223.
31. op. cit. para. 210.
32. John Burrell, *The Psychiatric Hospital as a New Community*; see also John Burrell, 'Taking the people to the patients', *The Times*, 16 December 1986; Kathleen Jones, *Mental Hospital Closures: The Way Forward?*
33. DHSS, *Government Response to the Second Report from the Social Services Committee, 1984–85 Session: Community Care with Special Reference to Adult Mentally Ill and Mentally Handicapped People*, Cmnd 9674, 1985, para. 3.
34. *Government Response*, para. 4.
35. *Government Response*, para. 9.
36. The Audit Commission for Local Authorities in England and Wales, *Making a Reality of Community Care*, Summary, p. 1.

37. *Audit Commission Report*, para. 17.
38. op. cit., Exhibit 4, p. 21 and paras 36–37.
39. op. cit., paras 72, 87–96 and Exhibit 11, p. 111.
40. DHSS, Sir Roy Griffiths, *Community Care: Agenda for Action: A Report to the Secretary of State for Social Services* (Griffiths Report): Letter to Secretary of State, para. 9, p. iv. .
41. *Griffiths Report*, para. 7.
42. op. cit., para. 25.
43. op. cit., para. 23.
44. op. cit., para. 26.
45. op. cit., para. 28.
46. Interdepartmental report: Secretaries of State for Health, Social Security, Wales and Scotland, *Caring for People: Community Care in the Next Decade and Beyond: Caring for the 1990s*, Cm 849, 1989, introduction.
47. *Caring for People*, op. cit., paras. 7.1–7.23.
48. op. cit., para. 7.5.
49. op. cit., para. 7.10.
50. op. cit., para. 7.1.
51. op. cit., para. 3.1. 3.
52. op. cit., para. 2.4.
53. Department of Health, *The Health of the Nation: Key Area Handbook – Mental Illness*, January 1993, p. 1.
54. op. cit., p. 11.
55. op. cit., p. 28.
56. op. cit., p. 29.
57. op. cit., pp. 33–42.
58. op. cit. pp. 127–30.
59. op. cit., pp. 49–53.
60. op. cit., pp. 57–64.
61. Good Practices in Mental Health, *Community Mental Health Teams/ Centres: Information Pack*.
62. John Black, *User Involvement in Mental Health Services: An Annotated Bibliography*; Althea and David Brandon, *Consumers as Colleagues*.
63. Marinus P. Klinsma, 'Patient Advocacy in the Netherlands', *Psychiatric Bulletin*, 17, 4, pp. 230–1, April 1993.
64. Anny Brackx and Catherine Grimshaw (eds), *Mental Health Care in Crisis*; Liz Sayce, *Waiting for Community Care*.
65. *NSF Today, NSF News* and other publications of the National Schizophrenia Fellowship.
66. Marjorie Wallace, *The Forgotten Illness*.
67. *Sunday Times Magazine* 3 May 1987.

CHAPTER 14   CONSEQUENCES

1. Correspondence from Sarah Steele in the *Independent*, 5 January 1993.
2. Comments taken from reports in the *The Times, Guardian* and *Independent*, 5 January 1993. Policy is increasingly explained to the public on television, which makes accurate documentation difficult. In this case, the reports in the serious newspapers are very similar, and the commentaries were on the whole responsible and well informed.
3. British Medical Association *News Review*, December 1992.
4. Bryan Silcock, 'Which way for Community Care?', *Sunday Times* News Review, 10 January 1993, p. 5.
5. *Government Statistical Services*, Cmnd. 8236, 1981, Annexe 2, para. 17.
6. Proposal from Sir Claus Moser, former head of Government Statistical Services, and Sir David Cox, former President of the Royal Statistical Society, reported in the *Independent* 9 October 1989.
7. S.R. Hirsch, 'Services for the severely mentally ill: a planning blight', *Psychiatric Bulletin* (1992), vol. 16, p. 673.
8. Julian Leff (ed.), 'The TAPS Project:' evaluating community placement of long-stay psychiatric patients, *British Journal of Psychiatry*, vol. 162, Supplement, 19 April 1993.
9. Department of Health, press release H93/698, 14 April 1993.
10. Abridged version reported in Kathleen Jones and Hugh Freeman, (eds), *Community Care and Schizophrenia: The Need for Social Research*, 1993, pp. 23–6.
11. Kathleen Jones, *After Hospital: a Study of Long-Term Psychiatric Patients in York*. Summary in K. Jones, *Experience in Mental Health*, pp. 107–28.
12. Alvin Schorr, *The Personal Social Services: an outside view*, pp. 46, 47.
13. House of Commons, Select Committee on Health, *Community Care: Funding from April 1993*, March 1993.
14. Department of Health ref. RDL/3/93, dated 1 March 1993.
15. Kathryn Ellis, *Squaring the Circle: User and Carer Participation in Needs Assessment*, February 1993, pp. 19–22.

Bibliography

PUBLIC GENERAL STATUTES

43 Eliz. c.2	Poor Law Act 1601
12 Anne(2) c.23	
[13 Anne c.26]	Vagrancy Act 1714
17 Geo. II c.5	Vagrancy Act 1744
14 Geo. III c.9	Act for Regulating Private Madhouses 1744
48 Geo. III c.96	County Asylums Act 1808 amended by:
	51 Geo. III c.79 [1811]
	55 Geo. III c.4 [1815]
	59 Geo. III c.127 [1819]
9 Geo. IV c.40	County Asylums Act 1828
9 Geo. IV. c.41	Madhouse Act 1828
2 and 3 Will. IV c.107	Lunatics Act 1832
4 and 5 Will. IV c.76	Poor Law Amendment Act 1834
5 and 6 Vict. c.87	Lunatic Asylums Act 1842
8 and 9 Vict. c.100	Lunatics Act 1845
16 and 17 Vict. c.70	Lunacy Regulation Act 1853
16 and 17 Vict. c.96	Lunatics Care and Treatment Amendment Act 1853
16 and 17 Vict. c.97	Lunatic Asylums Amendment Act 1853
25 and 26 Vict. c.111	Lunatics Law Amendment Act 1862
45 and 46 Vict. c.75	Married Women's Property Act 1882
49 and 50 Vict. c. 41	Idiots Act 1886
52 and 53 Vict. c.41	Lunatics Law Amendment Act 1889
53 Vict. c.5	Lunacy (Consolidation) Act 1890
54 and 55 Vict. c.65	Lunacy Act 1891
3 and 4 Geo. V c.28	Mental Deficiency Act 1913

19 Geo. V c.17	Local Government Act 1929
20 and 21 Geo. V c.23	Mental Treatment Act 1930
9 and 20 Geo. VI c.81	National Health Service Act 1946
7 and 8 Eliz. II c.72	Mental Health Act 1959
18 and 19 Eliz. II c.42	Local Authority Social Services Act 1970
30 and 31 Eliz. II c. 5	Mental Health Amendment Act 1982
31 and 32 Eliz. II c. 20	Mental Health Act 1983

OFFICIAL PAPERS

(Published by HM Stationery Office, London)

Parliamentary Papers

Hansard's Parliamentary Debates, 1804 to date.
House of Commons Journal.
House of Lords journal.
House of Commons: Select Committee reports
  on Private Madhouses in this Kingdom, 1763. House of Commons
  reprints, vol. 25, pp. 3–11.
All the subsequent Select Committee reports on the subject before 1890 are
contained in the Mental Health volumes of the Irish University Series of
Parliamentary Papers:
  on Madhouses, 1763.
  on Criminal and Pauper Lunatics, 1807.
  on Madhouses, 1815 (3 reports published May–July and subsequently
  reprinted in one volume)
  on Madhouses, 1816 (3 reports published April–June, and subsequently
  bound as one volume)
  on Pauper Lunatics in the County of Middlesex, and on Lunatic
  Asylums, 1827.
  on the Poor Law Amendment Act of 1834, 1836 (Irish University Series,
  Poor Law, 3 vols).
  on Lunatics, 1859–60
  on the Operation of the Lunacy Laws, 1877–8
  on Community Care: Funding from April 1993, March 1993.

Royal Commissions

Reports:
  on the Administration and Practical Operation of the Poor Law, 1834.
  on the Care and Control of the Feeble-minded, 8 vols, minutes of
  evidence Cd 4215–4202, Report Cd 4202, 1908 (Radnor Report).
  on the Poor Laws, Cmd 4499, 1909
  on Lunacy and Mental Disorder, Cmd. 2700, 1926 (Macmillan Report).

on the Laws relating to Mental Illness and Mental Deficiency, Cmnd 169, 1957 (Percy Report).

on Medical Education, Cmnd 3569, 1968 (Todd Report)

World Health Organization

Report of Third Expert Committee on Mental Health, Technical Report Series no. 73, 1953.

Central Statistical Office

Annual Abstract of Statistics (from 1935).
Social Trends (annual from 1970).

General Register Office

Registrar-General's Statistical Review: Supplements on Mental Health, 1952–3, 1954–6, 1957–8, 1959, 1960.
Studies on Medical and Population Subjects, no. 16: Area of residence of Mental Hospital Patients: admissions to mental hospitals in England and Wales in 1957 according to area of residence, diagnosis, sex and age, 1962.
Studies on Medical and Population Subjects, no. 18: A Cohort Study of Patients first admitted to mental hospitals in 1954 and 1955, by E.M. Brooke, 1963.

Ministry of Health (1919–69)

Annual Reports.
A National Health Service, Cmnd 6502, 1944.
Central Health Services Council, *Report on Co-operation between Hospital, Local Authority and Practitioner Services*, 1952 (Messer Report)
Health and Welfare: The Development of Community Care, Cmnd 1973, 1963 and subsequent revisions.
A Hospital Plan for England and Wales, Cmnd 1604, 1962.

Departmental committees, working parties, reports:
on the Administration of Public Mental Hospitals, 1922 (Cobb Report).
on Sterilization, 1934 (Brock Report).
on the Voluntary Mental Health Services, 1939 (Feversham Report).
on Social Workers in the Mental Health Services, Cmnd 8260, 1951 (Mackintosh Report).
on Co-operation between Hospital, Local Authority and Practitioner Services, 1952 (Central Health Services Council, Messer Report).
on Medical Staffing Structure in the Hospital Service, 1961 (Platt Report).
on Senior Nursing Staff Structure, 1966 (Salmon Report).
on the Organization of Medical Work in Hospitals, 1967 (Cogwheel Report).

on Social Workers in the Local Authority Health and Welfare Services, 1959 (Younghusband Report).

on Findings and Recommendations following Enquiries into Allegations concerning the Care of Elderly Patients in Certain Hospitals, 1968.

Interdepartmental Committees, reports:
on Social Insurance and Allied Services, Cmd 6404, 1942 (Beveridge Report). (Joint publication with Ministry of Labour, Ministry of Pensions, etc.).

on *Local Authority and Allied Personal Social Services*, Cmnd 3703, 1968 (Seebohm Report) (Joint publication with Home Office, Department of Education and Science, Ministry of Housing and Local Government).

on *Collaboration in Community Care: A Discussion Document*, 1978. (Department of Health and Social Security, Central Health Services Council, Personal Social Services Council).

Department of Health and Social Security (1969–89)

Allegations of Ill-treatment of Patients and other Irregularities at the Ely Hospital, Cardiff: Report of Committee of Inquiry, Cmnd 3795, 1971.
Farleigh Hospital, Report of Committee of Inquiry, Cmnd 4557, 1971.
Whittingham Hospital, Report of Committee of Inquiry, Cmnd 4861, 1972
Better Services for the Mentally Ill, Cmnd 6233, 1975.
Priorities for Health and Personal Social Services in England: A Consultative Document, 1976.
Review of the Mental Health Act 1959, Cmnd 7320, HMSO, 1978.
Collaboration in Community Care: A Discussion Document, 1978 (Central Health Services Council/ Personal Social Services Council).
Government Response to the Second Report from the Social Services Committee, 1984–85 Session: Community Care with Special Reference to Adult Mentally Ill and Mentally Handicapped People, Cmnd 9674, HMSO, November 1985, para. 3.
Community Care: Agenda for Action: a report to the Secretary of State for Social Services, March 1988 (Griffiths Report).

Circulars
HM (61) 25, March 1961.
Joint Care Planning: Health and Local Authorities, Circular HC (77) 17, LAC (77) 10, 1977.

Statistical Report Series
no. 3: The Activities of Psychiatric Hospitals: A Regional Comparison (Mental Hospitals and Units, 1964).
no. 4: Psychiatric Hospitals and Units in England and Wales: Inpatient

Statistics from the Mental Health Enquiry for the years 1964, 1965 and 1966.

no. 5: Psychiatric Hospitals and Units in England and Wales: In-patient Statistics from the Mental Health Enquiry, 1967.

no. 6: Facilities and Services of Psychiatric Hospitals, 1967.

no. 7: Pilot Survey of Patients attending Day Hospitals, 1967.

no. 8: A Psychiatric Case Register, 1969.

no. 9: Facilities and Services of Psychiatric Hospitals in England and Wales, 1968.

no. 10: Facilities and Services of Psychiatric Hospitals in England and Wales, 1969.

no. 11: Psychiatric Hospitals and Units in England and Wales: In-patient statistics for 1968.

no. 12: Psychiatric Hospitals in England and Wales: In-patient statistics for 1969.

no. 13: Nottingham Case Register: Findings 1962–9.

Department of Health (from 1989)

Care in Action: A Handbook of Policies and Priorities for the Health and Personal Social Services in England, 1981.

Caring for People: Community Care in the Next Decade and Beyond: Caring for the 1990s, Cm 849, November 1989 (Secretaries of State for Health, Social Security, Wales and Scotland).

The Health of the Nation July 1992.

Key Area Handbook: Mental Illness, January 1993.

Lunacy Commissioners

Annual Reports of the Metropolitan Commissioners in Lunacy, 1830–43.

Report to the Lord Chancellor, 1844.

Annual Reports of the Lunacy Commissioners, 1845–1912.

Board of Control:

Annual Reports, 1914–59.

Colonies for Mental Defectives, 1931.

Conference on the Mental Treatment Act, 1930.

Hypoglycaemic Shock Treatment in Schizophrenia, 1936.

Pre-frontal Leucotomy in 1,000 Cases, 1947.

Suggestions and Instructions for the arrangement of . . . mental hospitals, 1940.

Poor Law Commission

Annual Reports, 1835- 47.
Official Circulars (Poor Law Commission and Poor Law Board) 1835–54,
2 vols.

UNPUBLISHED PAPERS

Cornwall Asylum, records and minute books.
Eugenics Education Society, minutes of Council, 1907–12.
Lancaster Asylum, records and minute books.
Manchester Royal Infirmary and Royal Lunatic Hospital, records and
minute books.
Nottingham Asylum, records and minute books.
Pinsent, Dame Ellen, private papers.
Stafford Asylum, records, minute books and case-papers.
The Retreat, York: records, minute books, case-books, Visiters' Book.
Thane, Lectures of Sir George Thane, Professor of Anatomy in the
University of London, 1877–1919. Notes taken by Dr H.A. Harris, no date.

JOURNALS

Administration in Mental Health (USA)
Asylum Journal/Journal of Mental Science/British Journal of Psychiatry
Biometrika
British Journal of Social and Preventive Medicine
British Medical Journal
Community Care
Comprehensive Psychiatry
Edinburgh Quarterly
Gentleman's Magazine
Hospital and Community Care (USA)
Hospital and Social Services Journal
Human Relations
International Journal of Social Psychiatry
Lancet
Mental Health/MIND/MINDOUT/OPENMIND
Mental Hygiene (USA)
New Society
Practitioner
Social Problems (USA)
Social Work Today
Westminster Review

BOOKS AND ARTICLES

(Published in London unless otherwise stated)

Action for Mental Health (USA), see Joint Commission on Mental Health.

Alexander, F., and Selesnick, S., *The History of Psychiatry*, Mentor Books, New York, 1966.

Allderidge, Patricia, 'Management and mismanagement at Bedlam, 1547–1633' in Charles Webster (ed.) *Health, Medicine and Morality in the Sixteenth Century*, Cambridge University Press, 1979.

—— 'Bedlam: fact or fantasy?', in W.F. Bynum, Roy Porter and Michael P Shepherd (eds) *The Anatomy of Madness: Essays in the History of Psychiatry*, vol. II, Tavistock, 1985, pp. 17–33.

—— 'The foundation of the Maudsley Hospital' in G. Berrios and H. Freeman, *150 Years of British Psychiatry, 1841–1991*, pp. 79–88.

Alleged Lunatics Friend Society, Annual Report, 1851.

American Civil Liberties Union: Bruce Ennis and Richard C. Emery, *The Rights of Mental Patients*, 1977, based on *The Basic ACLU Guide to a Mental Patient's Rights*, Discus/Avon, Basic Books, New York, 1973.

Andrews, Jonathan, 'In her Vapours . . . [or] in her Madness? Mrs. Clerke's case: an early eighteenth century psychiatric controversy', *History of Psychiatry*, vol. 1, part 1, no. 1, March 1990, pp. 125–144.

—— 'Bedlam revisited: a history of Bethlem Hospital *c*.1634–*c*. 1770', Ph.D. thesis, University of London, 1991.

Anon., 'An Account of several Workhouses in Great Britain in the year 1732, shewing their original Number and the particular Management of them at the above Period. With many useful Remarks on the state of the Poor', 3rd edn, 1786.

Apte, R.Z., *Half-way Houses*, Bell, 1968.

Ashdown, M., and Brown, S. Clement, *Social Service and Mental Health*, Routledge and Kegan Paul, 1953.

Aspinall, A., *Politics and the Press, 1780–1850*, Home and Van Thal, 1949.

Association for Psychiatric Social Workers, *Training for Social Work*, no date, probably early 1950s.

Atlay, J.B., *The Victorian Chancellors*, Smith, Elder, 1906–1908.

Aubrey, John, *A Natural History of Wiltshire* (written 1656–91), ed. Britton, pub. by the Wiltshire Topographical Society, 1847.

Audit Commission for Local Authorities in England and Wales, *Making a Reality of Community Care*, HMSO, December 1986.

Baines, E., *History, Directory and Gazeteer of the County of York*, Leeds Mercury Office, Leeds, 1823.

Baker, A.A., 'Pulling down the old mental hospital', *Lancet*, 25 March 1961, pp. 656–7.

Baldwin, J.A., *The Mental Hospital in the Psychiatric Service*, Oxford University Press, 1971.

Barton, W. Russell, *Institutional Neurosis*, Wright, Bristol, 1959.

Basaglia, Franco, 'Problems of law and psychiatry: the Italian experience', Report of Fourth Congress on Law and Psychiatry, *International Journal of Law and Psychiatry*, 1980, vol. 3, pp. 17–37.

Battie, William, *A Treatise on Madness*, J. Whiston and B. White, 1758.

Beardshaw, V., *Conscientious Objectors at Work*, Social Audit, 1981.

Becker, Howard (ed.), *The Other Side: Perspectives on Deviance*, Free Press, Glencoe, Illinois, 1964.

Beedie, M.A., and Bluglass, R., 'Consent to psychiatric treatment: practical implications of the Mental Health (Amendment) Bill', *British Medical Journal*, vol. 284, pp. 1613–16).

Bentham, J., *Letters on the Management of the Poor*, Dublin, 1796 (includes the *Panopticon*). See also Bowring.

Berrios, German, and Freeman, Hugh (eds), *150 Years of British Psychiatry, 1841–1991*, Royal College of Psychiatrists/Gaskell, 1991.

Bethlem Hospital, *Brochure* prepared for the official opening of the new buildings, July 1930.

—— *Charters of the Royal Hospitals of Bridewell and Bethlem*, 1807.

—— *Sketches in Bedlam*, by A Constant Observer, Sherwood, Jones, 1823.

Bettelle, M., *Rapport au Conseil Général des Hospices de Paris sur les établissements aliénés d'Angleterre, et sur ceux de Bicêtre et de la Salpétrière*, Paris, 1848.

Bierer, Joshua, *The Day Hospital*, H.K. Lewis, 1951.

—— *Therapeutic Social Clubs*, no date, probably early 1950s.

—— 'A review of modern trends in psychiatry and their consequences for the psychiatric services', in *Proceedings of the Thirteenth International Hospital Congress* Paris, International Hospital Federation, 1963, pp. 161–3.

Bion, W.R., 'Experiences in groups', *Human Relations*, vols 1–4, 1947–51, published as a book with other papers under the same title, Tavistock,1961.

Black, John, *User Involvement in Mental Health Services: An Annotated Bibliography*, Department of Social Policy and Social Work, University of Birmingham, 1992.

Blacker, C.P., *Neurosis and the Mental Health Services*, Oxford University Press, 1946.

Bloom, Bernard, *Community Mental Health: A general Introduction*, Brooks/Cole Publishing Co., Monterey, California, 1977.

Bluglass, Robert, *A Guide to the Mental Health Act 1983*, Churchill Livingstone, Edinburgh, 1983. (See also Beedie and Bluglass.)

Booth, William, *In Darkest England: or, The Way Out*, Salvation Army, 1890.

Bosanquet, H., *Social Work in London: A History of the Charity Organization Society*, Murray, 1914.

Bowley, A.L., *Wages in the United Kingdom in the Nineteenth Century*, Cambridge University Press, 1900.

Bowring, J. (ed.) *The Works of Jeremy Bentham*, Tait, Edinburgh, 1843.

Brackx, Anny, and Grimshaw, Catherine (eds), *Mental Health Care in Crisis*, Pluto, 1989.

Brandon, Althea, and Brandon, David, *Consumers as Colleagues*, MIND, 1987.

Bristol Corporation of the Poor. (See Butcher.)

Brockbank, E.M., *A Short History of Cheadle Royal from its Foundation in 1766*, Sherratt and Hughes, Manchester, 1934.

Brooke, E.M. (See General Register Office; Tooth and Brooke.)

Brooke, John, *King George III*, Constable, 1972.

Brown, G.W., and Wing, J.K., 'A comprehensive clinical and social survey of three mental hospitals', *Sociological Review Monograph no. 5*, July 1962.

Browne, W.A.F., *What Asylums Were, Are, and Ought to Be*, Adam and Charles Black, Edinburgh, 1837. Reprint A.T. Scull (ed.) *The Asylum as Utopia: W.A.F. Browne and the Mid-Nineteenth Century Consolidation of Psychiatry*, Tavistock/Routledge, 1991.

Buckingham and Chandos, Duke of, *Memoirs of the Court of George III*, Hurst and Blackett, 1853, vol. I, p. 170.

Bucknill, J.C., 'An open letter to Samuel Trehawke Kekewich, Esq., MP', *Journal of Mental Science*, vol. V, pp. 421–430, April 1859.

Burrell, John, *The Psychiatric Hospital as a New Community*, Burrell-Foley Associates, 15 Monmouth Street, Covent Garden, London WC2H 9DA.

—— 'Taking the people to the patients', *The Times*, 16 December 1986.

Burrows, G.M., *Commentaries on the Causes, Forms, Symptoms and Treatment Moral and Medical, of Insanity*, Underwood, London, 1828.

Burton, Robert, *The Anatomy of Melancholy*, 1621, ed. Floyd Dell and Paul Jordan-Smith, Tudor Publishing Company, New York, 1955.

Busfield, Joan, *Managing Madness: Changing Ideas and Practice*, Hutchinson, 1986.

Butcher, E.E. (ed.), *Bristol Corporation of the Poor: Selected Records 1696–1834*, Bristol Record Society Publications (1932), reprinted Bristol Branch of the Historical Association, Bristol, 1972.

Bynum, W.F., 'Tuke's Dictionary and psychiatry at the turn of the century', in G.E. Berrios and H. Freeman (eds), *150 Years of British Psychiatry, 1841–1991*, Royal College of Psychiatrists, 1991.

Bynum, W.F., Porter, Roy and Shepherd, Michael, *The Anatomy of Madness: Essays in the History of Psychiatry*, Tavistock, vol. I, *People and Ideas*, 1985; vol. II, *Institutions and Society*, 1985; vol. III, *The Asylum and its Psychiatry*, 1987.

Carse, Joshua, *The Worthing Experiment*, Graylingwell Hospital, Sussex, 1958.

Carstairs, G.M., 'Advances in psychological medicine', *The Practitioner* Symposium on Advances in Treatment, no. 1, 1961, vol. 187, pp. 495–504.

Cartwright, Anne, *Human Relations and Hospital Care*, Routledge and Kegan Paul, 1964.

Cattell, J. McKeen, Address before the American Psychological Association, *Psychological Review*, vol. III, 2, 1896.

Chaplin, A., *Medicine during the Reign of George II*, Fitzpatrick Lecture, Royal College of Physicians, 1919.

Charlesworth, E.P., *Considerations on the Management of Insane Persons*, Rivington, 1828.

Cheyne, George, *The English Malady, or, A Treatise of Nervous Disorders of All Kinds*, Strahan, 1733.

Clark, David H., *Administrative Psychiatry*, Tavistock, 1964.

Clarke, Sir J., *Memoir of Dr Conolly*, Murray, 1869.

Cochrane, David, 'Humane, economical and medically wise: the LCC as administrators of Victorian lunacy policy', in Bynum, Porter and Shepherd, op. cit., pp. 247–72.

Cohen, Stanley, *Folk Devils and Moral Panics*, Martin Robertson, Oxford, 1972.

Conolly, John, *An Inquiry Concerning the Indications of Insanity, with suggestions for the Better Protection and Care of the Insane*, Taylor, 1830.

—— *On the Treatment of the Insane without Mechanical Restraints*, 1858. Facsimile edition, intro. R. Hunter and I. Macalpine, Dawsons of Pall Mall, 1973.

Cooper, David, *Psychiatry and Anti-psychiatry*, Tavistock, 1967.

—— *The Death of the Family*, Allen Lane, Penguin, 1971.

Conservative MPs' analysis: 'The Social Services – needs and means. *The Times*, 17 January 1952, 17j3c; leading article, 7b.

Constant Observer, *Sketches in Bedlam*, Sherwood Jones, 1823.

Crowther, Bryan, *Practical Remarks on Insanity, to which is added a commentary on the dissection of the brains of maniacs, with some account of diseases incident to the insane*, Underwood, 1811.

Crowther, Caleb, *Observations on the Management of Madhouses*, Simpkin Marshall, 1838.

Dain, Norman, *Concepts of Insanity in the United States, 1789–1865*, Rutgers University Press, 1964.

David, Henry C., *International Trends in Mental Health*, McGraw-Hill, New York, 1964.

Deutsch, Albert, *The Mentally Ill in America*, Columbia University Press, New York, 1937.

Dicks, H. V., *Fifty Years of the Tavistock Clinic*, Routledge and Kegan Paul, 1970.

Digby, Anne, 'Moral Treatment at the Retreat, 1796–1846', in Bynum, Porter and Shepherd (eds) op. cit., 1985, pp 53–55.

——*Madness, Morality and Medicine: A Study of the York Retreat*, Cambridge University Press, 1985.

Ditton, Jason (ed.), *The View from Goffman*, Macmillan, 1980.

Dugdale, R.L., *The Jukes: A Study in Crime, Disease and Heredity*, 1877. 4th edition, Putnam, New York, 1910.

Eden, Sir Frederick, *The State of the Poor, or, A History of the Labouring Classes in England*, etc., 1797, 3 vols.

Ellis, Kathryn, *Squaring the Circle: User and Carer Participation in Needs Assessment*, Joseph Rowntree Foundation, York, 1993

Ellis, Sir William C., *A Letter to Thomas Thompson, Esq., containing Considerations on the Necessity of Proper Places being provided by the Legislature for the reception of all Insane Persons*, Hull, 1815.

——*A Treatise on the Nature, Causes, Symptoms and Treatment of Insanity* Holdsworth, 1838.

Elwin, Malcolm, *Charles Reade: A Biography*, Jonathan Cape, 1931.

English and Empire Digest (Law Reports), Butterworth, London, 1919.

English Reports (Law Reports), Black, Edinburgh, 1900–32.

Ennis, Bruce and Emery, Richard D., *The Rights of Mental Patients*, 1977. (see American Civil Liberties Union.

Epistle to Mr Ewart, MP. see Hanwell.

Estabrook, A.H., *The Jukes in 1915*, Carnegie Institute of Washington, DC, 1916.

Eugenics Education Society, Annual Reports, 1926–54.

Farndale, W.A.J., *The Day Hospital Movement in Great Britain*, Pergamon, Oxford, 1961.

——(ed.), *Trends in the National Health Service*, Pergamon, Oxford, 1964. (See also Freeman and Farndale).

Ferriar, John, *Medical Histories and Reflections*, Cadell and Davies, 1810.

Finer, S.E., *The Life and Times of Sir Edwin Chadwick*, Methuen 1952.

Flinn, M.W., *British Population Growth 1700–1859*, Macmillan, 1973.

Foucault, Michel, *Folie et déraison: histoire de la folie à l'âge classique*, Plon, Paris, 1961. English version – *Madness and Civilization: A History of Insanity in the Age of Reason*, trans. Richard Howard, Pantheon, New York, 1965, and Tavistock 1967.

——*Surveiller et punir: naïssance de la prison*, Gallimard, Paris, 1975. English version – *Discipline and Punish: The Birth of the Prison*, trans. Alan Sheridan, Allen Lane, 1977.

——*Naïssance de la Clinique*, Presses Universitaires de France, Paris,

1963. English version – *The Birth of the Clinic*, trans. Alan Sheridan, Tavistock, 1976.

Foulkes, S.H. and Anthony, E., *Group Psychotherapy: The Psychoanalytic Approach*, Pelican, 1957.

Freeman, Hugh (ed.), *Psychiatric Hospital Care*, Ballière, Tindall and Cox, 1964.

—— and Farndale, W.A.J. (eds), *Trends in the Mental Health Services*, Pergamon, Oxford, 1963.

—— and Farndale, W.A.J. (eds), *New Aspects of the Mental Health Services*, Pergamon, Oxford, 1967.

Galton, Sir Francis, *Hereditary Genius*, 1869, reprint Watts, 1950.

Gardiner Hill. (See Hill, R. Gardiner.)

Garratt, F.N., Lowe, C.R., and McKeown, T., 'The institutional care of the mentally ill', *Lancet*, 29 March 1958, pp. 682–4.

—— 'Investigation of the medical and social needs of patients in mental hospitals', *Br. J. Prev. Soc. Med.*, vol. 11, no. 4, October 1957; vol. 12, no. 1, January 1958.

Gerard, James, and others, *An Address to the Magistrates of the County Lancaster on the Situation Proposed for the Intended County Lunatic Asylum*, Liverpool, 1810.

Goddard, H.H., *The Kallikak Family*, Macmillan, New York, 1912.

Godlee, Fiona, 'Aspects of non-conformity: Quakers and the lunatic fringe', in Bynum, Porter and Shepherd, op. cit., vol. II, pp. 73–85.

Goffman, Erving, *Asylums: Essays on the Social Situation of Mental Patients and Other Inmates*, Anchor Books/Doubleday, New York, 1961.

Gooch, G.P., *History and Historians in the Nineteenth Century*, Longman, 1913.

Good Practices in Mental Health, *Community Mental Health Teams/Centres Information Pack*, no date, early 1990s. Obtainable from GPMH, 380–384 Harrow Road, London W9 2HU.

Gore, C.P., Jones, K., Taylor, W., and Ward, B., 'Needs and beds: a regional census of psychiatric patients', *Lancet*, 24 August 1964, pp. 457–60.

Gostin, Larry O., *A Human Condition*. vol. 1, *The Mental Health Act from 1959 to 1975: Observations, Analysis and Proposals for Reform*, MIND, 1975. Vol. 2, *The Law Relating to Mentally Abnormal Offenders: Observations, Analysis and Proposals for Reform*, MIND, 1977.

—— *Is It Fair? The Mental Health Act, 1959*, MIND, 1978.

—— *A Practical Guide to Mental Health Law: The Mental Health Act 1983 and Related Legislation*, MIND, 1983.

Granville, J. Mortimer, *The Care and Cure of the Insane*, Reports of *Lancet* Commission on Lunatic Asylums, 1875–6-7, Hardwicke and Bogue, 1877.

Greenblatt, M., Levinson, D.J., and Williams, R.H., *The Patient and the Mental Hospital*, Free Press, Glencoe, Illinois, 1957.

Griffiths, Sir Roy. (See Department of Health and Social Security.)

Grob, Gerald, 'Marxian analysis and mental illness', *History of Psychiatry*, vol. 1, part 2, no. 2, pp. 223–232.

Halliday, Sir Andrew, *A General View of the Present State of Lunatics and Lunatic Asylums in Great Britain and Ireland, and in some other Kingdoms* Underwood, 1828.

Hammond, J.L. and Hammond, Barbara, *Lord Shaftesbury*, 1933. 4th edition, Penguin, 1936.

Hanvey, C., 'Italy and the rise of democratic psychiatry', *Community Care*, 25 October 1978, pp. 22–4.

Hanwell: 'An Epistle addressed to Mr Ewart, MP, on his withdrawing his notice of a Motion for an Enquiry into the Total Abolition of all Restraint on the Pauper Lunatics at Hanwell', by a Rev. Gentleman not under restraint, Hanwell, 1841. *Hume Tracts*, University College Library, London.

Harding, T.W., 'Not Worth Powder and Shot': a reappraisal of Montague Lomax's contribution to mental health reform, *B. J. Psychiat.* (1990), vol. 156, pp. 180–7.

Hart, H.L.A., *The Concept of Law*, Clarendon Press, Oxford, 1961.

Haslam, John, *Observations on Madness and Melancholy*, 1809.

——*Considerations on the Moral Management of Insane Persons*, 1817.

Hawkins, Rev. H. 'A Plea for convalescent homes in connection with asylums for the insane poor', *J. Ment. Sci* vol. XXIII, 1877, pp. 10–16.

——'After-care', *J. Ment. Sci.*, vol. XXV, 1879, pp. 358–67.

Heptinstall, C., 'Psichiatrica Democratica: Italy's revolution in caring for the mentally ill', *Community Care*, 1 March 1984, pp. 17–19.

Hervey, Nicholas, 'A slavish bowing down: the Lunacy Commission and the psychiatric profession, 1845–60', in Bynum, Porter and Shepherd (eds), op. cit., vol. II, 1985, pp. 98–131.

——'Advocacy or folly: the Alleged Lunatics' Friend Society', *Medical History*, vol. 30, 1986, pp. 245–75.

Higgins, Godfrey, *A Letter to the Right Honourable Earl Fitzwilliam respecting the Investigation which has lately taken place into the Abuses at the York Lunatic Asylum, together with various Letters Reports etc.*, Rivington, London 1814. This volume contains minutes of the Governors' Meetings of the York Asylum, newspaper correspondence and other relevant material.

Hill, R. Gardiner, *The Non Restraint System of Treatment in Lunacy*, Simpkin Marshall, 1857. (Abridged version in Hunter and Macalpine, *300 Years of Psychiatry*).

Hodder, E., *The Life and Work of the Seventh Earl of Shaftesbury, KG*, popular edition (1 vol.), Cassell, 1887.

Hoggett, Brenda, *Mental Health Law*, Sweet and Maxwell, 1983.

Howard, John, *The State of the Prisons in England and Wales, with Preliminary Observations and an Account of some Foreign Prisons* (1777), Everyman edition, Dent, 1929.

Howells, John G., 'The establishment of the Royal College of Psychiatrists', in Berrios and Freeman (eds), op. cit., 1991.

Hubback, Eva, *The Population of Britain*, Penguin, 1947, p. 20.

Hunt, H.C., *A Retired Habitation: A History of the Retreat, York*, H.K. Lewis, 1932.

Hunter, Richard, and Macalpine, Ida (eds) *A Treatise on Madness by William Battie, MD, and Remarks on Dr Battie's Treatise on Madness, by John Monro, M.D.: A Psychiatric Controversy of the Eighteenth Century*, Dawsons of Pall Mall, 1962.

——(eds.), *Description of the Retreat, by Samuel Tuke*, Dawsons of Pall Mall, 1964.

——(eds) *Three Hundred Years of Psychiatry, 1535–1860*, Carlisle Publishing Inc., Hartsdale, New York, 1982.

(See also Macalpine and Hunter.)

Jesse, J. Heneage, *Memoirs of the Life and Reign of George III*, 1867.

Jones, Kathleen, 'Problems of Mental After-care in Lancashire', *Sociological Review*, July 1954.

——*Lunacy, Law and Conscience, 1744–1845*, Routledge and Kegan Paul, 1955.

——*Mental Health and Social Policy, 1845–1959*, Routledge and Kegan Paul, 1960.

——*A History of the Mental Health Services*, Routledge and Kegan Paul, 1972.

——*After Hospital: A Study of Long-Term Psychiatric Patients in York*, York District Health Authority, 1985.

——*Mental Hospital Closures: The Way Forward?*, University of York, 1987.

——*Experience in Mental Health: Community Care and Social Policy*, Sage, 1988.

——*The Making of Social Policy*, Athlone, 1991.

——'The culture of the mental hospital', in Berrios and Freeman, op. cit., 1991.

——and Sidebotham, Roy, *Mental Hospitals at Work*, Routledge and Kegan Paul, 1962.

——and Fowles, A.J., *Ideas on Institutions: Analysing the Literature on Long-Term Care and Custody*, Routledge and Kegan Paul, 1984.

——and Freeman, Hugh (eds), *Community Care and Schizophrenia: The Need for Social research*, SANE, 199–205 Old Marylebone Road, London NW1, 1993.

—— and Poletti, Alison, 'Understanding the Italian Experience', *B.J. Psychiat.*, vol. 146, 1985, pp. 341–7; 'The Italian Experience Reconsidered', *B.J. Psychiat.*, vol. 148, 1986, pp. 144–50.

—— (ed.) *The Year Book of Social Policy in Britain, 1971*, Routledge and Kegan Paul, 1972.

—— (ed.) *The Year Book of Social Policy in Britain, 1973*, Routledge and Kegan Paul, 1974.

Jones, Richard, *The Mental Health Act 1983*, Sweet and Maxwell, 1983.

Jones, Maxwell, *Social Psychiatry*, Tavistock, 1952.

—— *Social Psychiatry in the Community, in Hospitals and in Prisons*, Charles Thomas, Springfield, Illinois, 1962.

—— *Social Psychiatry in Practice*, Pelican, 1968.

Jones, W.Ll. Parry, *The Trade in Lunacy*, Routledge and Kegan Paul, 1972.

Kamenka, E., and Tay, A.E.S., *Human Rights*, Arnold, 1978, pp. 15–31.

Kennedy, Ian, *The Unmasking of Medicine*, Allen and Unwin, 1971.

Kittrie, N.N., *The Right to be Different: Deviance and Enforced Therapy*, Johns Hopkins University Press, Baltimore, 1971.

Klinsma, Marinus P., 'Patient Advocacy in The Netherlands' *Psychiatric Bulletin* 17, 4, pp. 230–1 April 1993.

Knight, Paul Slade, *Observations on the Causes, Symptoms and Treatment of Derangement of the Mind* (Knight on Insanity), Longman, 1827.

Lacey, Ron, 'Where have all the patients gone?', *Guardian*, 4 July 1982.

Lader, Malcolm, *Psychiatry on Trial*, Penguin, 1977.

Laing, R.D., *The Divided Self*, Tavistock, 1960.

—— *The Politics of Experience and the Bird of Paradise*, Penguin, 1967.

—— and Esterson, A., *Sanity, Madness and the Family*, Tavistock, 1964.

Leff, Julian (ed.) 'The TAPS Project: evaluating community placement of long-stay psychiatric patients', *British Journal of Psychiatry*, 162, supplement 9, April 1993.

Levine, Murray, *The History and Politics of Community Mental Health*, Oxford University Press, New York, 1981.

Lomax, Montague, *Experiences of an Asylum Doctor*, Allen and Unwin, 1921.

Loudon, Irvine, *Medical Care and the General Practitioner, 1750–1859*, Clarendon Press, Oxford, 1986, pp. 14–17.

Macalpine, Ida and Hunter, Richard, *George III and the Mad-Business*, Allen Lane/Penguin, 1969. (See also Hunter and Macalpine).

MacDonald, Michael, *Mystical Bedlam: Madness, Anxiety and Healing in Seventeenth Century England*, Cambridge University Press, 1981.

McKeown, T., *Medicine in Modern Society*, Allen and Unwin, 1965. (See also Garratt, Lowe and McKeown).

MacLeod, Iain and Powell, Enoch, *The Social Services – Needs and Means*, Conservative Political Centre, 1954.

Main, T.F., 'The hospital as a therapeutic community', *Bulletin of the Menninger Clinic*, X, 1946, pp. 66–70.

Manchester Lunatic Hospital, *An Account of the Rise and Present Establishment of the Lunatic Hospital in Manchester*, 1778. Abridged reprint, J. Harrop, Manchester, 1971.

Manchester Royal Infirmary, *Rules for the Government of the Infirmary, Lunatic Hospital and Public Baths in Manchester*, 1791.

Martin, D.V., *Adventure in Psychiatry*, Bruno Cassirer, 1962.

Martin, F.M., (See Rehin).

Martin, J.P., *Hospitals in Trouble*, Basil Blackwell, Oxford, 1984.

Matthews J. (ed.), *The Mental Health Services*, Shaw and Sons, 1948 and subsequent editions.

Medical Services Review Committee, *Review of the Medical Services in Great Britain*, Social Assay, 1963, (Porritt Report).

Mellett, D.J., *The Prerogative of Asylumdom*, Garland Publishing, Inc., New York, 1982.

Mental After Care Association, Annual Reports.

Milbank Memorial Fund, *Steps in the Development of Integrated Psychiatric Services*, New York, 1960.

MIND publications: obtainable from Kemp House, 1st floor, 152–160, City Road, London EC1V 2NP. (See Brandon, Brackx, Sayce).

Mitford, J., *The Crimes and Horrors of Kelly House* and *The Crimes and Horrors of Warburton's Private Madhouses*. No date, probably 1828–30. Hume Tracts, University College Hospital Library, London.

Monro, John, *Remarks on Dr Battie's Treatise on Madness*, Bridewell, 1758.

Monro, Thomas, *The Observations of Dr Thomas Monro upon the evidence taken before the Committee of the Hon. House of Commons for Regulating Madhouses*, Bridewell, 1816.

Morris, Pauline, *Put Away: A Sociological Study of Institutions for the Mentally Retarded*, Routledge and Kegan Paul, 1969.

Morrissey, J.P., and Goldman, H.H., 'The enduring asylum: in search of an international perspective', *Int. J. Law and Psychiat.*, 4, 1981, pp. 13–34.

National Association for Mental Health, Annual Reports, and Reports of Annual Conferences. (See MIND).

O'Donoghue, E.G., *The Story of Bethlehem Hospital from its Foundation in 1247*, Fisher Unwin, 1913.

Olsen, Rolf, 'The case for giving more rights to the mentally ill', *New*

Society, vol. 59, pp. 347–8, 4 March 1982.

——(ed.) *Social Work and Mental Health: A Guide for the Approved Social Worker*, Tavistock, 1984.

Parry-Jones (See Jones, W. Ll. Parry).

Parsons, T., 'The mental hospital as a social system', in M. Greenblatt, D.J. Levinson and R. Williams (eds) *The Patient and the Mental Hospital*, Free Press, Glencoe, Illinois, 1957, pp. 108–29.

Paternoster, Richard, *The Madhouse System*, Patemaster, 1841.

Paul, Sir George Onesiphorus, *Suggestions of Sir George Onesiphorus Paul, Bart, to Earl Spencer*, 1806, published as Appendix IV to the Report of the Select Committee on Criminal and Pauper Lunatics, 1807.

Pearson, Karl, *The Life and Labours of Francis Galton*, Cambridge University Press, 1914, 4 vols.

Persaud, Rajendra D., 'A Comparison of symptoms recorded from the same patients by an asylum doctor and A Constant Observer in 1823', *History of Psychiatry*, vol. 3, part 1, no. 9, March 1992, pp. 83–8.

Porter, Roy, *A Social History of Madness: Stories of the Insane*, Weidenfeld and Nicolson, 1989

——'History of psychiatry in Britain', *History of Psychiatry* vol. 2, part 5, no. 7, September 1991. (See alse Bynum, Porter and Shepherd).

Powell, Enoch (See MacLeod).

President's Commission for Mental Health, *Report to the President*, US Government Printing Office, Washington, DC, 1978.

Ramon, Shulamit, 'The Italian job', *Social Work Today*, 14 December 1982, p. 14.

——*Psychiatry in Britain: Meaning and Policy*, Croom Helm, 1985.

——*Beyond Community Care: Normalization*, Macmillan, 1991.

Rand, Benjamin (ed.) *The Life, Letters and Philosophical Regimen of the Third Earl of Shaftesbury*, Swan Sonnenschein, 1900.

Rapaport, Robert, *Community as Doctor*, Tavistock, 1961.

Reade, Charles, *Hard Cash* (1863), Cassell, 1909 edition.

Rehin, George and Martin, Fred, *Patterns of Performance in Community Care*, Oxford University Press, 1968.

——*Psychiatric Services in 1975*, Political and Economic Planning (PEP), vol. xxix, no. 468, 1963.

Robb, Barbara (ed.) *Sans Everything: A Case to Answer*, Nelson, 1967.

Rooff, Madeleine, *Voluntary Societies and Social Policy*, Routledge and Kegan Paul, 1957.

Rose, George, *Diaries and Correspondence of the Rt Hon. George Rose*, ed. Vernon Harcourt, Bentley, 1860, 2 vols.

——*Observations on the Poor Laws and the Management of the Poor*, 2nd ed., Hatchard 1805.

Ross, J. Stirling, *The National Health Service in Great Britain*, Oxford University Press, 1952.

Rothman, D.J., *The Discovery of the Asylum: Social Order and Disorder in the New Republic*, Little, Brown, Boston, Mass., 1971.

——*Conscience and Convenience: The Asylum and Its Alternatives in Progressive America*, Little, Brown, Boston, Mass., 1980.

Royal Medico-Psychological Association, Report of Medical Planning Committee, *A Memorandum on the Future Organization of the Psychiatric Services*, RMPA, 1945.

Runwell Hospital, *Brochure* prepared for the official opening, 1937.

Russell, Richard, 'The lunacy profession and its staff in the second half of the nineteenth century, with special reference to the West Riding Lunatic Asylum', in Bynum, Porter and Shepherd (eds), op. cit., vol. III, pp. 297–315.

St Luke's Hospital, *Considerations upon the usefulness and necessity of establishing an hospital as a further provision for poor lunatics in London*, printed at the Hospital, 1817.

Sayce, Liz, *Waiting for Community Care*, MIND, 1990.

Schorr, Alvin, *The Personal Social Services: An Outside View*, Joseph Rowntree Foundation, York, July 1992.

Scull, A.T., *Decarceration: Community Treatment and the Deviant – a Radical View*, Prentice Hall, Englewood Cliffs, NJ, 1977.

——*Museums of Madness: The Social Organization of Insanity in Nineteenth Century England*, Allen Lane, 1979.

——(ed.), *Madhouses, Mad-Doctors and Madmen: The Social History of Psychiatry in the Victorian era*, University of Pennsylvania Press, Pa, 1981.

——'A Victorian alienist; John Conolly' in Bynum, Porter and Shepherd, op. cit., vol. I, 1985, pp. 103–50).

——*Social Order / Mental Disorder: Anglo-American Psychiatry in Perspective*, Routledge, 1989.

——'Psychiatry and its historians', *History of Psychiatry*, September 1991, vol. 2, part 3, no. 7, pp. 239–40.

Sedgwick, Peter, *Psycho Politics*, Pluto, 1982.

Selborne, Roundell Palmer, first Earl, *Memoirs, Political and Personal, 1865–1895*, Macmillan, 1898.

Semelaigne, René, *Philippe Pinel et son Oeuvre*, Réunis, Paris, 1888.

——*Aliénistes et Philosophes: les Pinel et les Tuke*, Steinheil, Paris, 1912.

Shepherd, Michael (See Bynum, Porter and Shepherd).

Sheridan, Alan, *Michel Foucault: The Will to Truth*, Tavistock, 1980.

Showalter, Elaine, *The Female Malady: Women, Madness and English Culture, 1830–1990*, Virago, 1987.

Sketches in Bedlam (See Constant Observer).

Skultans, Vieda, *English Madness: Ideas on Insanity 1580–1890*, Routledge and Kegan Paul, 1979.

Smith, Jef, 'Top jobs in the Social Services', in Kathleen Jones (ed.), *The Year Book of Social Policy in Britain, 1971*, op. cit., pp. 16–30.

Smith, Sidney, 'Mad Quakers', *Edinburgh Review*, 1817, pp. 431–71.

Sprigg, S.S., *The Life and Times of Thomas Wakley*, Longmans Green, 1897.

Stanton, A.H. and Schwarz, M., *The Mental Hospital*, Tavistock, 1954.

Stirling Ross (See Ross, J. Stirling).

Szivos, Sue, 'The limits to integration?', in Hilary Brown and Helen Smith, *Normalization: A Reader for the Nineties*, Tavistock/Routledge, 1992.

Surrey Asylum, *Rules*. Printed with *Reports of the Visiting Justices of the Surrey Asylum, 1844–6*, 1847.

Szasz, T.S., *The Myth of Mental Illness: Foundations of a Theory of Personal Conduct*, Dell, New York, 1961.

——*Law, Liberty and Psychiatry: An Inquiry into the Social Uses of Mental Health Practice*, Macmillan, New York, 1963.

——*Ideology and Insanity: essays on the Psychiatric Dehumanization of Man*. Anchor Books/Doubleday, New York, 1970.

——*The Manufacture of Madness: A Comparative Study of the Inquisition and the Mental Health Movement*, Routledge and Kegan Paul, 1971.

——*The Ethics of Psychoanalysis: The Theory and Methods of Autonomous Psychotherapy*, Routledge and Kegan Paul, 1974.

Thomas, Keith, *Religion and the Decline of Magic: Studies in Popular Beliefs in Sixteenth and Seventeenth Century England*, Weidenfeld and Nicolson, 1971.

Thomas, Neil, and Stoten, Brian, 'The NHS and local government: co-operation or conflict?' in Kathleen Jones (ed.),*The Year Book of Social Policy in Britain, 1973*, op. cit, pp. 48–70.

Thurnam, J., *Observations on the Statistics of Insanity*, Simpkin Marshall, 1845.

Timms, Noel, *Psychiatric Social Work in Great Britain*, Routledge and Kegan Paul, 1964.

Titmuss, R.M., *Commitment to Welfare*, Allen and Unwin, 1968.

Tomes, Nancy, 'The great restraint controversy: a comparative perspective on Anglo-American psychiatry in the nineteenth century', in Bynum, Porter and Shepherd (eds), op. cit., vol. III, pp. 190–225.

Tooth, G.C., and Brooke, E.M., 'Needs and beds: trends in the mental hospital population and their effect on future planning', *Lancet*, 1 April 1961, pp. 710–13.

Townsend, Peter, *The Last Refuge: A Survey of Residential Institutions and Homes for the Aged in England and Wales*, Routledge and Kegan Paul, 1962.

Tuke, D.H., *Chapters in the History of the Insane in the British Isles*,

Kegan Paul/Trench, 1882.

Tuke, Samuel, *Description of the Retreat, an institution near York for Insane Persons of the Society of Friends*, Alexander, York and Darton Harvey, London, 1813. (Facsimile edition, see Hunter and Macalpine).

Turner, Trevor, 'Henry Maudsley: psychiatrist, philosopher and entrepreneur', in Bynum, Porter and Shepherd, op. cit., vol. III, pp. 151–89.

—— 'Not worth powder and shot.': the public profile of the Medico-Psychological Association, c. 1851–1915', in Berrios and Freeman, op. cit., pp. 3–16.

Ullman, L.P., *Institution and Outcome*, Pergamon, Oxford, 1967.

Unsworth, Clive, *The Politics of Mental Health Legislation*, Clarendon Press, Oxford, 1987.

US Department of Health, Education and Welfare, Joint Commission on Mental Illness and Health, *Action for Mental Health*, Basic Books, New York, 1961.

Walk, A., 'Mental hospitals' in *The Evolution of Hospitals in Britain*, Pitman Medical Publishing Co., 1958.

—— 'The History of mental nursing', *J. Ment. Sci.*, 107, 446, January 1966.

Wallace, Marjorie, *The Forgotten Illness*, articles reprinted from *The Times*, 1985 and 1986, obtainable from SANE, 199–205, Old Marylebone Road, London NW1 5QP.

Walton, John, 'Pauper lunatics in Victorian England', in Scull (ed.) *Madhouses, Mad-Doctors and Madmen*, op. cit., pp. 166–97.

Webb, Sidney, *Grants in Aid: A Criticism and a Proposal*, Longmans Green, London, 1911, p. 43.

Webb, Sidney, and Webb, Beatrice, *English Poor Law History*, vol. I, *The Old Poor Law*, Longmans Green, 1910.

—— *English Poor Law Policy*, Longmans Green, 1910.

Webster, Charles (ed.), *Health, Medicine and Mortality in the Sixteenth Century*, Cambridge University Press, 1979.

Wesley, John, *Primitive Physick, or, An Easy and Natural Way of curing most Diseases* (1780) 9th edn, Strahan, 1912.

Wesley, John, *John Wesley's Journal*, ed. Nehemiah Curnock, Kelly, 1909.

Willcocks, A.J., *The Creation of the National Health Service*, Routledge and Kegan Paul, 1967.

Willey, Basil, *The Eighteenth Century Background*, Chatto and Windus, 1940.

Wolfensberger, Wolf *et al.*, *The Principle of Normalization in Human Services*, National Institute of Mental Retardation/Leonard Crainford, Toronto, 1972.

Young, Hugo, *One of Us: A Biography of Margaret Thatcher*, Macmillan, 1989.

Younghusband, Eileen, *The Employment and Training of Social Workers*, Carnegie United Kingdom Trust, 1947.
——*Social Work in Britain*, Carnegie UK Trust, 1959.
(See also Ministry of Health, Report on Social Workers, 1959).

Zeitlyn, B.B., 'The therapeutic community – fact or fiction?' *B.J. Psychiat.* vol. 113, 1967, pp. 1083–6.

Zilboorg, G. and Henrey, G., *A History of Medical Psychology*, Norton, New York, 1941.

Index

Action for Mental Health, 193
Admission procedures: see
    Certification, Voluntary patients,
    Temporary patients, Informal
    admission
Advocacy systems, 200–5, 235, 236
After-Care, 75, 127–8, 133, 139,
    144, 150, 210. See also
    Community Care
Alleged Lunatics' Friend Society,
    95, 102
American Civil Liberties Union,
    180, 200–1
Andrews, Dr Jonathan, 9
Anti-psychiatry, see Laing, Szasz,
    Scull
Appeal, patients' right to, see
    Mental Health Review Tribunals
Approved Social Workers, 206,
    209, 212
Ashley, Lord, see Shaftesbury, 7th
    Earl
Asset-stripping, 233
Asylum architecture, 74, 81, 119–
    20, 148, 149, 173, 174
Asylum doctors, 39, 67–71, 93, 95,
    97, 104, 106–7, 112, 124. See also
    psychiatrists
Asylum Journal, 93
Asylum system, rationale for, 34–5,
    38–40

Asylums, see Goffman
Asylums, cost of, 37, 60, 74–5, 81–
    2, 86–7, 149
Asylums, size of, 60, 91–2, 114–7,
    118–20, 129, 133, 145
Attendants, 42, 55, 65, 66, 67, 70,
    93, 96–7, 101, 102, 118–9. See
    also Psychiatric nurses
Aubrey, John, 7–8
Audit Commission, 197, 228–30

Baker, Dr A. A., 164
Barter, Percy, 129, 130
Barton, Dr W. Russell, 179
Battie, Dr, 17, 124
Bedlam, see Bethlem
Bedlam beggars, 7–8
Bentham, Jeremy, 34, 92, 176
Best, Dr, of York Asylum, 43–8
Bethel Hospital, Norwich, 82
Bethlem, 7–10, 23–4, 41–2, 55, 77,
    79, 97, 101, 138
Better Services for the Mentally Ill,
    190–3
Beveridge Report, 143
Binet-Simon tests, 122
Biometrika, 121
Bion, Dr W. R., 143, 152
Birth of the Clinic, 173
'Blanket patients', 49–50

Block grant, 155, 158, 197, 206
Bluglass, Dr Robert, 205
Board of Control, 123–4, 127–8, 130, 131, 133, 136–8, 141, 154–5, 156
Bodmin Asylum, 60, 61, 64
Bolden, Gilbert, 98
Bowlby, Dr John, 143
Braddock, Mrs Bessie, 163
Bridewells, 11–12
British Association of Social Workers, 197, 204, 205
Brooke, Eileen, 161, 190
Brooke, John, 19
Browne, Dr W. A. F. of Montrose, 69–70, 114
Bucknill, Dr J. C., 93, 95
Burrows, Dr George Man, 68, 69
Bynum, Dr W. F. 13

'Cardboard City', 225–6
Caring for People, 232–4
Carstairs, Prof. G. M., 150
Castle, Mrs Barbara, 190
Cattell, J. McKeen, 122
Certification, 38, 53, 83, 90–1, 102, 108, 113–4, 132, 133, 135, 136. See also Compulsory admission, Magistrate's order
Chadwick, Edwin, 34, 75
Charlesworth, Dr E. P., 64–5
Christian ethic, 26, 34, 105, 175–6, 177
Civil liberties, see Patients' rights
Clapham Sect, 34
Clark, Dr D. H., 162
Clerke, Dame Sarah, case of, 15–6
Closure of mental hospitals, 2, 193, 225, 226, 228, 232–3, 235–6
Cobb Committee, 128–9
Cochrane, David, 119
Code of Practice, 62, 206, 212
Cogwheel Report, 187
Collaboration, co-operation, co-ordination, 145, 186–7, 190–1, 222–4, 231, 233, 249
Community Care, 2, 131, 134, 141, 151, 155–6, 158, 159, 163, 183, 185–6, 212–3, 221–37, 238–55
Community Mental Health Centers (USA), 178, 194, 196
Community Support Program (USA), 195–6
Community Treatment Order, 239, 240, 241–2
Complaints machinery, 189–90
Compulsory admission, 157, 207. See also Certification
Conolly, Dr John, 66–8, 84, 97, 126
Cornwall Asylum, see Bodmin
'Cosmic Toryism', 33
County Asylums Act (1808), 33, 36–7
County asylums, rationale for foundation of, 34–5
Crew, Professor F. A. E. 124
'Crib-room cases of Bethnal Green', 56–8, 99
'Crossing-sweeper judgement', 104
Crowther, Dr Bryan (of Bethlem), 48–9, 68
Crowther, Dr Caleb (of Wakefield), 70–1
Culture of mental hospitals, 118–20, 136–8, 145–7

Day hospitals, 151, 152
De facto detention, 210
Definitions, see Terminology
Delarive, Dr, 26–7
Deprofessionalization, 163, 204, 215, 234, 249
Description of the Retreat, see Tuke, Samuel
Digby, Dr Anne, 31–2
Discipline and Punish, 173–4
District General Hospitals, 181–2, 191, 192
Duly Authorized Officers, 145
Duncombe, Thomas Slingsby, 73
D'Vebre, Mrs Deborah, case of, 16

Early treatment, 70, 102, 116, 126, 127, 134, 235

Earmarked grants, 155–6, 206, 231
Eldon, Lord, 54–5
Ellis, Dr William, of Wakefield, 68, 69
Entertainment programmes, 119, 134, 137, 167
Eugenic School, 121–2
Evangelical Movement, 34
Ewart, Dr Jack R., 193, 196
Exorcism, 6

'Feeble-minded', 120–3
Ferriar, Dr John, 25
Feversham Report, 139–40
Foucault, Dr Michel, 2, 12–13, 30–31, 165, 170–5, 176, 177, 180

Galton, Sir Francis, 121–2
Gardiner Hill, R., see Hill, R. Gardiner
General hospitals, psychiatric units in, see Psychiatric units
General medicine, psychiatry as a branch of, 132, 143–4, 164, 181–3, 184, 191, 192
General Nursing Council, 138, 184
General practitioners, 134, 183, 191
General View of Lunatics, see Halliday
Generalism, genericism in training, 184
Gentleman's Magazine, 16–17
George III, 14, 19–22, 39
Godlee, Fiona, 32–3
Goffman, Dr Erving, 2, 40, 113, 165, 166–70, 179, 180
Gordon, Robert, 56, 72, 89
Gostin, Larry, 200, 202–3, 205, 213
Grant-in-aid of pauper lunatics, 115–8
Granville, Dr Mortimer, 101–2, 105
Guardianship, 208, 212
Gulson, Edward, 74–5, 81

Habeas Corpus, 15, 16
Halliday, Dr Andrew, 36, 55, 62, 68
Halsbury, Lord, 106
Hansard, Luke James, 95
Hanwell Asylum, 58, 66–7, 84–5, 101, 119, 245
Hard Cash, 98–9
Hargreaves, Dr Ronald, 143
Haslam, Dr John, 42, 48–9, 55, 68
Health and Welfare: the Development of Community Care, 183
Health Services Commissioner, 189–90
Herschell, Lord, 106
Hervey, Nicholas, 72
Higgins, Godfrey, 41, 43–7, 99
Hill, Dr R. Gardiner, 64–66
Hornsby-Smith, Patricia, 149
Hospital Inquiries, 188–9
Hospital Plan (1962), 181–3
Howard, John, 11–2, 34
Human rights, see Patients' rights
Hunter, Dr Richard, 13, 19–20
Hunter, Dr (of York Asylum), 43

Idiots Act (1886), 120
Illegitimacy, 121, 123
'Increase in insanity', 114–5
Industrial therapy, 141, 151
Informal admission, 157
Information systems, 231, 242–5
Institutional Neurosis, see Barton
'Institutional psychiatry', 178
Intelligence testing, 122
'Italian Experience', 216–21, 225

Jones, Dr Maxwell, 152
Jones and Sidebotham, 164
Joseph, Sir Keith, 184
Juke family, 121
Justices of the peace, see Magistrates

Kallikak family, 122
Kennedy, Prof. Ian, 201–2
Key Area Handbook, 234–5
Knight, Dr Paul Slade, 64

Labelling, 122, 179
Lacey, Ron, 217
Lader, Dr Malcolm, 198
Laing, Dr R. D., 179, 188
Lancaster Asylum, 60, 61, 64, 79–80, 118
Lancet Commission, see Granville
Law, Liberty and Psychiatry, 177
Lay inspection, 40–59, 79, 89, 94
Learning disabilities, 4, 120–3, 206–7. See also Mental deficiency
'Least restrictive alternative', 201
Legal profession, legal views, 72, 78–9, 89, 94, 104, 105, 111, 113–4, 124, 132–3, 155, 156, 200–13
Licensed madhouses, see Private madhouses
Lincoln Asylum, 60, 64–6, 84
Local authorities (mental health care), 107, 141, 145, 155, 156, 158, 185–6, 206, 209, 222–35, 244–52
Local Government Act (1929), 134–5
Lomax, Dr Montague, 128–30, 189
Lunacy Act (1890), 106–11, 112–4, 120, 139, 148, 154, 203
Lunacy Commissioners, 68, 89–91, 95, 105–7, 109–10. See also Metropolitan Commissioners
Lunacy Laws Amendment Association, 103, 104
Lunatics Act (1845), 87–92

Macalpine, Dr Ida, 13, 19–20
Macdonald, Michael, 6–7
McKeown, Prof. T., 182
Maclay, Dr W. S., 147
Macmillan Commission, 130–4, 148, 154, 182

Madhouses Act (1774), 18
Madness and Civilization, 165, 170–3
Magistrates, 14, 35, 37–8, 59, 67, 70, 81, 83, 91, 95, 107
Magistrate's order, 98, 100–1, 102, 106, 154, 157
Main, Dr T. F., 143, 151–2
Manchester Lunatic Hospital, 23, 24–5, 32, 82
Manufacture of Madness, 178
Maudsley, Dr Henry, 126
Maudsley Hospital, 126–7
Mechanical restraint, 21, 25, 28–9, 52, 84–5. Abolition of, see Non-Restraint
Medical model of mental illness, 144, 184, 192, 193
Medical qualifications, 6, 93, 144
Medical superintendents, 62, 69, 70–1, 91, 146–7
Medico-Psychological Association, 93, 106–7
Mellett, Dr D. J., 76–7, 92
Men, as proportion of asylum patients, 116–8
Mental After-Care Association, 127–8, 139
Mental deficiency, mental handicap, 4, 120–3
Mental Health Act (1959), 156–8, 159, 202, 205
Mental Health Act (1983), 205–13
Mental Health Emergency Committee, 139
Mental Health Review Tribunals, 156–7, 202, 204, 207
Mental Treatment Act (1930), 135–6, 139
Mental Welfare Officers, 145, 209
'Messianic Christianity', 177
Metropolitan Commissioners in Lunacy, 18, 51–2, 53–4, 57–9, 70, 72, 75–9, 255. See also Lunacy Commissioners
Middlesex Asylum, see Hanwell
Milbank Memorial Fund, 153–4
Miles' House, Hoxton, 51–2, 58

Mills, Hannah, case of, 26
Milltown, Lord, 105
MIND, 199–200, 204–5, 236, 239, 249. See also National Association for Mental Health
Mind-body interaction, 3, 25, 69, 86, 102, 127, 131–2, 133, 176–7, 182
Mitford, John, 72, 76
Monro, Dr Edward Thomas, 55
Monro, Dr John, 24, 48–9, 55
Monro, Dr Thomas, 17–8, 52
Moral management, moral treatment, 25, 27–9, 33, 63, 172–3
'Moral panic', 188, 190, 193
Morison, Sir Alexander, 72
'Mortification of the self', 166
Myth of Mental Illness, 175–7, 193
'Myth of progress', 2–3

National Association for Mental Health, 139, 198–200. See also MIND
National Health Service Act (1946), 144–5
National Health Service and Community Care Act (1990), 234
National Institute of Mental Health (USA), 169, 193–4
National Schizophrenia Fellowship, 236–7, 239, 240
National Society for Lunacy Reform, 130–1
'Naval maniacs', 51–2
'New Communities', 227
Non-restraint system, 27, 64–8, 84–5
Normalization, 214–6, 245, 254
Norris, William (or James), case of, 41–2
Nottingham asylum, 42, 60, 118
Nurses, see Psychiatric Nurses

Occupational therapy, 134, 151
Office of Population Censuses and Surveys (OPCS), 246–7, 255

'Ombudsman', see Health Services Commissioner
Open door policy, 137–8, 151, 153, 154
Out-patient clinics, 127, 133, 134, 139–40, 141, 151, 161

'Packages of care', 231, 247
Paliamentary debate of 19 Feb. 1954, 149–50
'Parole' systems, 128, 138
Parry-Jones, Dr W. Ll., 14, 15, 52
Paternoster, Richard, 72–3, 76, 99
Patient education, 63, 67, 146
Patient entertainment, 119, 134, 137, 146
Patient labour, 30–1, 63, 119, 120, 134, 147, 151
Patient occupation, 30–31, 63, 120, 134, 146, 147
Patients' rights, 75, 95, 109–10, 137, 147, 156–7, 199, 200–5, 209, 210–11
Paul, Sir George Onesiphorus, 34–5
Pauper lunatics, 10–11, 50–3, 56–8, 74–5, 77, 79, 108, 115–8, 133, 134–5
Peel, Sir Robert (the younger), 42, 86
Percy, Lord (Eustace), 154
'Perverse incentives', 230, 231
Pharmacological revolution, see Psychotropic drugs
Phillips, Lewis, case of, 73–4, 76
Physician superintendents, see Medical superintendents
Pinel, Dr Philippe, 172–3, 174
Poor Law, see Pauper lunatics
Poor Law Act (1601), 10
Poor Law Amendment Act (1834), 74
Poor Law Commissioners, 74–5, 81, 92
Porphyria, variegated, 19
Porphyrian Tree, 176
Porter, Dr Roy, 3

Powell, Enoch, 159–60, 164, 190, 191
Press reportage, 44–8, 87–8, 95, 102, 103, 189, 237, 238–40
Prestwich Hospital Inquiry, 128–30
Primary care team, 191
Private madhouses, licensed houses, 15–8, 51–4, 55–9, 72–4, 75–7, 82–3, 90–1, 97, 101, 102–4, 106–7, 109
'Problems in living', 176
Psichiatria Democratica, see 'Italian Experience'
Psychiatric nurses, 128–9, 133–4, 136, 137, 138, 142, 184, 186–7, 189, 207, 249. See also Attendants
Psychiatric social workers, 134, 138, 140, 163, 184–6
Psychiatric units in general hospitals, 127, 133, 160, 181, 184, 217, 220
Psychiatrists, 127, 130, 138, 142–4, 150, 162, 164, 178, 181, 182–4, 192, 194, 197, 198, 201, 204–5, 219, 220, 249. See also Asylum doctors
Psychosomatic approaches, see Mind-body relationship
Psychotropic drugs, 3, 149, 150, 164, 179–80, 182–3, 198, 254
Public education, 140, 151

Quaker beliefs, 30, 31, 32. See also Retreat

Rake's Progress, 8–9
'Reality confrontation', 153
Reduction of mental hospital beds, 158–64, 185, 187, 191, 193, 223, 225, 226, 228, 232, 235–6, 242–4, 250–1, 253, 254
Rees, Dr J. R. (of Tavistock Clinic), 142–3
Rees, Dr T. P. (of Warlingham Park), 154

Regency Bill (1789), 21
Report to the President (USA), 194–6
Research in mental health, 134, 197, 245–8
Restraint, see Mechanical restraint
Retreat, York, 23, 26–33, 39, 42, 64, 82, 118, 172
Revisionism, vii, 2, 3, 174, 180, 254. See also Foucault, Scull, Szasz
'Revolving door', 188
Right to treatment, right to refuse treatment, see Patients' Rights
Robinson, Kenneth, 148–9
Romilly, Samuel, 35
Rose, George, 35, 42, 49, 51
Royal College of Nursing, 197, 204
Royal College of Psychiatrists, 184, 197, 203, 204, 205, 207, 240, 241–2
Royal Commissions: on the Care of the Feeble-Minded (1904–8), 121–3
on the Poor Laws (1905–9), 122
on Lunacy and Mental Disorder (1924–6), 130–4
on Mental Illness and Mental Deficiency (1954–9), 154–5
Royal Medico-Psychological Association, 138, 181, 184
Runwell Hospital, 138

St Luke's Hospital, London, 22–3, 32, 42, 82, 97, 101
St Peter's, Bristol, 10–1, 82
Salmon Report, 187
Sans Everything, 188–9
Sargent, Dr William, 182
Saumarez, Admiral, 98
Scapegoating, 175
Schorr, Dr Alvin, 251
Scientology Movement, 198–9
Scull, Dr Andrew, vii, 38–9, 54, 67–8
'Second opinions', 205, 208, 209, 210–1
Seebohm Report, 185–6

Selborne (2nd Earl), 105, 106
Select Committees: on Madhouses
  (1763), 17–18
  on Criminal and Pauper Lunatics
    (1807), 35–6
  on Madhouses (1815–6), 42–54
  on Pauper Lunatics (1827), 55–
    62
  on the Poor Law Amendment
    Act (1838), 74–5
  on Lunatics (1859–60), 96–8
  on Lunacy Law (1877), 98–101
  on Community Care (1985),
    224–6
Seymour, Lord Robert, 42, 55, 58
Shaftesbury, (3rd Earl), 7
Shaftesbury, (7th Earl) (Lord
  Ashley), 56, 72, 77, 78–9, 84, 86–
  9, 91, 92, 95–8, 100, 105, 106,
  114, 127–8, 211, 255
Shaftesbury's Act, see Lunatics Act
  (1845)
'Shell-shock', 126
'Shift' system, 152
'Ship of Fools', 170
Showalter, Dr Elaine, 117–8
Silcock, Ben, case of, 237, 238–42
Single lunatics, 77, 97, 110–1
Sites of county asylums, mental
  hospitals, 61, 82, 227
Size of county asylums, mental
  hospitals, 60, 91–2, 114–7, 118–
  20, 129, 133, 145
'Skill-mix', 197
Skorey, the Rev. Mr, case of, 46–7
Smith, Dr Stanley, 162
Smith, Rev. Sydney, 29
Smythe, Tony, 200
'Social degeneracy', 121–3
Social Services Departments, see
  Local authorities
Social Services Act (1970), 186
Social workers, 134, 138, 140, 163,
  184–6, 191, 192, 233–4, 249, 252
Social work model of mental illness,
  192
Somerset, Lord Granville, 78, 80
Stafford Asylum, 60, 61, 62

Statistics, deterioration in, 231,
  242–5
Stigma, 144, 147, 154, 221, 227
Sturges-Bourne, W., 42
'Submerged tenth', 123
Surrey Asylum, 71–2, 101
Szasz, Dr T. S., 2, 165, 175–8, 180

TAPS Project, 245–6
Tavistock Clinic, 142–3
Television, 188, 237, 250
Temporary patients, 135–6
Terminology, 3–4, 25, 86, 120–1,
  132, 135, 156, 206–7, 235–6
Therapeutic communities, 151–2
Therapeutic social clubs, 152–3
'Therapeutic state', 178
'Three Revolutions' (1950s), 148–
  58
Thurnam, Dr John, 117
Titmuss, Prof. R. M., 163–4, 234
Tom o'Bedlam, 7–8
Tomes, Dr Nancy, 68
Tooth, Dr G. C., 161, 190
'Total institutions', see Goffman
Tuke, Dr Daniel Hack, 26, 104
Tuke, Samuel, 27–30, 31, 32, 41,
  44
Tuke, William, 26, 31, 44
Turlington's House, Chelsea, 16

Unemployment, effects of, 136, 216,
  248
Unmasking of Medicine, 201–2
Unreason, Foucault's defence of,
  170–5
Unsworth, Clive, 113, 203, 204
USA, mental health services in,
  153–4, 165, 193–6
Utilitarianism, 34, 92

Vagrancy Act (1714), 14
Vagrancy Act (1744), 14, 35
Venables-Vernon, Archbishop, 44,
  48

Vickers, William, case of, 43–4
Villa-system, 129, 133, 138
Visiting justices, see Magistrates
'Voluntary boarders', 101, 132
Voluntary patients, 126, 127, 132, 133, 135–6, 142, 147, 157

Wakefield, Edward, 49–50, 52–3
Wakefield Asylum, 60, 71
Wakley, Thomas, 78, 85
Wales, Charles, Prince of, views on George III's illness, 19
Wales, George, Prince of (Prince Regent, later George IV) 20–21
Walker-Smith, Derek, 155
Wandsworth, see Surrey Asylum
War, effects of, 124–5, 141–4
Warburton's houses, 52, 56–8, 73–4, 76
Weldon, Mrs Georgiana, 102–4, 106

Wesley, John, 9–10
West Riding Asylum, see Wakefield
Westminster Review article, 86–7
'Whig history', 2
Whitbread, William, 35
Wilberforce, William, 35
Williams-Wynn, Charles, 35, 42, 72
Willis, Dr Francis, 20–1
Winslow, Dr Lyttleton Forbes, 102–3
Witchcraft, 6, 13, 175–6
Wolfensberger, Wolf, 214–6
Women patients, 116–8, 137
Workhouses, 10–1, 50, 74, 75, 77, 83–4, 97, 115, 118
World Health Organization Report (1953), 150–1

York Asylum, 26, 41, 42–8
Younghusband Report, 185